D1110459

Kelly provides a window on the most alluring destination in Italy. Anyone traveling to the Amalfi Coast must read this book. For those who have already discovered the Divine Coastline, it will rekindle cherished memories.

—Ralph Stern, Vice-President, Barclay International Group

The ache to visit the Bel Paese again becomes almost overwhelming while reading Chantal's gelato tales. I could feel the warmth of the sun and Italian men's gazes on me while the smell of the sea air wafted about. She brings to mind all of the elements that make a lady fall deeper in love with the people and places during each visit to Italy.

—Alison Turner, Senior Custom Travel Consultant, Select Italy Travel

Imagine traveling to the Amalfi Coast with your own personal guide whispering in your ear....Chantal Kelly takes you along as she conveys fascinating historical information mixed with humorous observations. After reading this book I can't wait to take my wife on a second honeymoon to one of the most romantic locations in Italy.

—Stefan Adelaar, General Manager, Euro-Connection

GELATO SISTERHOOD

on the Amalfi Shore

CHANTAL KELLY

Fenicia Press

Copyright 2011 Chantal Kelly

All rights reserved under International and Pan American Copyright Conventions.
No part of this publication may be reproduced, stored in a retrieval systems, or transmitted
in any form or by any means, electronic, mechanical, photocopying, recording or otherwise,
without the prior permission of the copyright owner.

Cover design and page layout: Anita Jones, Another Jones Graphics
Cover photo - Amalfi Coast © Chantal Kelly
Tiled pillar - Ceramica Casola by permission
Woman in chair - YinYang/iStock Photography

Maps by Chantal Kelly

Illustrations by Carine Cattrel
1. Pompeii   2. Paestum   3. Positano   4. Capri
5. Sorrento   6. Cooking Class   7. Amalfi

Text set in Adobe Garamond Pro 12/16

ISBN: 978-0-9832217-3-9

Library of Congress Number: 2011920618

Printed in the United States

Fenicia Press
PO Box 2326
Lake Oswego, OR 97035
www.feniciapress.com

DEDICATION

To my husband of thirty years,
my wonderful traveling companion.
For you I would cross another ocean.

To my parents.

To the people of Campania.

Contents

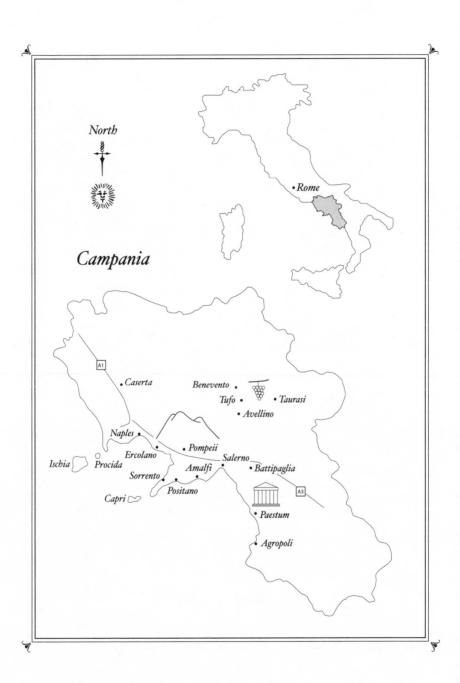

North

Campania

· Rome

· Caserta

Benevento ·

Tufo · · Taurasi

· Avellino

Naples ·

· Pompeii

Ercolano ·

Salerno

Ischia   Procida   Amalfi

Sorrento ·   · Battipaglia

Capri   Positano ·

· Paestum

· Agropoli

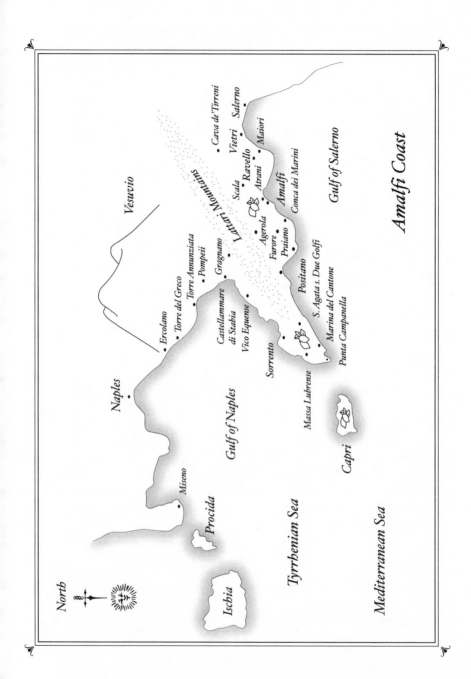

North

Vesuvio

Naples

Ercolano
Torre del Greco
Torre Annunziata
Pompeii

Gragnano

Lattari Mountains

Scala
Ravello
Atrani
Agerola
Furore
Praiano
Conca dei Marini
Amalfi

Cava de'Tirreni
Vietri
Salerno
Maiori

Gulf of Salerno

Castellammare
di Stabia
Vico Equense

Sorrento

Positano

S. Agata s. Due Golfi
Marina del Cantone
Punta Campanella

Massa Lubrense

Gulf of Naples

Miseno

Procida

Capri

Ischia

Tyrrhenian Sea

Mediterranean Sea

Amalfi Coast

viii

"One never really knows how much one is being

touched by a place until one has left it."

—THOMAS JEFFERSON

Introduction

 $\mathcal{W}$ hat I thought would be a simple winter business trip to Rome many years ago was actually the start of my love affair with Italy. Just three months later I flew with a girlfriend to Florence, took a train to Genoa and embarked on an Italian cruise ship bound for Venice. By the time we reached Naples, a charming Italian man had convinced me that Capri was definitely more romantic to explore than the excavations of Pompeii. With a sense of adventure I accompanied him to the island where in a sizzling red Fiat convertible he showed me the most spectacular sights. Without realizing it, that day—like Ulysses, Homer's hero of ancient times—I fell under the spell of Capri.

Over the next couple of decades, though I traveled back to Italy on numerous occasions, it was mainly to the northern part of the country without once venturing beyond Rome. Then one day I came across a picture of a smiling young woman with long chestnut hair standing against the railing of a ship. Capri was in the background. I longed to see the island again, only this time my husband was to be my escort.

We rented an apartment in the small village of Furore along the Amalfi Coast and invited my sister and brother-in-law to share it with us. For a week we occupied the top floor of a beautiful house perched on a cliff with sweeping views of the Tyrrhenian Sea. We toured ruins, discovered picturesque towns and explored the isle of Capri. The scenery was breathtaking, the inhabitants welcoming and warmhearted, and the local cuisine delicious. At the end of our sojourn we found it difficult to leave.

Since my reacquaintance with the southern part of Italy I have made several trips to its various regions. However, captivated by the beautiful landscape and infused by the enthusiasm of the inhabitants of the Amalfi Coast, I keep finding my way back there by escorting small groups on week-long vacations. Seven days award travelers the time to absorb the culture and the flavors of the area, to make friends, or simply to delight in the sweet life.

Here then, on the eve of my departure with a group of ten women, I invite you to come along with us and discover your own reasons to plan your trip to the Amalfi Coast.

Prelude in Rome

*W*ith only a one-hour delay we landed at Fiumicino Airport outside of Rome in the middle of the afternoon. Although tired and jetlagged, I was relieved to finally reach our destination for, in contrast to our smooth transatlantic flight to Frankfurt, the connecting flight to Rome had been quite bumpy. To divert my attention while we were in the air, I kept glancing at the off-duty pilot across the aisle and imagining that we were together on an island somewhere in the Pacific. Of course it helped that he was extremely good-looking. Perhaps sensing my unease, the pilot turned a couple of times to offer me a reassuring smile. My travel companions seemed unfazed. They were eager to tackle the city.

After disembarking we rapidly collected our bags—luckily they were all there—passed through customs and proceeded to the arrival hall where Marco, our transfer driver, waited for us. He led us outside the terminal to a white minivan where, one by one, we relinquished our suitcases. Effortlessly, Marco loaded them into the rear of the van while we stepped inside. The drive from the airport to the center of Rome took less than forty minutes. Had we landed in the midst of the rush hour, it would have taken us twice as long to reach our hotel and my group would likely have learned some Italian gestures from frustrated drivers.

The reception clerks expeditiously checked us in for two nights. The women took the elevator to their rooms. I climbed the stairs, for I have a phobia of being trapped in an elevator. On the first floor above the lobby I wheeled my carry-on down a long narrow hallway to my room, went inside and inserted my electronic key into the slot above the light switches to turn the power on. Many European hotels now use this system to save energy.

The bedroom was small but cozy. The queen-size bed, covered with a damask spread in similar tones to the ruby and gold striped drapes, took up most of the space. Two puffy pillows laid invitingly against the headboard. On either side was a nightstand, and on the nearest one to the entrance were an alarm clock-radio and a telephone. An antique writing desk, topped by an ornate mirror, and a chair had been placed in a corner for the convenience of the guests and in the opposite corner stood a small refrigerator. Right above it, attached to the wall, was a flat screen television.

As soon as I sat on the bed, I heard a knock at the door. The hotel porter was delivering my suitcase.

"Permesso, may I?" He asked.

From the bedroom wall closet he pulled a luggage rack, lifted my suitcase onto it and turned around to ask me if I needed anything. I shook my head and he departed a couple of euros richer. Finally, I took off my shoes and slipped into the white slippers graciously provided by the hotel management.

When I stepped into the bathroom, I could not refrain from laughing. The shower stall was so tiny, it looked liked I would barely fit inside. The thought crossed my mind that there definitely was not enough room for some hanky-panky in such a tight space. Just as I grabbed my toiletry bag and fresh clothes from my suitcase the phone rang. I dropped everything on the bed and picked up the receiver. I immediately recognized the caller.

It was Danilo, my Italian agent, in charge of coordinating the local arrangements for my group. He was calling from Sorrento to welcome me to Italy and to reconfirm the following morning's pickup time from our hotel for our private tour of "Ancient Rome." After we finished discussing some minor changes in the upcoming week's program, I thanked him, hung up and headed to the bathroom. One hour later I was ready to reacquaint myself with the "Eternal City."

As I crossed the lobby, three of the women in my group stepped outside the hotel. It was their first time in Rome and I could tell, as I watched them laughingly stroll away, that they were truly elated to be here. Engrossed by the sights around them, they were totally oblivious to the fact that I was following them down the street.

Since we were only staying in Rome for a couple of days, I selected our four-star hotel primarily for its location: right in the heart of the capital, around the corner from the Piazza Venezia and close to the city's main shopping street, Via del Corso. I wanted to grant my travel companions every opportunity to see and experience as much as possible during their leisure time. In the past nine months we had met on several occasions at a local restaurant to discuss and prepare for the upcoming trip. During our "get togethers," I shared my knowledge of Rome and the Amalfi Coast, handed out maps and brochures and showed them hundreds of pictures. What the women had been anticipating for so long was finally happening. Only I knew that Rome was just the prelude to an amazing week ahead.

It was a little before five in the afternoon and I was pleasantly surprised that it was still quite warm in Rome. I took off my sweater and tied it around my waist. I reached the corner of Via IV Novembre and the Piazza Venezia, then turned left. I continued toward the Vittorio Emanuele Monument and joined a small group about to cross the piazza. There are very few street lights in Rome. Although pedestrians have the right-of-way, whenever possible, it is preferable to cross a street amid a crowd of people. It sounds selfish but it is a "matter of survival in a busy environment," as my husband would say. After all, he would know—he grew up in New York City. Unlike car drivers, who generally stop, impatient Vespa drivers always try to sneak by. Thankfully, they appear to be more intimidated by a wall of pedestrians than by a few individuals.

Dozens of tired-looking tourists were sitting on the bottom steps of the edifice that has been dubbed "The Wedding Cake" or "Typewriter" by the American troops who entered Rome on June 4, 1944. The gigantic white structure was built in the beginning of the twentieth century as a tribute to Vittorio Emanuele II of Savoy, the first king of the Unified Italy. Though the building is a little out of place in its surroundings, it is a landmark that visitors always remember.

As I reached the middle of the structure I glanced up. An impressive equestrian statue of the king stood several feet above me. Right below, at the base of the goddess Roma, was the tomb of an unknown soldier who died during the First World War. Guarding the tomb and the eternal flame were two soldiers. Behind me was a clear view of the entire Via del Corso, which runs in a straight line to the Obelisk of the Piazza del Popolo, the People's Square. At the beginning of the via the name Bonaparte was written on top of a four-story nineteenth-century building, reminding us that the French Emperor's family once lived in Rome. Napoleon Bonaparte's mother Letizia died in the city in 1836.

Leaving the monument, I strolled through the Via San Marco, which eventually turned into the Via delle Botteghe Oscure, in the direction of the "Area Sacra." I was devilishly tempted to step inside one of the beautiful fabric stores that lined the street, as table linens are one of my three weaknesses. The other two are books and Italian ceramics.

Reaching the Largo di Torre Argentina Square, I paused at the Roman excavation site to read the informational panel. According to the historians, this was the location where the Roman Senate used to convene, in the "Area Sacra" or "Sacred Place," and where Julius Caesar was killed in 44 B.C. Today only the remains of four temples from the Republican era are visible. They were discovered in 1920, during reconstruction, and are simply known as Temple A, B, C and D. I snapped a picture, crossed Corso Vittorio Emanuele and entered a large bookstore.

Since I had resisted buying fabric, I decided to indulge myself with the purchase of a couple of books. I was particularly interested in learning more about the small, coned houses in the region of Puglia called the Trulli. Instead I found myself wandering to the history section in search of a condensed version of Italy's history. This section practically dominated the entire second floor. I felt a little overwhelmed, almost dizzy, being surrounded by thousands of books. All the books ever written about Italy's past were right there, on shelves, on tables, even on the floor. Completely lost, I did not know where to begin my search.

Noticing my distress, a smiling young clerk stepped forward to offer her assistance. I explained, in my rusty Italian, what I was looking for. She quickly narrowed the selection down to four books, then left me alone to skim through them. Within minutes my decision was made and I headed downstairs to the CD-DVD department. Whenever I visit Italy, I never miss an opportunity to buy a newly-released album from one of my favorite Italian singers, as every time I listen to Italian songs at home or in my car I fantasize that I have escaped to some beautiful Italian country-side. I browsed through the different music styles, found what I was looking for, then walked over to the cashier's desk.

As I was waiting in line, someone behind me moved furtively closer to my person. Believing that I was about to be robbed, I quickly turned around and confronted the individual. I was looking at a tall and skinny young man, probably not older that fifteen. By the startled look on his face I knew that I had caught him. I told him angrily in Italian to step backward a few feet, then reverted to English. "Back off."

He grumbled something and strode away. He would not have gotten much out of my travel purse, I thought, since I carried most of my money in a pouch under my blouse. Still, the situation reminded me to be cautious. I paid for my purchases and walked out.

The sunlight was fading and the street lights were slowly coming on. From every direction Romans were leaving their offices to head home. For a few minutes I watched them running to catch already crowded buses. Farther down the street a couple in their mid-thirties, standing at the edge of the pavement, was engaged in a passionate kiss. Passersby were smiling. Drivers tapped their horns. But mindless of the people around them, the couple kept on kissing as if alone in the world. It was a beautiful sight, extremely romantic, and I was smiling too. I admit, I was a little envious!

Checking my watch, I realized that the Despar Grocery Store would soon close, so I hurried my steps. Last minute shoppers were grabbing items on their way to the checkout register as I entered the store. Unfamiliar with the layout of the little supermarket, it took me several minutes to find what I needed before joining the queue. On the rolling counter I placed a large bottle of water, a wrapped prosciutto ham sandwich and a bag of Italian grapes. The person behind me deposited four bottles of expensive wine. Intrigued, I turned sideways and saw a strikingly handsome Italian man dressed in a famous designer suit, a snowy white shirt and a pale lavender silk tie. I wanted to say, "Hello gorgeous, may I join your party?" But that would have been a little too forward on my part, so I just smiled at him. I must be getting extremely tired, I thought. Time to get back to the hotel.

Still needing to purchase a phone card, I remembered that just a block away from the hotel, a small tobacco store was selling them. With the grocery bag in my arms, I headed in that direction. Inside the store, a couple of tourists carrying heavy backpacks were arguing with the clerk over some change. I waited patiently for them to resolve their issue, then decided to interrupt them. Ready to collapse, I placed a ten euro bill on the counter and ordered two five euro international phone cards. The clerk handed me the cards and I stepped out.

In my hotel room, I immediately noticed that a chocolate candy had been placed on one of the bed pillows, compliments of the management. I ate the prosciutto sandwich and the sweet treat, then readied myself for bed. The minute I closed my eyes I fell instantly asleep. At three o'clock in the morning, however, I was wide awake. I turned on the TV and flipped through the channels. As nothing caught my attention, I turned it off and began to read the Italian history book instead. Eventually, with the bedside lamp still burning, I dozed off for another two hours.

It was still dark outside when I awoke. Ready to take on the new day, I climbed out of bed, showered and dressed. Since it was too early for breakfast, I decided to walk to the Trevi Fountain. I pulled a long sweater from my suitcase, grabbed my camera and left the hotel. Outside, the streets were empty. Occasionally a car or a bus drove by. The sound of their wheels on the cobblestone pavement reverberated in an otherwise silent city and, in the far distance, the wailing sound of an ambulance could be heard. A fall sunrise blanketed the Eternal City in a glorious morning glow and I was glad that I had ventured out to witness it.

While I walked the short distance between the hotel and the Trevi Fountain, I counted how often I had seen it since my first visit to Rome. Each time the small square around the fountain had been crowded with hundreds of tourists. I hoped that in the early morning I would have the most popular Roman sight entirely to myself. When I reached it, I was not disappointed. Except for a handful of city workers busy sweeping up the coins, I was virtually alone.

For the next fifteen minutes I studied the various architectural elements of the illustrious eighteenth-century Baroque Fontana di Trevi, which to my greatest pleasure was still illuminated. The water basin was littered with coins thrown in by tourists wishing to ensure their return to Rome. There must be some truth to the legend; I was living proof. I made my first wish decades ago and had returned countless times to Rome. Not wanting to jinx my good luck, I turned around and, with my right hand over my left shoulder, tossed a small coin into the fountain. After one final glance at the fountain, I strolled away.

Gradually, as I walked back to the hotel, Rome came to life. Freshly baked breads and pastries were being delivered to a small boutique hotel. Newspaper and magazine stacks were dropped off in front of a tobacco store. Men in dark suits appeared on their way to the nearest caffè bar to enjoy their first espresso before going to work.

Rounding the corner of a church, I nearly collided with a jogger. He mumbled an excuse, then continued on as I crossed the street to withdraw money from an automated teller machine. Just as I finished my transaction, I heard the sound of approaching horses. A black motorcar surrounded by a group of cavalry men, dressed in pristine green uniforms and feathered helmets, was slowly coming up the street. It was an impressive sight. For a brief moment, I pondered who could be inside the vehicle. Must be somebody important, I guessed. I fumbled with my camera, but by the time I was ready to snap a picture, the cortège had already moved on.

Back at the hotel I went straight to the breakfast room. A perky young woman greeted me in English. Smiling, she asked for my room number before directing me to a large buffet. I picked up a plate, helped myself to some bread, scrambled eggs and cold cuts, then searched for a table. I scanned the room. Several persons were enjoying their breakfast, but as none of them belonged to my group, I just sat by myself. I had not realized how hungry I was until minutes later, when I looked at my plate; it was empty. After sipping a second cappuccino, I went back to my room.

)(

Two hours later I was standing in the middle of the Forum with my group. Our tour guide Sara, a history professor with a major in archeology, was talking to us from four feet away. Yet I was scarcely paying attention. Somehow her narration had triggered the memory of an event I had witnessed four years earlier. As Sara turned our attention to the Vesta Temple, I found myself thinking about the time I stumbled across a large gathering of people dressed up as Roman citizens.

It was at the end of April. I was strolling along Via di San Gregorio in the direction of the Circus Maximus when I heard someone on a loudspeaker announcing, "Five minutes." Something was about to start. Was it a game or some kind of demonstration? I was curious. As I rounded the corner of the Palatine Hill, I thought that I was dreaming. Lined up on top of the knoll in the center of the ancient hippodrome were hundreds of people dressed in Roman costumes. I was puzzled. Perhaps an Italian director was filming a scene from his new period movie and those were the actors.

When I reached the front of the line, I walked up to an Italian gentleman dressed in contemporary clothing and asked him what was happening.

"We are celebrating the birth of Rome." He smiled.

"How wonderful."

"Rome was founded on April 21 in 753 B.C.," he continued. "Every year, fans of Ancient Rome mark the anniversary with three days of festivities. Today, which happens to be the last day, they will march from here to the Coliseum and then along Via dei Fori Imperiali to the Piazza di Venezia."

For someone who loves pageantry, I could not believe my luck. Although there were thousands of tourists in Rome, there were but a few of them here. Looking around, I estimated that, besides a few cameramen and journalists, there were maybe only a hundred spectators in the Circus Maximus that morning. Those spectators had probably wandered on the scene just like I did. For once I did not have to fight a crowd. I had a front-row seat!

As we waited, I glanced over at a group of legionnaires, dressed in authentic accouterments from head to toe. They wore helmets, shining cuirasses over short red tunics and leather sandals. In one hand each held a sword and, in the other, a long shield. Since I was showing a special interest in their outfits, the gentleman offered to enlighten me.

"In front of the group is the Aquilifer. He carries the symbol of the legion: the gilded *aquila* (eagle). The one behind him is the Signifer. He carries the *signum*, the military emblem of the unit—which is composed of a number of *philarae* or disks mounted on a pole and topped with a replica of a human hand surrounded by a laurel wreath. The signum is the most recognizable icon of Ancient Rome. Both men are wearing mail armor instead of a breastplate called *lorica segmentata*. The Aquilifer is wearing the pelt of a *lupa* or wolf over his helmet and armor, and the Signifier is wearing the hide of a bear to show Rome's domination over nature."

Delighted by his explanation, I encouraged him to continue.

"At the head of the group of men is the Centurion, easily recognizable by his crested helmet. He is wearing a *subarmillis* (skirt made of leather straps) over a white tunic and a medallioned cuirass on top of a chain mail. His legs are protected by golden braces," he added. I was amazed by how authentic they looked.

While perusing his military uniform, one of the legionnaires noticed that the leather thong of his right sandal had come undone.

Since he was standing in an awkward position, he turned to his companion for assistance. The other legionnaire, a heavyset man, handed him his shield and sword, then bent down to retie the lace. Well, this might be interesting I thought. For, in the process, his tunic had traveled higher above his thighs, exposing more flesh. It appeared that I was about to find out what the Roman legionnaires wore under their tunics. Did they practice "going commando" like the Scots, I wondered. Grinning, I readied my camera. Regretfully, just at that moment the speaker announced the start of the parade and my line of vision became obstructed by a group of dancers. Oh well, some things are best left unseen.

I turned and transferred my attention to the Corteo Storico, the Historical Cortège. Leading the parade was Julius Caesar. Immediately after came the Senators in their white togas, the Patricians (Roman nobles), their wives, the Vestal Virgins, half a dozen gladiators, musicians, Egyptian dancers and Cleopatra carried by slaves. The next groups of people were introduced by the gentleman at my side. Emperor Augustus and Livia were followed by the Praetorian Guard (the Emperor's personal army), the Britannia Legion, a handful of dancers, a few archers and the Germania Legion.

Suddenly a touch on my arm interrupted my daydream. Sara, our guide, was looking at me. "Are you okay?" she asked anxiously. Glancing around, I discovered that I was still standing in front of the Vesta Temple while the rest of my group had moved on. Smiling, I quickly apologized and assured her that I was fine. We resumed our walk and she continued to identify the different structures as we moved along toward the Forum's exit and to the Coliseum. There we lingered for a short time before we finally boarded a minivan.

Close to one o'clock in the afternoon we returned to the hotel. While I looked for my room key, I asked my companions for their comments on Sara and our morning tour. They had thoroughly enjoyed their first history lesson thanks to the expertise of our guide. Now they were ready for some leisure time and looking forward to some shopping. Before we went our separate ways, I suggested that we meet in the lobby around seven to share a dinner together.

My plan for the afternoon was to lose myself for a few hours in Trastevere, the old district on the west bank of the Tiber and the most picturesque neighborhood of Rome. Since it involved public transportation, I asked the reception clerk which bus to take and where to buy the tickets.

After purchasing the tickets from the tobacco shop nearby, I made my way to the bus stop. Within minutes, the bus arrived and I hopped on board. I checked with the driver to make sure that he was actually driving to the location I wanted to see and, when he nodded, I claimed the nearest seat. Half an hour later, he shouted, "Trastevere," and I got off the bus.

Literally translated, the name "Trastevere" comes from the Latin *Trans Tiberium*, meaning "Across the Tiber." In ancient times, the community was located outside the city limits. Many important Roman figures built villas in Trastevere including Julius Caesar, who shared his with his mistress Cleopatra. Immigrants from the East—mainly Greeks, Syrians and Jews—also settled in the area. In the time of Emperor Augustus, it was a densely populated community and a melting pot of cultures, customs and cuisine. Under the emperor Aurelian, large walls were constructed around the community to incorporate it with the city of Rome. Over the course of time, Trastevere continued to develop its own character— a character that has been described in recent years as "authentically Roman"—and I was anxious to discover it.

For the next three hours, I meandered through a maze of narrow cobbled streets and alleys, listening to the banter of the locals, the laughter of teenagers walking home from school, the occasional purr of mopeds and the periodic sounds of church bells. Blessedly absent were the hordes of tourists. I found myself entirely captivated by the old Trastevere. Somehow the neighborhood had managed to retain a medieval atmosphere with russet and ochre building facades draped in ivy, freshly laundered clothing hanging from balconies, unique artisan boutiques and quaint little restaurants.

By the time I reached the Piazza Santa Maria in Trastevere, I was feeling the effects of jetlag again. I had also developed a little appetite. Dinnertime was still too far away but I needed some food and a strong coffee. Scanning the area, I located a small outdoor café, strode across the piazza, and sat down at a table where I could watch people go by.

Just as I grabbed the menu left on the table, a very tall and thin waiter in his late twenties appeared. "Sorry, we only serve ice cream in the afternoon," he said. So much for food, I thought, and simply ordered a coffee. He flashed me a smile and walked away. He reappeared a couple minutes later with my coffee and a small cookie. Before I could thank him, he had already moved on to serve another table a few feet away. Two very lovely young women were sitting at the table. By their white sneakers, I guessed that they were Americans and, by the books piled in front of them, that they were probably attending the private American University in Trastevere. Blondes in their early twenties, they reminded me of my nieces.

Leaning back in my chair, I watched them smile flirtatiously at the waiter as they each ordered an Italian soda. The waiter slowly walked away, but returned with their drinks in the blink of an eye. Instead of moving on, he dallied. I searched for a handkerchief to blow my nose and to hide a smile while I observed them. The young women kept grinning playfully while he talked to them teasingly. He was very good-looking with a sun-tanned face and dark eyes full of mischief. My nieces would probably have called him an ice cream—their private code name for a heartthrob. Their game of seduction went on for several minutes, until he was hailed by a group of newcomers. Reluctantly, he stepped away from the young ladies' table.

My gaze drifted over to the piazza and the octagonal fountain. Dozens of young people were sitting on the steps around its base. I gathered that the fountain was a popular meeting place. An Italian man in his mid-forties, impeccably dressed in a dark gray suit, was pacing in front of the fountain. Do Italian men ever wear anything other than suits? If white sneakers are an indication of the American culture, then suits are definitely an Italian one. He was holding his cell phone with one hand and gesturing with the other. He was too far away for me to eavesdrop on his conversation, but I could tell by his gestures that he was quite upset. Without sounds, he was actually funny to watch. I even recognized some of the hand signals. My only regret was that I did not have a camera to film him. I lingered awhile, then rose.

Leaving the outdoor café behind, I strolled to the opposite end of the square and entered the Church of Santa Maria in Trastevere, believed to be the oldest worship place in Rome. Although the church was originally constructed in 4 A.D., the present structure was built in the twelfth century. Once inside, I gazed at the beautiful mosaics and admired the granite columns that lined the nave. As I approached the altar, I noted that it was surrounded on three sides by several large bouquets of white carnations and red roses, while two red upholstered chairs had been positioned in front of it. The church was prepared for a wedding, I thought.

Just then, as if to confirm my guess, a young woman stepped from behind the altar and began to sing the first verse of "Ave Maria." Pleasantly surprised by the unexpected rehearsal, I sat down on one of the benches and listened to her melodious voice exploding in the church.

After exiting the church, I walked back to the bus stop. At the hotel, the reception clerk handed me three messages. Five of the women in my group had decided to skip dinner. They were too tired. I understood; I felt the same way. However, the easiest way to adjust quickly to the local time zone is by trying to stay awake as late as possible. Personally, talking and eating usually do the trick.

At seven, I was more than ready to have dinner. The small bag of M&M's I had found in my suitcase had barely satisfied my hunger. I was ravenous. Half of my group was waiting for me when I stepped into the small lobby. Grateful for their companionship, I told the women that I was going to introduce them to my favorite restaurant in Rome. I assured them that it was only a short distance away from the hotel. Delighted and in complete agreement, they followed me outside.

Vincenzo, the headwaiter at the Ristorante Abruzzi, greeted us at the door. I was glad to see him again and asked for a table for six inside, for it was a little chilly. Smiling, he motioned to a table in the corner of the main dining room and asked, *"Va Bene?"*

"Si," I answered. He helped us settle down, then disappeared. Almost immediately, he reappeared with multilingual menus, a basket filled with a variety of homemade breads, and a small dish of olives. I asked Vincenzo to bring us a liter of the house red wine and a carafe of water. By the time he returned, we had studied the menu and were ready to order. We all started out with some *antipasti*, hors d'oeuvres, then followed with a pasta dish.

Our food was served and as we ate the delicious meals, we discussed our afternoon. I told them about Trastevere and they related their shopping experiences. They particularly enjoyed peeking in the windows of the exquisite boutiques around the Spanish Steps, the Pantheon and the Piazza Navona.

After clearing our dinner plates, Vincenzo asked us if we cared for any dessert. I declined. I had savored every bite of my *Lasagna al forno* and could not have eaten another thing. Three of the women ordered an ice cream and the other two a tiramisu. Before turning away, Vincenzo smiled and winked at me. I chuckled, suspecting that he was going to bring us a surprise.

My suspicion was confirmed when he came back with two large bottles, one of Amaretto and one of Sambuca, and six small glasses. My companions gave me a questioning look.

"Now you know why this is my favorite restaurant. Help yourselves and I guarantee that you will have pleasant dreams tonight." I laughed.

After we had filled our glasses close to the rim, one of the women lifted hers and waited for us to follow suit. "To our Amalfi Adventure," she said, which was immediately chorused by the rest of the group.

This is a moment to remember, I thought. I took a sip from my glass and grimaced. The fiery mint sambuca slid down my throat to my stomach, all the way to my toes. That was some powerful after-dinner drink. We refilled our glasses a couple of times, settled the bill, and retraced our steps back to the hotel.

That night I fell asleep thinking how lucky I was to be going back to the Amalfi Coast.

Day One

Welcome to Campania

Still luxuriating in bed, I turn my head and gaze at the alarm-radio on top of the night stand. The illuminated clock reads five-thirty. Already I have been awake for an hour. Grateful for seven hours of uninterrupted sleep, but realizing that I will not manage to fall asleep again, I climb out of bed and head for the bathroom. At seven I am ready to tackle breakfast. I need coffee—a cup of freshly-brewed strong Italian coffee with steamed milk—or rather, a cappuccino.

Twenty minutes later, while nursing my second cappuccino, four of my travel companions step inside the breakfast room. One of the women approaches my table. "Finally, the day we have all been waiting for has arrived. It took forever." She smiles. Her delightful enthusiasm for the trip, a retirement gift from the company she worked at for nearly thirty-five years, had been present in each of our conversations. In anticipation, she had attended night classes to learn basic Italian, listened to CDs while driving back and forth to her job in the suburbs, and purchased several new outfits.

"Yes, I agree. In contrast, the upcoming week will fly by at the speed of a falcon. We will have to make every moment count," I remark, smiling back. She nods, then heads for the buffet.

After a third cappuccino, I return to my room just in time to hear the phone ring. In the dark, I rush to pick up the receiver, hitting my left foot against the bed frame in the process. The concierge is calling to inform me that our transportation has just pulled up in front of the hotel. I check my watch. It is eight o'clock. I quickly gather my last remaining articles of clothing and place them in my suitcase. Before closing the zipper, I inspect the room and bathroom to make sure that I have not accidentally left any items behind. Grabbing my shoulder bag and carry-on, I close the door and descend to the lobby. I ask the friendly reception clerk for assistance with my suitcase and exit the hotel to greet our driver.

It is a little nippy and windy this morning. I glance at the sky. Not a cloud. Warm temperatures have been forecast for the afternoon.

A woman in her mid-forties, dressed in a pair of black pants and a sky-blue shirt, steps off a thirty-three passenger bus and walks toward me to introduce herself. Her name is Francesca. She left her hometown of Naples at five o'clock this morning to pick up our small group of eleven women and transfer us to the Amalfi Coast. Thankful that she safely made it to Rome on time, I hand her my carry-on and return to the lobby to check on my fellow travelers.

They are coming down in the elevator one by one, dropping off their keys at the reception desk and exiting the hotel, rolling their suitcases and carry-ons behind them. After leaving their luggage with our driver, who quickly stores it in the cargo section, the women climb on board. And just as Francesca has nearly completed the loading process, the hotel porter shows up with my suitcase, which I nearly forgot about. I make one final check with the reception clerk to confirm that everyone has returned their keys, then step inside the bus.

"There will be no fighting for window or aisle seats," I announce loudly. "We have the entire bus to ourselves. There is definitely plenty of room for you to stretch, so go ahead and spread out," I add cheerfully. A chorus of laughter explodes as everyone gets up and moves about. I have always wanted to say those exact words, for there was a time in my life when I had hoped to become a flight attendant. Francesca slides back into her driver's seat as I claim mine next to the bus entrance. I sit down and buckle my seat belt. Our Amalfi adventure is about to begin!

After driving through Via Veneto, the Roman "Rodeo Drive," the Villa Borghese Park and one of the oldest plush residential areas of the city, Francesca reaches the entrance to the GRA.

The GRA, acronym for the Grande Raccordo Anulare—literally the Greater Ring Road—is the forty-two-mile circumference motorway surrounding Rome. Also nicknamed *Il Raccordo* or the "Junction" by the Romans, its official number is the A90.

Several miles later, she connects with the intersection to the A1 Firenze-Napoli and drives on, heading south, toward Napoli-Reggio Calabria. For several miles, the scenery can be described as a series of residential neighborhoods of houses, tall apartment buildings, manufacturing complexes and small farms, until finally we exit the outskirts of Rome and reach the open countryside of Lazio.

The bus is buzzing with chatter. I reach for the microphone, switch it on, test it with a light tap, then say: *"Buongiorno,"* the Italian word for greetings, which is quickly repeated. Not satisfied with the weak response, I repeat it a little louder and, again, it is echoed, but more assertively this time. This is fun! I introduce our driver, Francesca, then proceed to review the day's agenda: drive to Pompeii with a stop en route, then, after a three-hour tour of the excavations, we will continue on to our hotel. I pause for a moment to organize my thoughts and, after taking a deep breath, I continue.

"Rome is located in the region of Lazio, and the Amalfi Coast in the neighboring region of Campania. The region of Campania, with the Tyrrhenian Sea to the west, shares a border with the southern regions of Molise, Apulia or Puglia, and Basilicata.

"Campania—which means countryside or the 'Region of fields' in Latin—is, with a population close to six million, the second most populated region in Italy. The majority of the inhabitants live in and around Naples, its capital. The total area of 5,272 square miles includes the islands of Capri, Ischia and Procida. Campania is divided into five provinces: Napoli, Avellino, Benevento, Caserta and Salerno. The people of Campania have a common history and are generally known as the Campani. The people of Naples, however, refer to themselves as 'Napoletani' and the people of the province of Salerno as the 'Salernitani.' To understand them, one needs to know their tumultuous history.

"The first known inhabitants of Campania were three defined groups: the Osci, the Aurunci and the Ausoni. They belonged to the Ancient people of Italy who all spoke the Oscan language. In the eighth century B.C. the Samnites, another Oscan tribe from Central Italy, moved to the region. During that same century and the next, Greek colonists, in search of new fertile lands and new commercial outlets for their products, started to settle along the coastline of Southern Italy and in Sicily. The Greeks, who came from mainland Greece, Asia Minor and the Aegean islands, brought with them their culture and religion. They cultivated the land, produced wine and olive oil, created exquisite jewelry and painted beautiful vases and pottery that they exported along with textiles and weapons. They built several theaters and temples such as those in Paestum. The Romans often referred to the southern tip of Italy and Sicily as the Greater Greece, or *Magna Grecia* in Latin, for it was densely inhabited by Greeks. Their colonization of Campania and of the other surrounding areas brought prosperity to the region. This eventually attracted the attention of its northern conquering neighbor, the republican state of Rome.

"In the third century B.C. the Greek settlers tried to retain their independence. During the Pyrrhic War (280–275 B.C.) they engaged the Romans in a series of battles. With the assistance of mercenary troops under the command of Pyrrhus, Greek ruler of the Kingdom of Epirus (present-day Albania), the Greeks fought the Roman armies but could not beat them. Consequentially, Campania was entirely absorbed into the Roman Empire and Latinized.

"For the next one hundred years, during the Punic Wars (264 to 241 B.C., 218 to 201 B.C., 149 to 146 B.C.), which derives from the Latin term *Punici* for the Carthaginians and Phoenicians, the Greeks fought to regain control over Southern Italy and Sicily, this time with the help of the Carthaginians. However, they were unsuccessful and, in the end, totally defeated and devastated. The southern regions lost their importance.

"As a result, the main towns started to decline, losing their opulence. Farms owned by absentee Roman landlords using slave labor instead of peasants were run into the ground. Such was the desolation that in 73 B.C. a former gladiator named Spartacus started a slave uprising, which was initially successful, but eventually would be crushed. A couple of centuries later, Campania would be turned into a playground for Roman emperors and rich patricians.

"After the collapse of the Roman Empire, the following seven hundred years are very obscure. Certain parts of Campania were ruled by Germanic Goths and Lombards, while others and the town of Naples were governed by the Eastern Roman Empire, also called the Byzantine Empire after its capital Byzantium. Byzantium was the Greek name of the city that would become Constantinople and later Istanbul, in modern-day Turkey."

Pausing for a few minutes, I realize that it is very quiet in the bus. I probably have lulled everyone to sleep by now. I should take a peek. Nah, I'll just continue until I hear them snoring. Switching the microphone on again, I resume my narration.

"In the eleventh century, a Lombard prince and warlord hired Norman mercenaries to drive the Byzantines out. Known for their military prowess, the Normans swiftly won and reunified Campania. Their leader proclaimed himself king, and his descendants went on to gradually take control over the remainder of Southern Italy and Sicily. For the next 100 years or so, under the Norman rulers, Campania knew a second period of prosperity and stability. During his reign, King Renee II moved the capital from Naples to Palermo and the multiracial and polyglot people who inhabited the 'Kingdom of Sicily,' as it was then called, knew a time of religious freedom and enjoyed a great economic boom. Many magnificent cathedrals, monuments and castles were built and trade with overseas countries increased.

"With the marriage of Constance, the last legitimate descendant of the Norman dynasty, the kingdom of Sicily passed on to the powerful German house of Hohenstaufen of Swabia and eventually to her son Frederic II. While always in direct conflict with the Popes of Rome, Frederic established the Kingdom's laws, founded the University of Naples and improved the middle class. After his death, Pope Clement IV managed to put Charles Anjou, brother of the French king Louis IX (Saint Louis), victorious against the Swabians at the battle of Benevento in 1265, on the throne, and the capital was moved from Palermo to Naples. Under Charles' reign, Naples flourished. The port was enlarged and the Castel Nuovo

(New Castle) was built. While Charles and his descendants were concentrating on planning the conquest of the Byzantine Empire, King Pedro of Aragon seized the opportunity to capture Sicily. The kingdom was split into two halves.

"Wars between the two went on for years until, in 1442, the Angevins, burdened by political and royal scandals, lost against the forces of the Aragon monarch, Alfonso the Magnificent. King Charles VIII of France tried to regain control in 1495 by blasting his way in, but in the end had to retreat. In 1504, King Ferdinand the Catholic, married to Isabelle of Castile, united the kingdom of the Two Sicilies with Spain. For the next two hundred years Campania was ruled by the Aragon monarchs who appointed Viceroys, since they preferred to remain in Madrid. The Spanish monarchs lost the kingdom to the Austrians during the War of Spanish Succession, but reclaimed it in 1734. King Charles of Bourbon restored Sicily and Naples as an independent state.

"In 1800, having won a decisive victory against the Austrian Army in the north, the emperor Napoleon proceeded to a full occupation of Italy. He sent his brother Joseph to rule the south and appointed him King of Naples. He later replaced him with General Joachim Murat, his sister Caroline's husband. With the fall of Napoleon, Campania was once again ruled by a Bourbon monarch, this time until 1860, when an uprising to reunite all the Italian states finally succeeded. The unification of Italy actually took place at Teano, a border town between Lazio and Campania, on October 26, 1860, during a meeting between Guiseppe Garibaldi, the liberator of the two Sicilies and King Vittorio Emanuele II, elected ruler of Northern Italy.

"To summarize, for the last thousand years, Campania has been ruled by the Normans, the Germans (Swabians), the French (Angevins), the Spanish (Aragonese), the Austrians, the French

(Napoleon) and the Spanish (Bourbons) again until the reuni-
fication of Italy in 1860. Today, thousands of Germans, French,
Austrians and Spanish continue to invade, but only for a short
time. No wars are fought, as they just come for a nice vacation."

※

After the history dissertation, I turn off the microphone, reat-
tach it to the dashboard, pull out the Michelin map from my bag
and try to pinpoint our location. We have been traveling on the
A1 for the last two hours, heading south toward Naples and, with
every wheel turn, we are getting closer to our destination.

For the next thirty miles, I chat with Francesca. Since her English is limited, we communicate in Italian. She is quite a chauffeur,
I remark. She drives this large bus like it is a small Fiat. Her eyes
are constantly focused on the road, which is a good thing, as suddenly the driver of a black Volkswagen Jetta cuts her off sharply.
Fishtailing, as it is commonly called, is a move practiced by many
European drivers.

While sitting in the front of the bus, I watch drivers change lanes
constantly without using any turn signals. When I remarked upon
it to Aronne, the chauffeur for my last two groups on the Amalfi
Coast, he told me with a twinkle in his eyes that southern drivers
read minds. "Imagine that!" I marveled and burst into laughter.

It is intriguing to watch how some people actually manage to
drive on the dividing lines for miles, trying to decide which way
to go, left or right—a maneuver I have only seen in the south of
Italy, never in the north. Mercedes and BMWs are zooming by us,
their drivers going faster than the normal speed limit, obviously
unafraid of getting a traffic ticket.

Francesca is getting off the freeway. Instead of stopping at one
of the crowded and overpriced rest stops, she is driving us to the

quaint little restaurant and self-service bar of the Hotel Liola, located right across from the freeway's exit toll booths, in the small town of Castrocielo. It is a friendly place where we can get something to drink and eat, and I confess that I am looking forward to a coffee and a small *panino* even though I had a full breakfast. Francesca is pulling into the hotel's driveway and parking next to a large tour bus. We quickly alight and head for the entrance. Thankfully, as we enter, the tour bus passengers are exiting, leaving the restaurant entirely to us.

As I step up to the cashier, I realize how good it feels to stretch my legs. In Italy it is customary to pay in advance for food and beverages if one will consume them standing up. I turn over the receipts to the barista who, after tearing them, promptly sets a large cup of coffee with cream on the counter, grabs a ham and cheese panino and wraps it in a napkin before placing it on a plate in front of me. I move to the end of the counter and watch my companions go through the same process. Some of the women are walking around the little gift shop section of the restaurant. Besides wines and limoncello liqueur, the Hotel Liola sells candies, travel guides and local souvenirs. During my last stop I bought a wonderful book here: *The Guide to the Archeological Site Pompeii* (Marius Editions). Unfortunately, the English version is out of print. I glance at my watch—our twenty minute stop is over. We step outside and reboard the bus.

The border crossing between Lazio and Campania is about ninety miles from Rome, or just a few miles south of the town of Cassino. A mile and a half west of Cassino, perched on a rocky hill, is the monastery of Monte Cassino, which was founded by Benedicte of Norcia in 529 A.D. In Monte Cassino, where he lived and died, he wrote the Benedicte rules that became the foundation for the Benedictine Order. Originally built on the site of a temple dedicated to Apollo, the Abbey was destroyed and rebuilt in 581, 883 and 1389, each time larger and grander. In 1799, the site was sacked by Napoleon and in 1866 it became a national monument after the dissolution of the Italian monasteries.

On February 15, 1944, and for the next couple of days, under the assumption that German troops were stationed at the monastery, Monte Cassino was bombed by the US air forces and reduced to rubble. Three hundred monks and many civilians who had taken shelter at the Abbey were killed. Weeks prior, thanks to the foresight of two German officers, thousands of documents, books, ancient manuscripts and art treasures had been removed to the Vatican in Rome in order to prevent them from being destroyed. The battle for Cassino and Monte Cassino, also known as the battle for Rome, resulted in many casualties: 54,000 Allied and 20,000 Germans. The Americans are buried in the nearby town of Anzio, on the Tyrrhenian sea.

After the war the Abbey of Monte Cassino was totally rebuilt. Funded entirely by the Italian state, the reconstruction took ten years to accomplish. Though visitors are welcomed and can also attend masses, they need to be respectfully dressed and are requested to keep silent during their visit. No pictures are allowed.

As we continue along the A1 we pass Caserta, where Bourbon King Charles VII started the construction of his palace in 1752. The king had selected the wooded valley at the foot of Mount Virgo as the perfect location for his royal residence while on a visit to Caserta Vecchia—called simply Caserta at the time. Built to rival the Palace of Versailles, it took nearly one hundred years to complete. Some 3,000 workers participated in the construction of the Palace. Among them were people from Caserta and the surrounding area as well as convicts sentenced to hard labor and slaves kidnapped from the coast of Africa. During the construction process, many free laborers migrated from the old town to their job site, which resulted in the creation of a new Caserta. Over time, the population of Caserta Vecchia, as it was renamed, dwindled to a small number.

Easily seen from the freeway, the eighteenth century Palace dominates the town. It has 1200 rooms—including summer and winter apartments for the royal family—1790 windows, thirty-four stairways, four inner courtyards, an art gallery, an outdoor theater and a church. The stunning park behind the royal residence includes formal gardens, fountains and waterfalls. The entrance to the Royal Palace is one of the numerous locations where scenes from Star Wars Episodes I and II were filmed. Now the property of the Italian government, the grandiose palace and the magnificent gardens are open to the public.

The hill town of Caserta Vecchia, located just five miles from Caserta, is a gem for people who are interested in medieval architecture. The town and its castle were built by the Lombards on the site of Roman ruins in the eighth century. In the eleventh century, the Normans invaded. Under the new conquerors the town prospered. A cathedral was built as well as several Romanesque-styled houses. In the fifteenth century the town started to gradually decline under the Aragonese regime, and two centuries later Caserta Vecchia was practically abandoned by its inhabitants for the construction of the royal palace.

The town's misfortune suspended it in time. Caserta Vecchia is now one of Italy's best preserved medieval towns and a lovely tourist attraction, especially in the summer when locals present performances in front of the cathedral.

On the eastern side of the freeway, in the distance, a portion of the Appian Way is visible. In Roman times this road, flanked on both sides by tall parasol-shaped cypress trees, was strategically the most important road as it connected Rome to Brindisi, in the region of Puglia.

We must be getting closer to Naples, for suddenly Mount Vesuvius is looming in front of us. Although I have seen it several times, I'm still overwhelmed by its size. Soaring 4,203 feet to the sky above the Gulf of Naples, the mountain dominates the landscape. My first glimpse of the volcano was years ago, on the morning the Italian cruise ship Flavia docked in Naples harbor. I had studied the sleeping volcano in my high-school geography and history classes and had stared at a dozen pictures and drawings over the years. But nothing can compare to actually seeing it in person.

There are two other active volcanoes in Italy, Etna and Stromboli, both located in Sicily. But Vesuvius is the most famous one, known worldwide for its eruption in 79 A.D. that buried Pompeii and Herculaneum. Vesuvio as the Italians call it, was formed at least 25,000 years ago as a result of the collision between the African and Eurasian tectonic plates. It has erupted at least once every century since that fatal date, six times in the eighteenth century, eight times in the nineteenth century, and in 1906, 1929 and 1944. What we see today is the result of those eruptions and the accumulation of the debris.

The last eruption, witnessed by American pilots and filmed by the Allied forces while they were liberating Naples, destroyed the *funiculare,* the cable car, which had been built in 1880 to carry passengers on the final thousand feet to the summit. The lyrics "Funiculi Funicula," written by journalist and poet Peppino Turco and set to music by Italian composer Luigi Denza, were created that same year to celebrate the opening of the funicular. The song, first introduced at the Hotel Quisisana, which no longer exists, in Castellammare di Stabia, Denza's hometown, is now one of the most recognized Neapolitan melodies. It has since found its way into the repertoire of famous Italian tenors such as Mario Lanza, Luciano Pavarotti and Andrea Bocelli.

Mount Vesuvius was declared a national park in 1995. From its summit, open to the public, visitors can enjoy magnificent views of the Bay of Naples and the vast land of Campania. Hikers may also descend into the interior of the crater with a certified guide. While the volcano is dormant, seismic activities are being monitored by the Vesuvio Observatory in Naples.

Construction within a certain perimeter of the mountain is not allowed and evacuation procedures have been established in case of an eruption. If it does occur, however, it is unlikely that everybody will be saved in time. People living within a 4.3 mile radius of the mouth of the volcano, referred to as the "Red Zone," have been offered financial incentives to move away but they have refused. They prefer to live in Vesuvio's shadow rather than relocate.

As we connect with the A3, heading south in the direction of Reggio Calabria, we find ourselves driving beside the Gulf of Naples. Further afield, out in the Tyrrhenian Sea at the edge of the Sorrento Peninsula, the isle of Capri, basking under the sun, has caught my eye. It feels wonderful to be gazing once again at this beautiful panoramic scenery. This reminds me of another famous Neapolitan song titled "O' Sole Mio" which translates literally to "My Sun." It was composed in 1898 by two natives of Naples: the poet Giovanni Capurro and singer-songwriter Eduardo di Capua. The English version of the song, "It's Now or Never," is also well known, having been recorded by many singers—most notably by Elvis Presley.

Along the bay that bears its name lies the large city of Naples, or Napoli, from the Greek *Neapolis* meaning new town, the capital of Campania. With a population of one million inhabitants in 45.3 square miles, Naples is the third largest city in Italy after

Rome and Milan. The Greater Naples, including the suburbs, has a population of close to four million. At present we are breezing through several of those suburbs and gazing at small tended gardens and large greenhouses that are lining both sides of the freeway.

The advantage of living in the proximity of a volcano is that you get a rich fertile soil and excellent drainage—perfect for growing vegetables, fruits and flowers. Benefiting from a favorable climate, the region of Campania grows a large variety of agricultural produce that is exported to other regions of Italy. Every year tons of goods are being processed through the docks of the port of Naples, the largest in Southern Italy, while thousands of people come and go through its passenger facilities.

The Napoletani live mostly in apartments—some having a frontal view of the volcano and others of the Gulf of Naples. They still hang their laundry to dry on their balconies as electricity is too costly in Italy to use in drying clothes. It's nearly four times more expensive than in the US. Only a small number of families own electric clothes dryers, and by the large number of satellite dishes encroaching everywhere, it appears that they are addicted to television like the rest of the people in the world. We pass the exit sign for Ercolano, the Italian version of the Latin name *Herculaneum,* on the outskirts of Naples. We whiz by Torre del Greco, where beautiful cameos are still being manufactured in the traditional way. Finally, the sign for Pompeii appears and Francesca exits the freeway.

Pompeii versus Herculaneum

$\mathcal{A}$t the end of the A3 off-ramp, Francesca turns left toward the town of Pompeii. We will stop for a three-hour visit of the Scavi, the excavations of the ancient Roman city. The main road to the Scavi is always crowded with a long line of cars and tour buses. Today is no exception. Although there are plenty of parking lots to choose from, a local man is trying to steer the cars to his lot with the promise of "free parking" in exchange for buying a lunch at his restaurant next door. It might actually turn out to be a good deal if visitors are hungry, for the hourly parking fee at the Scavi is quite exorbitant. Francesca will drop us off in front of the Porta Marina—one of the two main entrances to the ancient city of Pompeii—then drive farther down the road to park in a lot reserved for the buses.

Known worldwide as a time capsule created by Mount Vesuvius nearly two thousand years ago, Pompeii is one of the most visited archeological sites in Campania. Each year thousands of people from every nation wander through the streets of the Scavi. While tour groups come with their own guides, it is possible for individuals to hire one locally, or, for a small fee, they can rent an audio.

For a good overview of the area, a minimum of two hours is recommended. However, people who are passionate about the

Roman period will likely spend more time. Comfortable walking shoes are a must, as well as a hat on a hot summer day and a bottle of water. Although there are plenty of street vendors that sell sandwiches, drinks and souvenirs outside the boundaries of the old city, there is only one small cafeteria available inside.

Once we alight from the bus, we quickly step up to the ticket booth to purchase our tickets, collect a brief guidebook and a site map, then walk uphill to another booth to rent the audios. After a last visit to the facilities, as there are only a few inside, we are ready to go.

We are about to step back in time, the Ancient Roman time that is. . .

)(

Pompeii was originally founded by the Oscan people in the seventh century B.C. a short distance from the edge of the Gulf of Naples on top of a hill at the mouth of the Sarno River. A century later, the Osci were joined by the Etruscans, then subsequently conquered by the Greeks, the Samnites and in 80 B.C. by the Romans.

In 79 A.D., the year of the eruption, Pompeii was a small town with a population of about fifteen to twenty thousand inhabitants, surrounded by a two-mile wall. It had a thriving economy based on the export of commodities produced in the surrounding countryside such as wheat, vegetables, wine and olive oil. The population was multi-racial as wealthy Roman patricians, the nouveau-riche and merchants, all owned slaves that had been captured in different parts of the Roman Empire. Several languages could be heard while tradesmen negotiated the purchase of imported goods, which were later sold at open-air markets and in the shops. Pompeii was busy and noisy. Its inhabitants honored Egyptian gods as well as the

Roman divinities that had been introduced by the Greeks. The most venerated—Venus, the goddess of love and beauty—was represented in many of the homes, on frescoes and in mosaics. A temple was even built in her honor.

In 62 A.D., Pompeii experienced a strong earthquake that scientists have established to have been a "six" on the Richter scale, followed by a series of aftershocks. For the citizens of Pompeii, quakes were not unusual. They were often felt in the area. In fact, several small seismic tremors had previously been recorded. But the 62 A.D. earthquake was different, for it did extensive damage to the Roman city and many people died. Restorations were still under way seventeen years later when Mount Vesuvius erupted.

On the western slopes of Mount Vesuvius, at the edge of the sea, was Herculaneum, named by Greek settlers for their mythological hero Herakles or *Hercules* in Latin. Unlike the commercial city of Pompeii, Herculaneum was more of an upscale resort town. Historians estimate that it had a population of about 4,000. In the earthquake of 62 A.D., the coastal town suffered some damage, and in 79 A.D. Herculaneum would share the same fate as Pompeii.

The residents of Pompeii and Herculaneum were unaware of the fact that Mount Vesuvius was a volcano. There wasn't even a word in Latin for "volcano." Scientists estimate that Mount Vesuvius had erupted 1500 years prior to 79 A.D., thus the people living in this region had never witnessed an eruption. They were totally unprepared for the sequence of events that would shatter their lives.

What happened during that fateful day was described in two letters written by Pliny the Younger to the Roman historian Tacitus. The seventeen-year-old witnessed the event from across the bay at Misenum while his uncle Pliny the Elder, admiral of the Roman fleet, was sailing up closer in an attempt to rescue a friend and his family. The sequence of events has been confirmed by hundreds of historians and archeologists who have excavated the site since its discovery and by scientists who have analyzed the different layers covering it by using modern technologies.

⚹

On the morning of August 24, 79 A.D., the people of Pompeii and Herculaneum were going about their daily routines of visiting the baths, negotiating business deals, listening to the speeches of politicians, meeting friends and visiting relatives. Slaves were busy buying fresh food and wine for the day's meals and refilling water containers at the public fountains.

Vesuvio's first warning was a sequence of tremors, which people ignored. At one o'clock in the afternoon, Mount Vesuvius, waking up from a long sleep, exploded in a fury, spewing ashes in a column twenty miles up into the air. As the volcanic cloud flattened, taking on the shape of an umbrella pine, it moved in the direction of Pompeii, obscuring the sun in the process. The day turned into night. People thought that it was just an eclipse. Reaching a cooler atmosphere, the burning ashes quickly hardened into small pebbles that pounced onto Pompeii. Rocks ejected from the center of the earth became even deadlier projectiles as they rained down on the city.

Thousands, believing the gods were angry, tried to escape. Others stayed indoors, thinking it would be safer. By mid-afternoon, Vesuvio had already spurted millions of tons of debris. Roofs were collapsing, trapping people inside.

In the beginning of the evening the full force of the volcano was released, sending volcanic rocks over Pompeii and Herculaneum. And in the early hours of August 25th a huge stream of gas mixed with ashes and rocks descended toward Herculaneum and the sea, its intense heat killing everything instantly. According to his nephew, the admiral died from asphyxiation on the beach of Stabiae and his body was carried back to Misenum.

Quakes kept shaking the earth, unleashing another flow of magma bursting into the air and descending this time on Pompeii. While the flow stopped short of the city, a toxic gas engulfed it, depleting the remaining oxygen and killing the people who had stayed behind.

Ultimately, a cataclysmic wave of volcanic rocks came down at 100 mph, destroying everything in its passage, burying Pompeii and the surrounding plain, even killing those who had escaped into the countryside. In twenty-four hours, covered with tons of volcanic mud, Pompeii, Herculaneum, Stabiae and Oplontis were erased from the map. The site of Stabiae is presumably near the town of Castellammare di Stabia while Oplontis is today almost entirely buried under the buildings of the city of Torre Annunziata.

At first nobody wanted to believe Pliny the Younger, as a catastrophe of this magnitude was unimaginable. But his observations were subsequently proven accurate and a new word entered the book of science—Plinian—to describe volcanic eruptions of such violence.

When the news reached Rome, Emperor Titus sent a rescue mission. It proved to be an impossible task. The damages were so great. No roads or trees were visible—only a wasteland. After a while, Pompeii faded into legend, a city shrouded in mystery and its location forgotten. Until its discovery close to seventeen hundred years later, people wondered if it really did exist.

While I have wandered through the Scavi of Pompeii numerous times, I have only seen the excavations of Herculaneum once, which was years ago during the week I rented a house in Furore with my sister and our husbands. I remember my single exploration like it was yesterday.

On a rainy Sunday morning we drove from the house to Ercolano, the new Herculaneum. Upon exiting the freeway we followed the signs to the archeological site, right to the center of town. Unlike Pompeii, where the new town developed outside the Roman city, the modern Herculaneum developed on top of the old one. We quickly found a parking spot across the street from the Scavi, near the police station.

After purchasing a single day ticket for both Herculaneum and Pompeii combined, we descended an incline leading to the site's main entrance. The road offered us an overview of the excavations, as well as a vista of the sea with its shoreline a quarter mile further out than prior to 79 A.D.

Since the first phase of the eruption spared Herculaneum, many of its structures had retained their upper floors and roofs. The site resembled an unfinished Ancient Roman movie set, void of any living creature. For almost two hours we walked through empty streets, gardens and buildings. I recall how quiet it was. Very few people visit Herculaneum. At times, I had the eerie feeling that we were not alone on that Sunday morning. Were eyes from the past looking at us, I wondered. I felt the same emotions when I walked through Ephesus, Turkey, years prior. It is true that the rain added an air of sadness to the place.

The old Roman town of Herculaneum was discovered quite by accident in 1579 when a farmer digging in a convent courtyard stumbled onto large stones. But it was not until 1738 that serious excavations began under the orders of the Bourbon King Charles VII. Then, in 1748, the location of Pompeii was discovered. The news traveled around Europe like wildfire and the potential for finding invaluable treasures was discussed in every circle.

Digging through twenty yards of hardened mud was proving to be a difficult task. Shovels and picks kept breaking, so much so that after the discovery of the House of Papyrus in 1750, the excavation work stopped, but it continued extensively at Pompeii. A century later renewed interest reopened Herculaneum.

Archaeology buffs will want to see the House of Papyrus, which was named for the many charred papyrus scrolls found inside. Historians have attributed it to Julius Caesar's father-in-law. In 1954 the millionaire JP Getty built a close replica of the house in Pacific Palisades, California. Part of a museum complex, it is open to the public with advance reservation.

At first it was thought that the majority of the people of Herculaneum had escaped by sea. Unfortunately that theory was proven untrue as new excavations in 1982 uncovered 250 skeletons in the boat houses. Archeologists keep finding treasures. Just recently a charred wooden throne was unearthed. Only one quarter of the Roman resort town has been excavated, as the new town of Ercolano sits on the rest.

✕

On this sunny afternoon we are slowly walking up the steep Via Marina, stepping through the city walls of Pompeii. On our right we pass the Temple of Venus and the Basilica and on our left the Temple of Apollo on our way to the Forum. At the edge of the Forum, the heart of Pompeii's daily life, we stop to regroup. Capturing everyone's attention I indicate the Temple of Jupiter, at the opposite end of the Forum, and behind it the mighty Vesuvio with its two summits, the tallest one 4,203 feet high.

"Now that we are here, it is easy to envision the pyroclastic flow of hot gas and rock that spewed out of the volcano," I begin. "Wall paintings uncovered at Pompeii suggest that prior to 79 A.D. Mount Vesuvius had a pointed summit, similar to the one of Mount St. Helens in the state of Washington, which was 9,852 feet high before its eruption in 1980.

"We can only imagine what the volcano looked like after the eruption, for what we see nowadays is the result of another great eruption that took place in 1631, which was nearly equal in violence to the one of 79 A.D. It caused the deaths of approximately four thousand people." I then proceed to explain the layout of the site while pointing in the appropriate directions. "Pompeii can be separated into four sections: the public areas around the Forum, the theater districts, the shopping streets, and the residential neighborhoods."

Glancing at my travel companions for their reactions, I notice that some of them are holding their breath. For many this is their first visit. Prior to our trip I had shown them pictures of the ruins, but the reality of that terrible day really hits when you stand in the middle of the Scavi. My first impression of Pompeii was that a nuclear bomb had blown up, killing every living creature, ripping walls, floors and roofs off practically every building around. If you see an aerial picture of the site, you'll know what I mean.

Each time I wander through Pompeii, I think about the people who lived here two thousand years ago. What they experienced that day must have been horrific. It might be hard to conceive, but if it weren't for the unleashed power of nature we would not have this historical testimony of their lives.

Scanning our booklet and map, we each select the areas and the buildings we want to see and go our separate ways. Only one building is on my list, for I have already seen the House of Mystery with its beautiful frescoes, the House of the Fawn, the Roman baths, the large theater and the amphitheater, the little shops and tavernas along the Via dell'Abbondanza and the luxurious villas lining the Via di Nola with their oversized doorways, atriums and private running water. And I have been through the House of Vettii on Vicolo di Mercurio, the most luxurious villa in Pompeii, twice, as it is my favorite.

One building has eluded me. And it is not for lack of trying to find it. It is very easy to get lost in Pompeii even though the streets are laid out in a grid pattern. Streets are sometimes cordoned off to protect visitors from unstable structures. During one of my previous visits I found myself on top of the Porta di Nola, an area not yet excavated, at the opposite side of the city, from where I had difficulties finding my way back as scaffolds and barriers were blocking the streets. However, my little adventure gave me the opportunity to capture an aerial shot of an empty street.

One third of Pompeii is still buried; forty-four of the sixty-six hectares have been exposed and only a quarter of those are open to the public. Of Herculaneum's twenty hectares only four and a half have been excavated. In the excavated section of Pompeii many of the buildings are barred from entry with metal doors and chains. The Scavi employs a staff of skilled workers who are constantly busy repairing and preserving the structures.

The building I wish to see is a *lupanar,* or a brothel. *Lupa,* meaning wolverine in Latin, was the nickname for a prostitute, and her place of business was called a *lupanar.* The Roman society of Pompeii was very liberal. The city had twenty brothels. The biggest one was located on Vicolo del Lupanare, Bordellos Lane. The lupanare of Pompeii did such a brisk business catering to both residents and visitors that Emperor Caligula imposed a tax on their services.

Leaving the Forum behind, I direct my steps toward the Via dell'Abbondanza, Pompeii's main shopping street. Since I read in one of the souvenir books that phallic symbols could be found in the paving stones pointing the way, I am closely paying attention to the pavers. So far, I have not seen one. Still it is a clever incentive to watch my steps, for the pavement is quite uneven. It wouldn't be the first time I kiss the ground of a European country.

Pausing at the Fontana di Via dell'Abbondanza, one of the forty fountains uncovered at Pompeii, I pull my map from my shoulder bag. Four feet away a tour guide, holding a folded umbrella up in the air, is explaining the layout of Pompeii to a group of Dutch tourists. "As the archeological site is quite large, it was divided into nine neighborhoods or *regio,* each numbered in Roman numerals from I to IX in 1858 by Giuseppe Fiorelli who was the director at the time.

"Each regio contains several *insulae,* or islands—blocks of houses and shops within two parallel streets, north, south and two east, west—also individually numbered. Each dwelling inside the insula was given a number and a name by the archeologists as they discovered them. The marble sign on the side of the building behind us reads: REG VII INS XIII. We are standing at the corner of regio seven insula thirteen."

Circling the group, I continue and turn left on Vicolo di Lupanare, passing one of many stray dogs that seem to have taken residence in the ancient city. I am getting closer, just around the corner . . . Whoopee! No pun intended, I have finally found it.

And so it seems did forty-plus German senior citizens who are blocking half the street while waiting for their turn to step inside. Suddenly there is an explosion of laughter. My guess is that the men are engaged in making colorful innuendoes. What is it that attracts people to this place, I wonder. The frescoes on the walls depicting various sexual scenes, the explicit graffiti left by satisfied customers, still visible today, or the fact that most of us have never visited such a place and are simply curious? Assumably, a little of each.

This recently-restored brothel was apparently the most famous and successful of the lupanare in Pompeii for it had two floors and ten stone beds. One can only imagine the discussions between the Italian masons and fresco painters as they were working on this building. I suspect that it was likely one of their most challenging restoration jobs and that they had fun doing it.

Many of the explicit sexual frescoes that were discovered at Pompeii have been transferred to the National Archeological Museum of Naples where they are displayed in *il Gabinetto Segreto,* or the Secret Room. Up until the first part of the twentieth century, only the male population was allowed to view them as they were considered too sensitive and offensive for the female population.

Since it does not appear that I will enter the lupanar within the next twenty minutes, for another large group of French people has just arrived with their own sense of humor, I decide to leave. This building is so popular that the Scavi should consider selling an extra entrance ticket. Oh well, maybe some other time. Today I would rather amble through the modern Pompeii.

Walking toward the Porta Nocera I find myself once again envisioning what the town must have looked like two thousand years ago. Sadly an unknown number of treasures of antiquity from Pompeii were lost to looters right after the eruption, then later to unscrupulous scavengers searching the area.

When artifacts were found, quite often they would be sold to wealthy and private collectors, scattering them around Europe. Prime pieces were selected by the Bourbon king for his own collection, and later Caroline Bonaparte, Napoleon's sister, helped herself as well. Over the years, tourists have taken hundreds of small pieces here and there from frescoes and carved marbles. It is no wonder that in order to protect the remaining artifacts of Pompeii and Herculaneum from robbers and severe weather, they were moved to the National Archeological Museum of Naples, which is open to the public every day except Tuesday. There, hundreds of statues, frescoes, two thousand pieces of jewelry and other exquisite items are displayed in several rooms.

Upon reaching Pompeii's main shopping street, I stop to retrieve my bottle of water. The afternoon is turning out to be quite warm. All this walking is making me thirsty. While passing behind me, a dark-haired boy, who looks to be about eight years old, asks his mother in French, "Why is everything closed, Mummy?" I smile. Funny that he should notice that, too.

A few feet away a young man is kneeling down awkwardly at the edge of the sidewalk to take a picture of his girlfriend as she poses on one of the stepping stones in the middle of the street. What a strange angle to snap a picture! Since Pompeii had a very limited sewage system, large cut stones were placed in streets with no drainage to allow pedestrians to cross without getting wet and dirty. The space between the stones allowed the wheels of vehicles to pass. Their ruts are still visible.

Along the way to the Porta Nocera I visit the House of Venus, named for the monumental mural of the "Venus of the Sea" that was found in the garden. I walk through a baker's house, one of the thirty bakeries of Pompeii where the ovens are practically intact, and the House of Three Arches with its peristyle garden.

It seems that the most lucrative profession in Pompeii, besides prostitution, was "fresco painting." Many dwellings had lavishly decorated walls with brightly colored paintings. Popular designs included *amoretti* or cupids, winged cherubs—the offspring of Bacchus and Venus, Roman gods and deities, clothed or naked, mythological scenes, vegetation, animals and hunting scenes, rich optical illusions, and faux marble, garlands and doorways.

Closer to the Porta Nocera I pass the garden of the fugitives, named for the plaster casts of the thirteen bodies of women, men and children who met their death trying to escape. These casts were produced by an ingenious method invented by Guiseppe Fiorelli in 1860. Plaster of Paris mixed with water was injected into empty cavities left behind by the natural decomposition of the burned bodies. There are numerous casts displayed in dwellings throughout Pompeii. It is estimated that most of the citizens of Pompeii did escape to neighboring towns. So far, close to two thousand bodies have been found.

After stepping through the Porta Nocera I stroll along the main avenue of Pompeii's necropolis, which is lined on both sides by the tombs of wealthy Roman families. I exit the Scavi and reenter the twenty-first century at the Piazza Amfiteatro and continue to the town center. How peaceful the old city was compared to the new one. Church bells are ringing. Music is escaping from a second floor window. Cars and Vespas are whizzing by, their roaring engines nearly deafening my ears. What a contrast!

The modern Pompeii, founded less than two hundred years ago, is home to twenty-five thousand inhabitants. The Piazza Bartolo Longo, the town's main square, is dominated by the Shrine of the Blessed Virgin of the Holy Rosary, a beautiful basilica with an attached convent and a bell tower. The new Pompeii is, in fact, a place of pilgrimage. Each year, four million pilgrims visit the Basilica, the most important Shrine dedicated to Mary in Italy.

With some time to spare, I decide to follow a small group of nuns into the shrine. I never get tired of stepping into churches in Italy, for you never know what treasures they might hold. Once inside, I am completely caught off guard by the magnificent marble decorations, the mosaics and the paintings, of which the most impressive is the Image of our Lady of the Rosary above the central altar.

Back outside, I glance around the large Piazza. In its center are various shaped patches of lawn. A young woman is pushing a stroller and four elderly men in dark suits are sitting on a bench. They have come to watch and gossip. Numerous hotels and restaurants on either side of the basilica denote the town's reliance on the tourism industry. I also count half a dozen ice cream parlors, or *gelaterie* in Italian.

"One scoop of chocolate and one of strawberry," I request of the attractive man with blazing blue eyes that contrast against dark olive cheeks and thick black hair a little longer than it should be, at Gelateria Maccarone. Behind me people gleefully wait for their turn to order their favorite flavor. On a sunny afternoon nobody can resist the lure of a creamy *gelato*. Italians and tourists, young and old, all want their cup of heaven. Italian ice cream is to die for.

"Prego bella, please beautiful," he flashes me a smile, handing over the waffled *cornetto,* or cone. I chuckle, strangely flattered. Italian men have a unique talent for making every woman feel special. I sample the chocolate; it is unquestionably the best in the world. Stepping outside, I burst into laughter, catching the startled stare of passersby. What if gelato meant something entirely different?

Checking the time, I realize that I only have a few minutes before catching up with my group and Francesca. Striding back to the Porta Marina along the fence that surrounds the excavations, I catch a glimpse of a large panel near a gated entrance. The text on the panel reminds us that the discovery of Herculaneum and Pompeii in the eighteenth century sparked the birth of modern archeology, a science that studies material remains of past civilizations in order to reconstitute its environment, society and economy.

Today, away from the public eye, scientists, historians and archeologists at both sites are still busily working, trying to solve new findings and puzzles of the past. And they are focusing on the preservation and restoration of buildings for the future.

The Blue Ribbon

Back inside the bus everyone is breathing a sigh of relief. It feels wonderful to be sitting again, for there are virtually no benches in the ancient city of Pompeii and, although my companions are grateful to have seen it, they are still a little jetlagged. After buckling my seat belt, I turn to Francesca and give her a nod of approval to depart. If the late afternoon traffic is not too heavy, we should reach our hotel in Sant'Agata sui Due Golfi, on the Sorrento Peninsula, within an hour.

For a short time Francesca reconnects with the Autostrada A3, then eases onto the Strada Statale SS145, the state road to Sorrento, on the outskirts of Castellammare di Stabia—the gateway to the Sorrentine Peninsula. Renowned since ancient times for its thermal and mineral springs, the seaside resort of Castellammare di Stabia owes its name to its position at the foot of a castle overlooking the sea and from the Roman settlement of Stabiae, which was also buried by the eruption of Vesuvio in 79 A.D. The location of Stabiae is still unknown, but it is presumed to be near the seashore. The only testimony to its existence is the archeological excavations of sumptuous patrician villas in the countryside nearby.

As the SS145 curves around the Gulf of Naples and reveals a succession of small villages and beautiful beaches, a chorus of

"Whoa" fills the air around me and I smile, delighted that the women are enjoying the ride. We peek at the charming town of Vico Equense, also known for its thermal baths, before the road becomes tortuous as it follows the slopes of Mount Faito—one of the highest summits of the Lattari Mountains. Suddenly, after passing the small summer resort of Seiano and driving around Punta Scutolo, we are staring at a splendid panoramic view of the Sorrento Coastline with the Sorrentine Peninsula and the isle of Capri in the backdrop. From a distance, those two seem to be connected.

Meta, Piano di Sorrento, Sant'Agnello and Sorrento are all visible right on the edge of a wide fertile plain, or *piano,* on top of sheer cliffs descending dangerously to the sea and surrounded by sheltering mountains. Through the ages, these towns have been a favorite retreat for wealthy Romans, European nobility, famous writers and celebrities.

We drive through Meta, an ancient town of Greek and Roman origins, which at one time had an important port with an impressive shipyard. At the entrance of Piano di Sorrento, Francesca turns left on Via Cavone, right on the Via dei Platani, then starts to ascend the Via Meta-Amalfi. As we slowly progress higher and higher through a string of hamlets, I recognize familiar details in the landscape—the scattered two-story houses, the little hotel with its large terrace where the locals hang out, the pink chapel on top of the hill, the four-foot plastic statue of Jesus at the entrance of a graveled path and the small grocery store with a green awning right before the sharp bend in the road. These images must be stored in my memory, for it feels as if I were here only yesterday.

We are almost there. At the Positano-Sant'Agata intersection, Francesca continues on the Nastro Azzurro, which will ultimately lead us to our hotel. Literally translated, the Blue Ribbon derives its name from the profusion of blues that is seen along the road, from the deep waters of the Tyrrhenian Sea on either side to the clear sky above.

The hills are covered with hundreds of olive trees, introduced to the region by the Greek colonists. They are a sight to behold—their foliage now silver-gray, now green as the breeze blows, their trunks gnarled with age. Each year the groves of the Sorrento Peninsula and the Amalfi Coast combined yield close to two thousand tons of olives. Three different kinds are produced: the Ogliarola, Rotondella and Frantoio. Local people still harvest them by hand. It is a tedious job, but the ancient method keeps the fruits undamaged.

Black and green nylon netting has been deployed around each trunk to collect the falling olives blown off the trees by the wind. At harvest time, which will soon begin, the netting is lowered to the ground and the hand picking begins. Sometimes the nets are left in place to catch the olives while the tree branches are being slapped with long crooks. Within twenty-four hours of being picked, the olives are washed and pressed to produce the wonderful fruity extra virgin oil essential to the preparation of many local dishes.

For miles now Francesca has been following a small three-wheeler truck known as the Ape, the Italian word for bee, when at last the road widens giving her the opportunity to pass. Pronounced Ah'pee, the Ape vehicles, which are made by the Italian Piaggio Company, the fourth largest producer of scooters and motorcycles in the world, are a common sight in Southern Italy and Sicily. Local farmers favor these miniature trucks. Not only are they practical for the transportation of small loads and ideal for buzzing around the countryside and in the small towns, they also don't take up a lot of parking space.

Finally the hotel comes into view. The Grand Hotel Due Golfi, where we will spend the next seven nights, is just a stone's throw away from the charming little town of Sant'Agata, often referred to as "Sant'Agata sui Due Golfi" or "Sant'Agata on the Two Gulfs" for it lies on top of an incline facing the Gulf of Salerno on one side and the Gulf of Naples on the other. Built on a hillside, the six-story hotel was completely remodeled a few years ago. Every newly-redecorated room has a balcony that either looks out over the front of the hotel, at the parking lot and the swimming pool or over the rear of the hotel, at Sorrento and the Bay of Sorrento.

After Francesca pulls to a stop in the parking lot of the hotel, we quickly retrieve our suitcases, thank our tired-looking driver who woke up at the crack of dawn to ensure our transfer from Rome, then climb a short flight of steps and walk through a set of double glassed doors into the lobby.

From behind an amazing seven-foot-long green alabaster reception counter two young women graciously greet us with their warm Italian smiles. They have been expecting us. As we approach the counter the petite blond, Ornella, mentions that she remembers me from a previous stay. Is that good or bad? I reflect, trying to remember if something out of the ordinary occurred during that time. I don't seem to recall anything in particular. It must have been something I said then.

While Ornella and her assistant Amelia are handing the women their electronic room keys I glance around. The classic style marbled lobby is spacious. It can easily accommodate a group of fifty people, including their luggage. Off to the side, through an open archway, is an elegant bar area. Beyond is an immense lounge, with floor-to-ceiling windows surrounding two sides of the room and comfortable leather couches and chairs, where guests can relax and enjoy breathtaking views of the Bay of Sorrento.

Ornella is calling my name. The women have all gone to their rooms. It is my turn to check in. "We have assigned you a lovely room on the third floor. The view from up there is quite beautiful. The room you stayed in the last time is occupied by an elderly lady. She was supposed to vacate this morning but she is not feeling well and asked us if she could remain for another couple of days," she explains apologetically, for I had requested my previous room on the same floor as the lobby.

I don't mind taking the stairs really. After all it is only three floors. It would be good exercise since I plan to enjoy many of my favorite Campania dishes and desserts in the upcoming days. But what about my luggage? Maybe I should place it in the elevator, press the third-floor button, then run up the steps to collect it as the door opens. I have done this a few times in European hotels. Still it was always in the wee hours of the morning when no porters were available and I had an early flight to catch. Up to now, my stratagem has worked without a glitch.

Although I do recall an awkward encounter in Rome at the end of a tour. As I was reaching the lobby, the elevator doors were closing. I rushed over. Inside, a man and a woman were fondling each other. I apologized and quickly grabbed the handle of my suitcase. The couple didn't even noticed me as I was pulling it out. The doors closed and I burst into laughter. My eyes burned for a long time after witnessing that scene.

Now faced with the choice of accepting the room or asking for another, I hesitate. As if she had been reading my thoughts, Ornella offers to bring my luggage up to my room. Relieved, I accept.

Once in the room, I drop my shoulder bag on the bed, take off my shoes and socks, eager to walk barefoot on the tile floor, then step through an open glass door onto a balcony where two chairs and a small table have been placed for the enjoyment of the guest. The view of the Gulf of Naples bathing in the glow of the setting sun is just as mesmerizing as I remember. Immediately, my eyes are drawn to the unmistakable profile of Vesuvio, to the surrounding open plain and to the path we traveled on today. In the lush valley below the hotel lies Sorrento, at the edge the sea. Directly across the deep blue of the Bay of Sorrento is Naples. Does anyone ever get tired of looking at this panorama I wonder, jealous of the people living here.

Stepping back inside, I have the impression that, in comparison to my previous room, this one seems more spacious. The sand-sea color scheme used for the walls, drapes and flowery bedcovers is similar, as are the cobalt blue Vietri tiles on the floor. Instead of a queen bed, there are two twin-size beds with a night stand on either side. Across the room is a custom-made wooden desk that extends nearly the entire length of the wall. A 32" flat screen satellite television has been mounted above, and tucked in the corner at the end, is a mini-bar.

The floor and walls of the bathroom are completely covered with Vietrisi tiles chosen for their beautiful blue and copper arabesque pattern. The European shower-tub is deep, ideal for soaking in. I purposely packed lavender-scented oils in my toiletry bag to pamper myself after some of the long days ahead. Facing the bathroom entrance are double mirrored doors hiding a large closet with plenty of room for hanging pants and dresses and six drawers to store small items.

Within seconds of sliding the closet doors back into place, Ornella knocks at the front door. Her timing is impeccable. I just finished my inspection. "Do you like your room?" she asks, pulling my suitcase and carry-on inside.

"*Si, grazie.* It's perfect, and I love the view. Did anybody in my group ask to change theirs?" I query, hoping for a negative response. Ornella shakes her head.

"Wonderful. If the women are happy, I am happy, too!" I reply, escorting her out.

I quickly unpack my entire suitcase, store it under one of the beds, then grab a fresh set of clothing from the closet and step inside the bathroom to get ready for our first group dinner in the redesigned dining room of the hotel.

Day Two

Paestum

As daylight is starting to color the sky the stillness of my room is suddenly jarred by the ring of the phone at my bedside. Expecting a call from my husband, I prop myself up against the pillows and pick up the receiver. Whenever one of us is abroad, our conversations tend to be brief as they generally revolve around the news at home, the weather and a couple anecdotes from the trip. This time I have one that will surely make him shake his head and smile.

Last night, as we were eating and drinking wine around an elegantly set dinner table, our group loosened up and started talking about Italian men. Most of our discussion was about their reputation and sex appeal. When one of the women asked me if it was true that Italian men love to pinch, unable to swallow a laugh, I shook my head. Finally catching my breath, I told my companions: "I don't know who started that rumor but it has never happened to me." Although I am not an expert on Italian men, I have worked with enough of them over the years to know that some of their behavior clichés have sometimes been exaggerated.

When the women quizzed me for Italian words to describe them I gladly obliged, but stumbled at the translation for "hunk." Then, remembering my nieces' private code and the attractive ice cream waiter, I suggested that if anyone of us saw a good-looking man we should refer to him as a "gelato." Amid giggles they all agreed and lifted their glasses to cheerfully toast the idea.

After saying goodbye to my husband, I replace the receiver and check my alarm clock. With his laugh singing in my head, I climb out of bed, quickly shower, dress and walk down the staircase for breakfast.

Standing in the doorway, my gaze scans the dining room for an empty table. Surprisingly, nearly all of them are occupied by the members of two large German groups that checked in late last night. Not willing to deal with a crowd this early in the morning, I step forward, grab a yogurt from the buffet, pour myself a cup of coffee and retreat to the quietness of my room to review my notes for today.

Aronne will be our driver. Danilo told me three days ago that I was lucky to have him again since he recently returned from a ten-day driving engagement in Tuscany. My timing is perfect. I thoroughly enjoy teaming up with Aronne. His sense of humor is refreshing and contagious, plus he speaks English with an Italian accent that I am sure the women will find quite charming.

An hour later, glancing through the lobby's glass doors, I watch a tall attractive man in his late twenties, dressed in a dark suit and a light blue shirt unbuttoned at the neck, crossing the parking lot with an easy stride. Recognizing Aronne, I step out to meet him. As we greet each other with kisses on the cheek, I realize that it has been a little more than a year since I last saw him. Curious, I ask him if he is married to his longtime girlfriend now. His brown eyes twinkle as he replies that they just recently moved in together. Out of the corner of my eye, I spot my group slowly strolling up to us. I turn around and introduce Aronne to the women.

Walking beside him, I catch sight of our ride—a brand-new twenty-passenger van. "They let you drive this?" I ask Aronne. He shrugs and smiles. I study the vehicle, paying particular attention to the sexy mermaid painted on the side, with hair cascading past her waist in thick waves. I laugh at the new company motto: "Pleasure on wheels."

"That is quite a statement," I blurt out.

"Angelo's idea." He grins. At the mention of Aronne's boss, my memory travels back to my first tour. Angelo was my chauffeur then. Of course I remember him. He gave me a mountain of inside information on the Amalfi Coast in his own amusing and witty way.

While Aronne gallantly assists the women on board, I open the passenger door and settle myself comfortably on the tan leather upholstered seat that still smells like new. In case something catches my photographic eye, I retrieve the camera from my shoulder bag and place it on my lap. Seconds later, Aronne climbs behind the wheel and hands me the microphone before starting the engine and driving onto the Blue Ribbon Road heading back to the A3 freeway.

Miles down the road, I flip the microphone on to welcome everyone with Buongiorno. After it is loudly echoed, I proceed. "Since both Greek and Roman civilizations have left their marks on Campania, it is only logical that after visiting Pompeii we see the three magnificent Greek Temples of Paestum. Mister Pino Schiavone will guide us through the archeological site, and after lunch we will stop in the small town of Vietri for some shopping.

"According to historians, Posedonia was founded on a travertine plateau on the fertile plain of the Sele River at the end of the seventh century B.C. by Greek colonists from the city of Sibari, one of the oldest cities of Magna Grecia on the Gulf of Taranto. Named in honor of Poseidon, the Greek god of the sea, the settlement quickly flourished to become the greatest city along the Gulf of Salerno.

"At the end of the fifth century B.C. the city was conquered by the nearby Lucani—the local branch of the Italic Samnites—and the name of the town was changed to Paistom. During the first Punic War Paistom allied itself with Rome and, in exchange, received the right to strike its own coins. In the second Punic War the Lucani sided with the enemy. After their defeat, the city was captured in 273 B.C. by the Romans who renamed it Paestum. For the next two centuries, the city continued to expand. New streets were laid out and numerous buildings were added. Then it fell into a long decline.

"The slow deforestation of the plain, caused by wars and commerce, contributed to a shift in the landscape, which eventually turned the terrain into marshes, bringing diseases to the area and putting an end to trade. After the Saracen incursions in the late ninth century, people abandoned it. Stones, columns and other building materials were moved from Paestum to other construction sites and the city was forgotten. Overgrown and immersed in swamplands, it was rediscovered in the eighteenth century during road construction. However, serious excavations did not begin until 1940. Today, tourists come to Paestum primarily to see the three splendid Doric temples from the fifth century B.C. They are among the best preserved of Classical antiquity."

Noticing that Aronne is about to get off the freeway at Battipaglia, I conclude. "We should be arriving at the site in fifteen minutes. You can leave any belongings you don't want to carry on your seat. Aronne will lock the van and remain nearby so it is completely safe." I turn off the microphone, hand it over to Aronne, lean my head back and close my eyes.

"Allora, dimmi qualcosa," says Aronne, encouraging me to speak in Italian. I glance at him and reply, "What would you like to know?" For the next few miles, while passing through a handful

of small modern towns, we exchange stories of our lives. And then our conversation turns to "What's happening on the Amalfi Coast?" Since he lives near Sorrento, I like to quiz him about the local gossip.

)(

As we file out of the van into the bright sunlight at the north entrance of the excavation site, we are met by our guide Pino, a retired history professor with a passion for Paestum. He immediately directs us to the Temple of Ceres. One of the many pleasures of escorting people to foreign lands is to see the element of surprise as they discover famous landmarks for the first time. The look of awe on the women's faces is well worth the trip.

Twenty-five hundred years, how can someone grasp that length of time when the average life span is seventy years? The concept of "century old" is not new to me since I grew up in a country that has many churches and castles dating back to the thirteenth, fourteenth and fifteenth centuries. The majority of what we saw yesterday in Pompeii is two thousand years old. Yet centuries beyond that are difficult to perceive, even for me. It is a marvel that those temples are still there for us to see.

In the proximity of the Temple of Ceres, gathering our attention with *"Allora,"* Pino spreads his arms wide, emphasizing the size of the dig. "It is estimated that the ancient city covered about one hundred twenty hectares, of which only twenty-five have been excavated. Unfortunately, we will probably never know how many people lived here during the Greek colonization, the Lucani period and the Roman period, for most of the remaining land is privately owned," he says with a sigh.

"The city walls are nearly intact. They were constructed with square blocks of limestone from a quarry nearby. They included four main gates, located on the cardinal points known in Latin as *Opus Quadrum Terra,* and forty-five smaller gates that served for accessing the city and for defensive purposes. Of the twenty-eight watch towers, very few remain intact," Pino continues, pointing to the ancient city wall in the distance.

"The Greeks constructed three Doric temples here in the span of a hundred and fifty years. They built them in their standard east-west orientation with the entrance facing the rising sun, unlike the Roman temples, which were built in the north-south direction. This is often referred to as the Italic direction for the shape of Italy. The best Roman example is the Temple of Jupiter in Pompeii.

"We have in front of us the building commonly known as the Temple of Ceres. It was built around 500 B.C., on the highest part of the town, with stone blocks from quarries south of Paestum. It contains both Doric and Ionic columns. When it was first discovered, the scholars attributed this temple to Ceres, the Roman goddess of vegetation and fruitfulness. But many statuettes found nearby prove, in fact, it was the Temple of Athena, the Greek goddess of wisdom, science and arts. During the middle ages this temple was transformed into a Christian church. The single column close by is where the plebeians would vent their complaints."

While walking along a Roman cobblestone road toward the other temples, Pino explains that since the Romans adopted the Greek divinities, to which they gave a Latin name, it is not uncommon to see in Paestum Greek and Roman structures next to each other.

We stop for a brief moment at the Roman forum, the hub of the ancient city—built on the site of the Greek agora, then at the Roman foundations of the gymnasium and swimming pool, before entering the southern side of the Amphitheater.

"The eastern side is buried under a road built in 1930. The civil engineer responsible for the construction of that road was actually sentenced for wantonly destroying a historical site" Pino relays.

Standing in front of the largest temple in Paestum, Pino waves a pestering fly away from his face and resumes. "The Temple of Poseidon—Neptune to the Romans—is the best preserved of all the surviving temples of Magna Grecia. It was built using the local limestone around 450 B.C., twelve years before the Parthenon in Athens, which is similar in style. From a distance the columns look straight and the temple proportioned, but as we get closer we see that the top and bottom sections of the columns are oval instead of round. The upper and lower columns of the inner room or *cella* are visible. Only a few of the small upper columns have survived. Many of the missing columns from the temples, as well as large marble pieces, were scavenged a thousand years ago to build the cathedral of Salerno. Even sarcophagi that were unearthed here have found their way to the cathedral.

"Scholars are still debating about to which divinity this temple was dedicated. At first it was said to have been consecrated to the god for which the city was named, then to Hera and Zeus, her husband, but recent studies might prove that the temple could actually have been dedicated to the god Apollo, the twin brother of Artemis and the son of Zeus and the Titaness Leto. You know Zeus was the biggest Casanova."

My gaze drifts over the women who are laughing at Pino's last comment. I hope that they have not started to overdose on Greek architecture for there is still the museum to visit. One woman seems very interested. She is feverishly writing in her small journal. Another is drawing in a sketchbook. Two are slowly moving away to take close-up pictures of the temple. Four are sitting on large limestone blocks embedded in the soil, while the others are standing close by. Glancing beyond our small group, I notice that there are less than two hundred people walking through the ruins at the moment. The majority of them are probably on a tour from Sorrento or Naples. Only a small number of visitors come by car.

Pino turns our attention to the last temple. "The Temple of Hera, the protector of the good earth, is the oldest temple, built in 550 B.C. Often referred to as the Basilica by the archeologists, as they first believed it to be a Roman building, the temple was dedicated to Hera, the Greek goddess of marriage and fertility. Childless couples would visit the temple at night in hope that Hera would answer their prayers and bless them with a child."

Upon leaving the ruins Pino stops near a Stone Pine tree, removes a reddish-brown piece of bark from its trunk, then explains as he rubs it between his fingers that the Greeks made use of its powder to paint frescoes. "Ground ashes mixed with water and the blood of animals were also used," he adds. These are small details that the artists in our group will likely remember.

We enter the National Archeological Museum of Paestum. For the next half hour we admire the many treasures that were found at Paestum. Among them are Roman coins, Greek vases, jewelry, imported pottery, bronze pots filled with soft honey—the food of the gods, metopes of the Temple of Hera and several figurines of the goddess.

The most famous artifact in the museum is the Tomb of the Diver, found in an incredible condition, in a small necropolis nearby in 1968. This ornate tomb, decorated with frescoes, dates back to 480–470 B.C. when the Lucani ruled. Depicted on the long sides are an all-male banquet and a funeral cortège. Painted on the short sides are a naked man enjoying wine and a couple of guests escorted by a female musician. On the covering slab the naked diver is jumping from a platform into a sheet of blue water, which has been interpreted as the after-world.

As we emerge in the warm sunshine, I look at my watch. It is already one o'clock. For lunch I suggest the Basilica Café, a small restaurant in an enviable position, around the corner from the museum, near the Church of the Annunciation. Recent renovations have revealed that the church was an early Christian basilica from the fifth or sixth century A.D.

Immediately after we sit down around beautiful ceramic tables under a covered patio in the rear of the restaurant, a young waitress appears and hands us menus. I quickly peruse mine and order my favorite pizza, the *Frutti di mare,* while Pino selects the *Fiori di zucca.* The seafood and the zucchini blossom pizzas are just two among the nineteen pizzas available, most of which have been named for Greek deities. For fun, I try to identify them. Pointing to the Eolo, I glance questioningly at Pino, who answers. "He is the god of the wind. The next one Ares is the god of war, the Romans called him Mars. Crono is a Titan, the father of Zeus. Dionisos is Bacchus, the Roman god of wine."

While we are enjoying a glass of red wine from the nearby Cilento Valley, I ask Pino in French if he would not mind explaining the Grand Tour to me. Guidebooks make reference to it without giving a lot of details. "The term Grand Tour is primarily associated with the British elite from the seventeenth and eighteenth centuries," he explains.

"Throughout that period, young wealthy English aristocrats often traveled to the continent to broaden their horizons and to further their education by visiting the wonders of the ancient world. Many left accounts of their tribulations in diaries. Their journeys frequently took more than a year or two, for the transportation systems at the time were not ideal. Lodgings were not too clean back then, either. Safety was a big issue, as well as illnesses. In the nineteenth century, transportation improved.

With the arrival of steam powered ships and the spread of railway lines on the continent, Europe's upper class started to move about faster and in a safer environment. Comfortable hotels began to open their doors. In the second half of the nineteenth century, affluent Americans joined poets, writers and painters on their quest of discovery. Young women with chaperones, usually widowed grandmothers or spinster aunts, began to venture out. Rome, Pompeii, Herculaneum and Paestum were the most popular stops on their Italian journey."

"Fascinating. In essence, our trip is a deluxe modern-day mini-version of the Grand Tour with a tall, dark Aronne as an escort. How times have changed!" I reply, laughing, at the same time thinking of other questions I could ask the professor. The waitress reappears with our pizzas, freshly baked in a traditional wood-burning oven, and slides them deftly onto our table. They look delicious. The crust is not too thick, not too thin, just right. But then it is to be expected since the people of Campania have been making pizzas for centuries. Neapolitans even profess to have invented the bread-like dough topped with garlic and olive oil.

"This is very good, " I say approvingly to Pino, after he graciously offers me a taste of his pizza. I could almost get addicted to the delicate flavor of the zucchini blossoms coated with mozzarella cheese. The genuine mozzarella is made from the rich milk of the black water buffalos that graze on the fertile plains of the Sele River between Paestum, Eboli and Salerno, and the Volturno River, to the northwest of Naples. Although there are contrasting theories as to who introduced the Asian buffalos to Italy—either the Goths during their migration, the Normans on their return from the crusades, or the Saracens as they found a base near Agropoli—records show that mozzarella cheese has been produced in Campania since the sixteenth century.

The Mozzarella di Bufala usually comes in single round clumps or in cherry-sized pearls. Sometimes the cheese is molded into braids, gourd-like vessels and other shapes, as Maria, whom I met several years ago while escorting my first group, demonstrated. Every morning, in front of tourists, Maria produces fresh mozzarella in her small farm on the outskirts of Sorrento. She learned the process from her mother, who learned it from hers. Over heat, the milk is brought to a boil to be separated, with the use of rennet, then left to rest for twenty minutes. After the crumbling curd, drained of whey, has been transferred to another bowl, she submerges it in hot water and, with a long wooden spoon, she evenly exposes the curd to the heat. When the cheese has achieved the right texture, Maria kneads and stretches the steaming mass, then cuts it by pinching it between her thumb and index finger. This last step, called *mozzatura* or "cutting off," actually gives the cheese its name.

"*Scusa, ma ora devo andare. Ci vedremo ancora, no?*" Pino says, waving his hand in front of my eyes as he is getting up, ready to leave.

"I am sorry. I was just lost in thought. Yes, of course we will see each other again," I reply. Goodbyes are exchanged and after retrieving my camera and shoulder bag I settle my bill with the cashier. As I glance at the ice cream display below the counter, an elderly woman steps behind it.

"My son Marco is absent today." She smiles.

"He is the owner. My husband and I are just here to help," she volunteers, pointing to a man in his late seventies who is relaxing in a chair near the front door under a shaded terrace. She reminds me of my paternal grandmother, petite and fragile, with soft brown eyes and only a touch of gray hair. While I enjoy a small cup of *limone gelato* she tells me that her name is Aida and her husband is Ottavio. The family Volza moved to Paestum at the beginning of the nineteenth century, and two decades ago they started the restaurant, which is open daily from February to December. I express my gratitude for the ice cream and hurry back to the van where Aronne is chatting with the women.

⚜

After catching a glimpse of the modern town of Paestum, a popular summer seaside resort along the Gulf of Salerno, we pass the beautiful sandy beaches where the Allied Forces landed on September 8 and 9, 1943, under the code name Operation Avalanche. Here and in the surrounding areas, they encountered fierce fighting for several days. Many of the casualties are buried in a small war cemetery that lies between Battipaglia and Pontecagnano. As the gentlemen from my previous group expressed an interest in that period of history, we stopped at the cemetery to pay our respects to fellow Americans. It was an emotional visit.

Driving through the main street of the impeccably maintained Salerno, the capital of the largest province of Campania, in the early afternoon is a breeze. Most of its 145,000 inhabitants are still busy at work. Often ignored by the tourists, Salerno, which lies between the Picentini Mountains and the Bay of Salerno, is a pleasant city with an impressive history. It was founded as a military outpost in 197 B.C. by the Romans who gave it the name of Salernum for the two rivers nearby, the Sele and Irno. It quickly developed as an important trade center connecting the southern region of Calabria with Rome.

During the following centuries, Salernum would be occupied by the Goths, the Byzantines, the Lombards (or Longebards) and the Normans, each of them enriching its culture and traditions. Most historians attribute the foundation of the Medical School of Salerno to the Lombard Prince Arichi II in the eighth century, making it the oldest medical institution in Europe. In 1076 the

Norman Robert Guiscard conquered Salerno, putting an end to the Lombard dominance. He ordered a cathedral to be built and expanded the medical school. After the Normans came the Hohenstaufen emperors, and in the sixteenth century the Spanish took control. The city suffered considerably in the seventeenth century with the plague and earthquakes causing many deaths. In the eighteenth century an urban development, which is still expanding, began outside the ancient city walls.

Salerno is a vibrant city with a splendid cathedral that dominates a restored historical center and a French-style five-mile-long promenade lined with many rare palm trees, several lovely public parks and gardens, and a string of centuries-old noble palazzos. Its port is one of the most important on the Tyrrhenian Sea. Close to seven million tons of goods move through its facilities each year. The city is a major hub between two beautiful coasts: the Amalfi and the Cilento.

Conversations are floating inside the van as Aronne drives along the bustling port and beyond, on a winding road that climbs to a small plateau overlooking the glittering blue waters of the Tyrrhenian Sea. Suddenly, at the sign of Vietri, a collective cheer of delight bursts through the air. I glance at Aronne. He, too, is smiling knowingly.

Vietri

*A*t the heart of Italian style is a refined passion for beauty and a devotion to the pleasures of the visual sense. Its expression can be as classical as the marble statue of Venus by Canova or as modern as the hand-painted ceramic pottery of Vietri. At the mere mention of Vietri, women's eyes light up with a sudden brightness, for the name is evocative of a distinctive Italian tableware.

The name derives from Vietri sul Mare, the easternmost town on the Amalfi Coast, which dominates the small Valle di Bonea. Vietri sul Mare is considered the ceramic capital of Campania. The original settlement, known as Marcina, was founded by the Etruscans, conquered by the Samnites and subsequently expanded by the Lucanians and the Romans. The village was attacked by Vandals in 455 A.D. and repeatedly sacked by new conquerors during the following centuries. In the Middle Ages survivors restored the town and gave it the name Vetere, from the Latin word *Vetus,* meaning old.

As Aronne pulls into the parking lot of the Piazza Matteotti, in the center of the old town, right off the SS163 highway, there is a bustle inside the van as the women prepare themselves to quickly step down. Our time here is limited to one hour. Outside

Aronne and I watch the women stride hurriedly across the square in different directions, straight into the ceramic shops. Having witnessed this scene before, we look at each other and burst out laughing. "Don't get between women and their ceramics for they will run you down," I comment good-humoredly, and we laugh again.

While I set out to reacquaint myself with Vietri, I am reminded by the scores of boutiques surrounding the piazza and the nearby streets of how much the economy of the town depends on the tourism industry. Everywhere I glance, ceramic pottery is spilling out of shops, beckoning the tourists to enter, to look around and to buy a souvenir piece to display back home. Prices here are four times less than in the States, so why not take advantage of it? Plus there is always the chance to meet an artist personally.

Besides being renowned for decorative ceramic wares, Vietri sul Mare is famous for the Vietri or Vietrisi hand-painted tiles. Tile production in Vietri and in the nearby town of Cava de' Tirreni can be traced back to antiquity. Archeological finds suggest that mosaic floors were first introduced to Southern Italy by the Greeks. The Romans, who favored more colors, extended the use of marble with decorative terra cotta. For several centuries artisans, generation to generation, painted the same designs. In the fifteenth century we begin to see the influence of the Islamic world in the patterns painted on opaque tin glaze or enamel and in the use of tiles for external decoration of patios, gardens and terraces. Cava de' Tirreni and Vietri's tile production increased considerably in the sixteenth century as a new enamel was introduced, a faience much thicker and whiter than previously used.

In the eighteenth century the surrounding towns of Nocera, San Severino and Giffono stepped in to satisfy the increasing demand for Majolica tiles in new constructions. However, a century later, feeling the competition from China, they began to reduce their production. Only Vietri and Cava continued to maintain the same level to fulfill orders coming from Sicily and the Mediterranean basin. In the last century German artists and entrepreneurs settled in the area, bringing with them new ideas and revitalizing a dormant industry. Today, Cava de' Tirreni, Salerno and Nocera produce tiles on a more industrial level in medium-sized companies that employ about three hundred people each. In Vietri, a half dozen companies with fewer than thirty employees and the small artisan workshops specialize more in tableware and decorative pieces.

At the entrance of a tiny workshop, on a narrow street, a thin-faced elderly man with a long gray beard is outlining a familiar scene with a fine paint brush on a large tile resting on an easel. While he is deeply concentrating on his design, amid a dozen paint colors, a portable radio on a small square table behind him is playing one of my favorite Italian tunes. I approach him.

"*Sarà bellissima,* it will be beautiful," I comment.

He peers over his eyeglasses and acknowledges me with a faint smile, then returns to his work. For a brief moment I watch him as the image of Vietri sul Mare appears against the white background on the tile.

The tiles of Vietri and of the nearby towns are made of local clay, hand cut with a steel wire or machine cut, and put in dryers for a few days. The dried pieces, which are still gray, are baked in a kiln and emerge a reddish terra cotta color. When the tiles have cooled off, they are dipped in a thin chalky white liquid glaze. After drying naturally, the tiles are ready to be painted. Artists have a choice of several painting techniques. Sometimes they apply a single color evenly with a large brush or a sea sponge. Alternatively, like the gentleman in front of me, they paint the designs freehand from memory as they recreate them often enough, a method referred to as *Fatto a mano* or "Hand painted." However, the most commonly used technique, favored for repetitive patterns and for large quantities, involves some type of pounce. The artist reproduces a design on a glossy paper and pierces its outlines with a needle. The paper is then placed on top of the tile and graphite is pressed through the holes. At that stage artists can add colors. The painted tiles are baked one last time for twenty-four hours at a constant high temperature. When emerging from the kilns, the tiles have a brilliant and glossy surface.

The Italian Government recently passed a law providing a designation of origin or DOC brand for the Vietri ceramics in order to protect their production as well as the material used, the painting techniques and the designs. Most companies producing ceramic wares and tiles in the Salerno province are adhering to a strict code and follow stringent regulations in exchange for the right to use the Vietri label.

I continue to amble through the main street toward the church while keeping one eye on the clock. Throughout the town, the craftsmanship of the local artisans is visible on large murals. Many of the store fronts are tiled from the street level to the second floor with vistas of Vietri and scenes of village life. At the intersection of an alley leading to the church, a large ten by fourteen tile composition depicts two fifteenth century Spanish galleons on the Tyrrhenian Sea during a storm.

Close by is a scene depicting a lively grape harvest featuring a group engaged in barefoot winemaking. In Via San Giovanni, a cartoonish mural above a small tiled fountain shows a humorous side to life in Italy. My favorite panels are on the facade of a grocery store in the winding Diego Taiani Street. On either side of its entrance is an eight-tiled composition, both depicting young women holding baskets overflowing with fruit. The one on the left, with a translucent scarf covering her brown hair and surrounded by wisteria, is standing on a terrace that dominates the old town, while the one on the right, a blond girl, is on a balcony that overlooks the marina of Vietri in the forefront and the port of Salerno in the distance.

The Chiesa di San Giovanni Battista, which dates back to the seventeenth century, stands at the highest point of the old town. Its Moorish style dome is entirely covered with bright blue and yellow majolica tiles. The word "majolica" is often used to describe fine glazed earthenware. The most common explanation that I have found for the term is that it comes from the medieval Italian for the isle of Majorca, off the Spanish coast, where Hispanic-Moorish ceramic imports would transit en route to Italy. In the Campania region, a tile is generally called a *riggiola*, which appears to have derived from the Catalan term *rajola* when referring to an Arabic tile.

The most impressive building in Vietri, besides the church, is the Ceramica Artistica Solimene Factory on the southern edge of town on Via della Madonna degli Angeli. It was built on solid rock in the mid-fifties by the Solimene family, who has been working in the ceramic business for more than a century. The facade of the six-story building is unique. It appears as if it is made of ice cream cones covered with green and terra cotta ceramics separated by banks of windows. Ceramica Artistica Solimene exports its production of crockery—floor and wall tiles entirely made and painted by hand—all over the world. The company craftsmen have combined ancient techniques with new technologies to create durable tableware that can be put in modern dishwashers, and they offer a large selection of decorative pieces with lead-free glaze. Ceramica Solimene holds annual courses to teach young people the art of ceramic production.

While strolling back toward the piazza, I notice that the majority of the houses in Vietri are whitewashed, and their numbers are displayed on charming Vietri tiles. Small religious panels adorn several entryways. Here and there fresh laundry, hanging from second-story balconies, demonstrates that this town is very much lived in. Wonderful aromas emanating from the kitchens along my path are making me hungry.

Thinking about dinner, I decide to stop at a small grocery store. As I enter, one of my companions spots me and asks for my help with translation. "Of course. Be glad to," I reply. In the rear of the store, behind a large counter, a stocky older man in a flamboyant red cotton shirt is pouring limoncello into tiny plastic cups. When he looks up, with a courtly gesture he motions for us to taste the yellow liqueur. His face is jovial. I never say no to limoncello, the nectar of the Amalfi Coast. After thanking him, I lift one of the cups and sip it while I watch my companion's face for her reaction.

"Wow, this is strong," she says, grimacing.

"No English," the balding shopkeeper informs, "only Italian."

"No problem," I answer and, for the next few minutes, I translate. This is his homemade limoncello, he explains, made with the lemons that grow in his backyard. "It has a fiery punch," I inform him. He chuckles, then disappears below the counter.

"This one is a little sweeter," he announces as he opens a new bottle and refills the cups. I look at my companion. Her cheeks are a little rosy. I am sure mine are too. Once again, we drink from our cups. One, two, three, down it goes. Instinctively we slap each other on the back as we both start coughing. "Not only is the last one sweeter, but its alcohol content is even stronger," he confesses with a grin that suggests he was playing a joke on us.

"I would like one of each," my companion says to the shopkeeper as she regains her breath. While he is wrapping them up, I grab a couple of cans of beer from one of the shelves behind me then glance at the deli section. When it's my turn, I order a ham sandwich.

"Grazie mille, thank you so much," I tell him after settling my purchase.

"Per piacere." He smiles and we hurry out eager to continue our exploration of Vietri.

Down the street I stop in front of a ceramic shop that features some of the most striking examples of pottery I have ever seen. As I peek through the window, two tall middle-age American men walk out.

"They may have gotten my wife's attention but they got my money," one of them says dryly. "She already has a closet full of that stuff. I am lucky she did not buy the entire store."

I turn my head to hide a smile as the other man chuckles. Vietri sul Mare does create havoc in a relationship, I realize, laughing quietly. There is no doubt that this town is every woman's dream and every man's nightmare.

Inside the Ceramica Falcone shop I suddenly become giddy by the sight of the hundreds of objects displayed on the walls, on the shelves and on the floor. Scanning the room, I see at least a dozen items that would fit quite nicely in my home. The selection is astounding: sets of dishes, lamps, wall plates, umbrella stands, bowls of every size, candle holders, pitchers, wine goblets, small and large tiles representing Vietri, and the list goes on and on. At the back of the store, I spot the original Vietri dinnerware with the whimsical animal motifs. Every farm animal is featured in vibrant and pastel colors in a childish pattern.

"Those are hand-painted by our artisans in our workshop in Cava de' Tirreni," says a young woman next to me, "We also have the elephant, the octopus and the fish designs if you prefer." As I remain silent she points to an entirely different pattern on a shelf above. "On these our artists have painted an ancient intricate arabesque pattern around the border of the plate and a little crown of lemons in the center, combining old and new designs, which have become very popular among the American tourists."

After a few minutes of indecision, I select four coffee mugs with a chicken motif on a pale green background and hand her my credit card.

Leaning against the concrete ledge at the far end of the Piazza Matteotti and squinting in the late afternoon sun, I gaze at the modern town of Marina di Vietri below, at its popular beach dominated by a tower recently transformed into a villa, and in the distance, at an expansive westward view of the Amalfi coastline. I quickly snap a series of pictures and turn just in time to watch the women trickling back to the van, each of them holding at least one bag. I am sure they wish that they had more time here, but there will be plenty of opportunity to buy additional ceramics in the days to come. I am pretty confident that by the end of the week our group will have an inventory large enough to open a small ceramic shop back home.

Halfway to our hotel, Aronne asks me in a conversational tone about my evening plans. I blink, realizing that I got lost in my thoughts. "There is no group dinner tonight," I inform him. "The women are on their own. I have recommended to them a couple of restaurants, one near the hotel and the other in the center of Sant'Agata. I plan on enjoying the view from my balcony while eating my sandwich; then later I will go over my notes for tomorrow."

"Domani andiamo a Positano, si?" he queries.

"Yes, tomorrow we are going to Positano."

Day Three

The Amalfi Coast

*T*his morning as I switch on the television to the channel RAI Uno, Italy's premier television station, to check on the weather forecast, I realize that for the first time since we arrived in Italy I managed to sleep comfortably until six forty-five. Thinking back to the previous evening, I remember returning to my room very late, pulling back heavy drapes, opening the glass door to the balcony and staring in the moonlit night for a while at the sleepy town of Sorrento and at the dimming lights of Naples before climbing into bed. Upon our return from Vietri a woman in my group had not been feeling well, so I offered to escort her to the little pharmacy in the center of Sant'Agata. Unlike in the U.S., medications are only sold in pharmacies in Italy. By Italian law, pharmacists are allowed to supply health advice, prescribe and dispense medicine.

The tiny shop was crowded with several women of various ages. When my companion and I glanced at the pharmacist, we understood why. "Definitely a gelato," she whispered at my side and we both laughed. Indeed he was, with damp curly jet-black hair, brown eyes, a straight nose, and a hint of a dark beard along his jawline. He wore a black suit and a pearly-white shirt opened at the collar as if he had just left a wedding party. He looked more Greek than Italian and more like a Renaissance painter than a pharmacist.

None of the women seemed to be in a hurry to be served and I could not help but wonder how many were really sick. They were probably feigning some kind of ailment for an opportunity to talk with the handsome pharmacist, I thought, glancing at the young woman sitting in a corner. She was patiently waiting to have her blood pressure taken. I suspected that it was higher than normal.

The pharmacist looked at us and smiled. Apparently we were next in line. After my companion described her symptoms, he quickly picked up several little boxes from the shelves behind him and placed them on the counter, then proceeded to give her instructions while he tallied the bill. Thanks to socialized medicine, the total was less than a co-payment for a specialist in the States.

Hopefully, by now, with the appropriate medication and a good night's sleep, she is well enough to join us. My intuition tells me that she would not want to miss today's program, which will start with a visit to a unique ceramic shop, followed by some leisure time in Positano and end with a wine tasting in the late afternoon.

After hearing that the next couple of days will be sunny, with temperatures in the mid-seventies, I hurriedly select an outfit from the closet and enter the bathroom. Half an hour later I settle myself at my desk with a cup of coffee and a croissant, carried with me from the breakfast room, and open a thick folder to read my historical annotations and personal observations on the Amalfi Coast.

The Amalfi Coast is simply spectacular, divine, stunning, fascinating, splendid and breathtaking. These adjectives are often used to describe this stretch of the Campania coastline, considered one of the most impressive in Italy, if not in all Europe. However, dazzling words cannot begin to arouse the feelings that only a visit can inspire. On site, you will simply succumb to the alluring charms of the Amalfi Coast just as I did, and your sojourn, after you leave, will linger forever in your memories as one of the most wonderful in your life.

Extending from the Campania Apennines westward to Punta Campanella, at the tip of the Sorrentine Peninsula, the Lattari Mountains provide the backbone for the dramatic coastal landscape that separates the Gulf of Naples from the Gulf of Salerno. The mountain range is often jokingly referred to as the "Milky Mountains" by locals, for its name derives from the milk—*lactis* in Latin—supplied by the flocks of goats grazing on its slopes. At 4,737 feet, the highest point, Monte Sant'Angelo a Tre Pizzi or Mount Sant'Angelo and the Three Peaks, overlooks both the Bay of Naples and the Bay of Salerno. In many places the rugged limestone cliffs of the Lattari Mountains dive perpendicularly into the clear blue waters of the Gulf of Salerno. Picturesque villages, intertwined with terraced lemon groves and vineyards, hang from hillsides, and delightful secluded bays and coves beckon for your attention.

According to the storyteller Homer, it was off the shores of the Amalfi Coast and the Sorrento Peninsula that Odysseus—*Ulysses* in Latin—resisted the alluring songs of the Sirens, who were described in Greek mythology as half bird-half woman, then by later writers as sea-nymphs and mermaids, half fish-half woman. The three islets near Positano, known as Li Galli—literally The Roosters in Italian—were believed to be the Sirens' dwelling. Their enchanting songs enthralled passing mariners to shipwreck on their rocky shores. Odysseus, warned by the enchantress Circe, escaped such a fate. On his homeward voyage, he filled his mens' ears with beeswax and asked to be bound tightly to the ship's mast so that he could hear and resist the Sirens' call. Legend has it that Parthenope, one of the Sirens who failed to bewitch Ulysses, drowned herself in the Bay of Naples. Naples is still known today as the "Parthenopean city."

Thirteen towns and small villages line up along the Amalfi

Coast: Positano, Praiano, Furore, Agerola, Conca dei Marini, Amalfi, Atrani, Ravello, Scala, Minori, Mairori, Cetara and Vietri sul Mare. Some were founded by the Greeks, others by the Romans more than two thousand years ago, and for many centuries, their residents were completely isolated. Their only link was the sea. Seeking refuge up in the hills from Barbarian invaders, the villagers began to trace overland trails and pathways interconnecting villages, farms, churches and monasteries. The most famous trail is the Path of the Gods or Il Sentiero degli Dei, which runs from Positano to Praiano on to Agerola and Amalfi. The ancient track ascends along ridges high above the coastline, offering spectacular and breathtaking views of the villages below. The trail passes through lush Mediterranean vegetation, small farms, vineyards and lemon groves.

Donkeys played an essential role in the development of the small villages along the coast as they were a practical mode of transportation for the uneven terrain. They carried people and their belongings, as well as loads of building materials and goods from the docks up narrow paths to the town centers and beyond. Farmers and wine growers used them in "terrace-cultivation" introduced to the region by the Greeks. They plowed the fields and transported the produce to the markets. With their help the inhabitants built stairs, allowing villages to grow vertically and rendering easier access to secluded beaches. The donkeys are still used for agricultural purposes. In construction and restoration projects they have been replaced by mules. Some years ago I witnessed them being used to restore the Hotel Luna in the town of Amalfi.

Managed since 1822 by the Barbaro family, the luxurious hotel, which was originally a monastery, founded in 1222 by St Francis, has undergone some renovation recently. Illustrious personalities from around the world left their autographs in the register of the hotel.

Bismarck, Mussolini, Ingrid Bergman, Simone de Beauvoir and Tennesse Williams are just a handful.

As I was walking along the main coastal road, I caught sight of something coming down a steep staircase on a side of the hotel. I stopped, looked more closely and got my camera ready. Descending the steps were three mules and a construction worker. At the street level, the worker loaded bags of cement onto the mules and then guided them back up the stairs while riding the leader. I took several pictures as they progressed up two ramps of stairs shaped like a reverse seven at a forty-five degree angle and disappeared through an archway.

Around fifty defensive towers are still visible along the coast, from the tip of the Sorrentine Peninsula to the edge of the town of Salerno. Norman rulers began to construct them in strategic places in the eleventh century to warn villages of possible invasions. Five hundred years later the Spanish monarchs were still building them as sentinels against Turkish pirate attacks.

The watch towers, with windows facing east and west, standing at sea level, a short distance from one another to facilitate communication, were manned twenty-four hours a day. The watchmen lit fires and rang bells to warn villagers of impending danger. People would immediately leave the coastal areas and climb up to the hills to seek refuge.

Several of the fortified Norman and Saracen towers, as they are sometimes called, have been restored to their original condition. Some have been incorporated within other buildings while a few were converted into hotels, bed and breakfasts, house rentals, restaurants, and one even into a disco.

X

The most notorious Turkish raider was Kheir-ed-Din, also known as Barbarossa, who, for more than forty years, was the scourge of the Mediterranean. His name alone was enough to put fear into the hearts of the people. In fact, parents frequently used it to make their unruly children behave.

Born under the name of Khizr on the isle of Lesbos circa 1478 to a Turkish father and a Greek mother, Barbarossa was the youngest of four sons. In his youth he followed his oldest brother, Aruj, to sea: initially as an oarsman on one of his galleys, then later as a privateer as they sought their fortune on the Barbary Coast of Africa. By 1515, Aruj was the richest man in the Mediterranean, which he ruled with Khizr, from the Gulf of Tunis, through the Straight of Sicily, to the coast of Calabria, by preying upon trading vessels and seizing scores of ships from their enemies. The warehouses of Algiers, where he established a kingdom for himself, were filled to capacity with tapestries and linens from Flanders, gold and silver from the New World, spices and silks from Asia and grain from Sicily and Campania.

Aruj was the first to have been called by the surname Barbarossa. He sported a vivid red beard, and the title given to him by his men, which was "Baba Aruj" or "Father Aruj," sounded very much like Red-Beard to the Italians and the Spanish. After he was killed in 1518, in a battle against the Spaniards, Khizr inherited his brother's Christian nickname, even though his beard was auburn. To the Turks and Moslems, however, he was known as Kheir-ed-Din, "The Protector of the Faith," an honorary name bestowed on him during the next few years by the Sultan of the Ottoman Empire.

To secure the kingdom his brother had founded, Barbarossa (Kheir-ed-Din) organized a powerful fleet, which he kept increasing by capturing every enemy ship in his path. He continued to plunder the coastal towns and islands on the Mediterranean Sea, slaughtering and enslaving, in the process, thousands of Christians, who were sold off at slave markets in Algiers. Only a small number were ransomed. The women ended up in the harem of a rich Turk, in the kitchen or in the fields. Men would be sent to the oar benches of the galleys or to the rock quarries and the foundries of his commanding base until the end of their lives.

Barbarossa had become so powerful that, in 1532, Sultan Suleiman the Magnificent appointed him Admiral of the Ottoman Navy. In 1534, he ruthlessly destroyed Reggio Calabria, at the tip of Italy, then sailed northward, under the cover of night, up the Tyrrhenian Sea, with a fleet of a hundred ships. There, he sacked the islands of Procida and Capri before attacking the ports in the Gulf of Naples. In 1538, Barbarossa succeeded in defeating the fleet assembled by the Pope, comprising the Knights of Malta, Spain, the Republic of Venice and the Holy Roman Empire, under the command of Andrea Doria, the Imperial Admiral from Genoa. The Sultan's admiral remained the master of the Mediterranean until he retired in Constantinople—present-day Istanbul—in 1545, where he died a year later.

Looking back, I am fortunate to be living in the twenty-first century instead of the sixteenth. I would rather read stories about harems than be enslaved in one. Although I studied the Barbary Corsairs and the Ottoman Empire in my history classes, visiting the area where they left their imprint puts it all in perspective.

The Amalfi Coast received the honor of becoming a "Unesco World Heritage Site" in 1997. To protect its beauty and environment, new construction is forbidden unless the land is family owned and building rights grandfathered in. The same rule applies to the Sorrentine Peninsula. This encourages many to renovate and enlarge existing dwellings, giving the towns an even more pristine look. Abandoned convents and monasteries are transformed into luxurious resorts, and it is not unusual to see shops and apartments carved deeper into the mountains.

The *Costa Amalfitana,* as Italians call it, benefits from a Mediterranean climate. It rarely snows in the winter except at certain locations in higher altitudes. Temperatures are mild, but it does get cold and a little damp in the evenings once the sun goes down. It rains on occasion, but only for a few days, not months on end, and it can be pretty windy at times. The summers are hot—sometimes sizzling, and crowded. The ideal time to visit is in the spring and fall. The coastline is bathed in sunshine from sunrise to sunset as the sun rises near Salerno and sets behind the isle of Capri. Its southern exposure gives it a great advantage for growing citrus and grapes on the multi-terraced hillsides.

Quickly, I glance at the alarm clock on the nightstand, then lean back into the desk chair and continue reading.

To Drive or not to Drive

*T*he Amalfi Coastal Road, or the SS163 Costiera, is described in travel magazines as one of the most scenic roads in the world. Its construction was commissioned in 1807 by Joseph Bonaparte, appointed King of Naples by his younger brother Napoleon, to facilitate transportation between the coastal towns, and ceremoniously opened in 1853 by the Bourbon King Ferdinand II. For forty-six years men carved and drilled out the limestone cliffs and seaside hills of the Lattari Mountains. In this dangerous and backbreaking project, they were aided by hundreds of donkeys and mules that transported building equipment and hauled off the debris.

The forty-three mile-long Amalfi Drive, as it is called, officially starts a short distance west of Positano and ends right after Vietri sul Mare. Driving it is neither for the fainthearted nor for those easily distracted. The narrow road demands your full attention as it is winding and tortuous in many places. Visibility around the curves is limited—even to the point that road mirrors have been placed in key positions to assist drivers. Traffic tends to be heavy during the summer months, holidays, weekends and at night with nightclub fans.

During the tourist season, from March to October, buses more than thirty-four feet in length are only permitted to drive one way along the Amalfi Coast, in the west to east direction, from Sorrento to Positano and onward to the town of Amalfi. Their height cannot exceed 13.12 feet and their width 8.2 feet. Those standards are set by the officials of the Campania Region and the local authorities who are responsible for regulating traffic along the coast. Many tourist coaches are double decker buses, and the German buses seem to be the biggest of them all. They totally dwarf the cars behind and in front of them. Barely passing through tunnels and archways, they transform the road into a single one-way lane when making turns.

The public Sita buses, easily recognizable by their blue color, are the only ones allowed to travel in both directions. They link all the towns, along the coast from Sorrento to Salerno, and on the Sorrento Peninsula. Their frequencies vary from one season to another. Used by the locals and the tourists alike, they tend to be more crowded during the peak travel season, on weekends and holidays. The tickets "Unico Costiera" can be purchased at hotel reception desks, bus stations, news agents, *tabacchi* or tobacco stores and bus stops. Single trip tickets are available as well as twenty-four hour and three-day passes.

Instead of taking the bus, why not travel by sea as the inhabitants did in past centuries? The Metro del Mare Company offers a regular summer boat service between Salerno, Amalfi, Positano, Capri and Sorrento. Water taxis provide quick access to the towns, isolated beaches and caves along the coast.

For those preferring the flexibility of driving anywhere along the coast and who are up for the challenge, by all means rent a car. Make sure that it is fully insured and that parking is available at your lodging. Parking is a very big problem on the coast. There are limited parking lots in the small towns and the hourly fees are often over the top. In Positano, drivers are required to hand over their car keys when they park. Space is so tight that attendants try to squeeze in as many cars as possible.

The locals tend to park along the main road to avoid paying and then walk long distances to their jobs. Oftentimes, they double park on the town streets or leave their vehicles in unexpected locations, rendering navigation even more difficult. Side mirrors are turned in as a precaution, as they can easily get damaged by passing vehicles, and quite a few cars are actually missing one.

Besides watching out for buses and other cars, keep an eye on the many Vespa or scooter drivers around you. They do not respect normal traffic rules. Instead of driving behind you or in front of you, they tend to drive on your left or right side, always trying to overtake you. Be prepared for Vespa drivers to slither in front of buses and cars at red lights and at other times when traffic is stopped. Locals are used to their behavior and drive accordingly. Incidentally, Vespa—the Italian word for wasp—is manufactured by Piaggio, the maker of the Ape 50.

On a positive note, drivers do have a habit of warning oncoming traffic by a light touch on the horn when rounding curves. At several hairpin locations, along the Amalfi Drive, the flow of traffic is controlled by transportation employees wearing safety jackets and talking into walkie-talkies. In the summer months traffic is a little lighter around lunch time, early afternoon and during the siesta. It is important to remain calm and to always be ready for the unexpected.

When my sister and I reminisce about our wonderful time together in Furore, we frequently recall how crazy the traffic was. Of course, it did not help that our vacation coincided with April

25th, which is the day the Italians celebrate the liberation of their country by the Allied Troops in World War II. The entire country was on a three-day holiday. To my husband's greatest relief, our brother-in-law offered to drive. During that week he repeatedly played the game of stops, back ups and yields. We kept shaking our heads at the local drivers' antics and even came close to "kissing" a couple of them.

The same thing nearly happened during my first group tour. I still smile at the memory. We were returning to our hotel from Amalfi. After ignoring the stop sign at the Furore intersection, the driver of a small white van, who came barreling down the road, would have hit us if not for our chauffeur's slamming his foot on the brake. Swearing, Angelo opened his window, swooped the fingers of his left hand tight together toward the reckless driver— a typical Italian gesture meaning "What is the matter with you?" then turned to us and asked mockingly:

"Have you ever seen the face of a stupid animal?" My group members dissolved into gales of laughter at Angelo's delicate sense of humor. After glancing at the driver of the other car, a man in his late sixties who was smiling sheepishly, I joined them, too. "The mother of a stupid animal is constantly laughing," he commented seriously and his remark was met with a second round of laughter. In the center of Praiano we almost got side-swiped a second time. This one by an Ape pulling out of a parking space. "Another stupid animal," said Angelo, and we chuckled again.

X

I throw another glance at the alarm clock. Twenty minutes remain before the arrival of Aronne. Enough time to brief the women in the hotel lounge. From the back of my chair, I retrieve a white sweater, slip it over my pink cotton blouse, gather my camera, notes, water bottle and shoulder bag and step out of the room.

Positano – The Romantic

*T*here is a general feeling of trepidation and great excitement in the air this morning as we greet our chauffeur and step into the van. Aronne is grinning, delighted by our enthusiasm. Soon my companions will catch what the people here call "The Amalfi Fever." Really, no one is immune. Even I must confess to feeling its effects. The beauty of the coastline is simply too mesmerizing.

This time, as we drive on the Blue Ribbon toward the SS163 junction, Aronne stops at several key locations along the way to let us admire fantastic simultaneous vistas of the Gulf of Naples and the Gulf of Salerno. At the intersection, he turns right, around an orange three-story building, in the direction of Positano. Leaving the hotel early has its advantages. The big tour buses haven't left Sorrento yet, and we have the Costiera almost to ourselves.

For the next few miles, as the road constantly twists and turns along the edge of the mountains, we are rewarded with breath-taking views of steep limestone cliffs diving precipitously into the shimmering sea, rocky beaches, deep gorges and fabulous ravines. Now and then, looking through the right side window of the van, I have the impression that we are floating in mid-air between the sea and the sky. The curves are so tight and narrow that one false maneuver from an oncoming driver could send us flying with the seagulls; although Aronne is too competent to let that happen. Since his favorite pastime is to drive his motorcycle at high speeds on the Costiera, he navigates each bend with practiced ease.

At the first viewpoint, we alight. Standing high above the sea level, we gaze at the coastline's western slopes under the morning sun, at the isle of Capri in the far distance, and at the individual islets of the famous Li Galli Archipelago nearby, also known as the isles of La Sirenuse and the dwelling of the mythical Sirens: Leucosia, Parthenope and Ligeia. These little islands, bearing the official names of Gallo Lungo, La Rotonda and Castelluccio— Long Rooster, the Round One and Small Castle—were once the refuge of pirates, the Russian choreographer Leonida Massine, and the ballet dancer Rudolf Nureyev. They now belong to an anonymous owner from Sorrento.

As we continue on the serpentine road, our eyes seem to view the archipelago differently. Its contour resembles a floating siren with a head, chest and tail. Angelo once told me jokingly that the locals visualize the body of a famous Italian movie star who grew up in Pozzuoli, near Naples. After rounding the next bend, Aronne motions to a unique rock formation at the edge of a cliff. This rock is called "Garibaldi Rock" for it favors a profile likeness of the famous hero's face.

Our next stop is at the Belvedere Della Madonnina, a large terrace that overlooks Positano. It is named for the beautiful statue of the Madonna, which is standing in a little garden at the top of the stairs, looking down protectively over the town below. The women step closer to the railing to soak in the view of the eastern hillsides of Positano and of the quaint village of Praiano, clinging onto a promontory further afield.

This spot tends to be overcrowded and chaotic at times. Large tour buses stop at the Belvedere as they are not allowed to drive into the heart of Positano. Vendors, who have set up shop at this location, persistently hawk linens, postcards and citrus produce to distracted tourists. The best chance to have the place to yourself is around lunch time or late afternoon.

Elbowing our way through a crowd of Japanese onlookers, we make it back to the van and drive on through the upper level of Positano to the ceramic shop. The road curves around the New Church of Saint Mary of Graces—the Chiesa Nuova—easily recognizable by its elliptic-shaped silver dome. Perched on top of a hill, the Baroque Church was totally restored in the eighteenth century, hence the name. The Moorish-style dome was built with concentric layers of bricks, covered with tar and painted silver to deflect sunshine and to block heat penetration.

On the eastern outskirts of Positano, about a mile and an half from the town center, we pass the entrance to the five-star luxury Hotel Il San Pietro. Named for the chapel at the top, this hotel is considered to be an architectural masterpiece, as it was entirely carved out of the rugged cliffs of the Lattari Mountains. A few years ago I had the pleasure of touring it.

The reception desk is only accessible via an elevator that travels through the rock several feet down from the roadside level to an elegant lobby, walled by tall French doors. When guests step through one of those doors, they emerge onto a magnificent terrace with breathtaking views of Praiano, the Bay of Positano, Li Galli and the entire coastline as far as the isle of Capri. The terrace is bordered by eleven gorgeous tiled benches. The back panels of the benches, painted with warm tones and in the style of the seventeenth century, depict country and maritime scenes. The spacious rooms with private balconies have been skillfully designed, their floors and bathrooms covered with exquisite Vietri tiles; no two are alike.

A private beach, set in a quiet natural cove where newlyweds and the elite can relax and enjoy endless views of the shimmering sea, is reachable by elevator. The Il San Pietro is very popular with celebrities from around the world as it offers them the privacy they are looking for when vacationing on the Amalfi Coast.

)(

There is only one other car in the Casola Factory parking lot as Aronne pulls the van to a stop. Standing to the side of the black Mercedes, a young couple is discussing rather loudly the purchase of a large item, while their chauffeur is talking on his cell phone a few feet away. My guess is that they are probably honeymooning in Positano to be here so early, as Casola is only a short taxi drive from its center.

Quickly I grab my shoulder bag, step out and open the side door of the van. While I confirm our allotted time here with Aronne, the women walk around. I watch them inspect the beautiful tiled benches, similar to the ones on the main terrace of the Hotel Il San Pietro, and the tiled columns that separate the gravelled area from a lovely garden where huge planters are displayed. Listening to their comments, my instincts tell me that they are glad their husbands are at home today, for they are about to help the Italian economy.

The woman I accompanied to the pharmacy yesterday squeals with delight.

"This is almost as good as drooling over a gelato."

I cannot hide a smile. After all, who can resist Italian ceramics? I sure can't. The same can be said for the two men who, on a previous tour, were so impressed with the Ceramica Casola's craftsmanship that, in front of their startled wives, both ordered large tables for their patios back home.

Like many businesses along the coast Ceramica Casola is a family enterprise, in operation for three generations. The grandfather started out in a little shop, producing small hand-painted pieces and selling them to passing tourists. As business flourished, the store expanded and new products were developed. Twenty years ago the artisans of Casola began painting on volcanic rocks, transforming thick slabs of hardened lava into lavish outdoor tables, which are today their best sellers.

Inside the store we are greeted by Franco and Luca, who with their brothers Vito and Luigi, Luca's twin, manage the operations at Casola with a staff of fourteen. But before we can drool over the gorgeous items displayed in the showroom, we are given a quick tour of the factory at the back of the shop.

In the large workshop a half dozen virgin lavic slabs are pressed against the wall already sanded and chalked and ready to be painted. A few steps away, completed items are being prepared for shipment. A forty-two inch round table is going to Boca Raton, Florida, a small tiled galvanized iron bench to Palm Springs, California, and two big umbrella stands to Chicago, Illinois. Several other items, including a large rectangular table split into two pieces, are being shipped to a buyer in Dallas, Texas.

On the opposite side of the room, two artists wearing white smocks are sitting at small work tables. On the tables are ceramic paints in an array of colors and jars filled with brushes of various-sized bristles. Both artists are totally absorbed in their work. Each is painting a different view of Positano on a large tile. Once their designs are completed, the tiles will be fired in a large kiln. The brightness of the colors will be determined by the kiln's temperature and the firing time.

As we step back into the showroom, the women are dazzled by the beautiful masterpieces displayed on the shelves and the walls. Some of them proceed slowly, carefully examining each collection of dishes, large platters, serving bowls and trays, while trying to visualize which ones would best accent their dining room table when entertaining. Others are looking at gorgeous tables, imagining one of them in their backyard. Two of the women are seriously considering the purchase of one and are in the process of selecting the pattern. Suddenly, Franco lets a heavy stone drop on top of one of the tables, making us all jump. His gesture is to demonstrate how extremely shock and scratch proof they are.

As tiles are my weakness, I walk over to a display rack against the wall and gently slide out large trays to reveal sets of tiles in a variety of patterns. On the first tray I recognize the one I purchased during a previous visit, a set of six tiles depicting Positano, which is now covering part of the backsplash of my remodeled kitchen.

Glancing at the pretty ceramic clock on the wall, I note that we have been at Casola for nearly two hours. Thankfully, Graziela is wrapping up our orders. One of the great benefits of traveling with a small group of people from the same area is that you can share the shipping costs. All of the magnificent pieces we have selected will be shipped in a large box to just one address. Merchandise is usually received within sixty days after purchase. I smile, thinking that it will be a good excuse to get together again. Before leaving Casola, I recommend that the women quickly peek into the restrooms. The pink and blue tiles that decorate the restrooms are by far the prettiest ones along the coast.

X

Back on the SS163, a short distance from Positano, I flip the microphone on to indicate the several rows of little white chapels amid Italian pine trees nestled on a ridge high above the road. "It is the last resting place for the inhabitants of Positano," I remark. And after cruising around the curve, the group is rewarded with a magnificent view of the town's western side. Aronne slows down, allowing us to take pictures through the van's windows.

To avoid traffic jams, people are only allowed to drive through the center of Positano in the west to east direction, and we quickly understand the reasoning behind this policy as we enter the town. As we descend, the road is getting narrow and narrower and the turns tighten. In several spots, pedestrians have to plaster themselves against the sides of buildings to let large vehicles pass through. Drivers who park their cars in a wrong spot definitely risk damage. Here and there, street vendors are selling produce from the backs of their Apes. We continue our drive through Via Pasitea, which is lined on both sides with boutiques, hotels and small restaurants. I glance at Aronne who is cursing softly as he tries to avoid distracted pedestrians. I swallow a giggle. Patience. We are almost there. The town center's main parking lot is just meters away.

While the women enjoy some leisure time in Positano, Aronne is taking me to the restaurant La Tagliata in Montepertuso, a perilous twenty-five minute drive up the mountains. He recommended it during my last visit, and I am in the mood to try it. As we are climbing the steep road to Nocelle, Aronne is telling me that the new van is equipped with a GPS and a rearview camera and sensor system which allows him, when gears are in reverse, to safely turn around or back up in a tight situation. A very convenient little system for this excursion, as the road is getting windier and narrower. At several locations there is barely enough room for a single car to pass. Every so often Aronne needs to back up to give way. My heart beats loudly in my ears each time I peek through the side window. We are so close to the rim. Although the view is breathtaking, the drop is long and scary.

The rear parking lot is completely full. By chance, there is enough room for Aronne to park the van near the front entrance, along the side of the road. He had warned me that the family-run Trattoria La Tagliata is often crowded with tourists during lunch time and always packed in the evenings with the locals, as this restaurant is famous for its antipasti.

As we step inside, Enzo, one of the owners' sons, recognizes Aronne and motions us to the last remaining table available by a window. Within seconds, he appears at our side with a bottle of *aqua frizante,* carbonated water. Familiar with the regional dishes, Aronne places the order for both of us. When I ask him about it, he replies, "Wait and see." Lunch, or *Pranzo,* tends to be the biggest meal of the day in Campania. And if the food tastes as wonderful as the aromas emanating from the kitchen, I am in for an unforgettable treat.

Leaning back into my chair, I study our surroundings. The restaurant is nestled into the rock at the edge of a cliff. A stone wall separates two large rooms. At least two dozen tables, covered with flamingo-pink cotton cloths, occupy the one we are in. Behind us, next to an open bar, is a large grill. Garlic, dried peppers and kettles in various sizes hang from the ceiling. The happy hum of conversation is floating around us. Slowly my gaze scans the patrons— the majority are tourists. I turn toward the window, right into the blinding sun. Lifting my hand to block the glare, I stare at the view below. Wow, impressive. The ride was well worth it.

"These are prepared by Mamma Dora, Enzo's mother," Aronne informs me as her son places seven little antipasti dishes in front of us. On them are slices of *prosciutto crudo,* cured ham, and salami, marinated olives, grilled eggplant, roasted peppers, cherry tomatoes, miniature mozzarella balls, little onions and artichoke hearts. "I don't eat vegetables," Aronne confesses.

"You are kidding, right?" I exclaim, realizing that this is the first time we are sharing a meal together. Who has ever heard of an Italian that doesn't eat vegetables? Amusement glints in his eyes as he shrugs.

"Mangia," he orders amiably.

"It is a good thing I only had a croissant for breakfast," I chuckle, thinking *here goes my waistline.*

Minutes later Enzo reappears with the *primo piatto,* the first course, which is always a pasta dish of some kind. The large plate is still steaming as he sets it on the table. I quickly take a look at its contents and smile. There are five different types of pasta: gnocchi, manicaretti, mozzarella-stuffed cannelloni, ravioli and penne, all covered with a rich tomato sauce. No vegetables. I glance up at Aronne and tell him, "Now you eat," and we both laugh.

Shortly after I savor a few bites, Peppino, Enzo's brother, arrives with the *secondo platto,* the second course, an oversized platter with a wide range of grilled meats. *"Carne alla brace"* as it is called in Italy, is another specialty this restaurant is known for. A side dish of tomatoes and green salad sprinkled with olive oil and a touch of vinegar is served.

And just when I am thinking that after this there is no way I will eat another meal today, Enzo brings us a dessert plate with an assortment of mini-pastries. Looking at our choices, I cannot resist eating my favorite regional dessert: the *Babà al Limoncello,* a spongy little cake soaked in limoncello.

Outside, Aronne asks me if I know the story of Montepertuso. When I shake my head, he points to a gigantic hole in the Montepertuso Peak and to an adjacent cave.

"According to legend," he begins, "the Devil challenged the Madonna to pierce the top of the mountain when they were both competing for the protection of Positano. While the Devil only managed to scrape the mountain, the Madonna, with a simple touch of her finger, successfully bored through it and in the process chased the Devil away."

"Every summer," he continues, "on the morning of August 15th, during the 'Festival of the Assunta,' a statue of the Madonna is placed inside the mountain gap by the town's inhabitants. The celebrations in her honor include a parade of hundreds of boats in the bay, a reenactment of a failed Saracen invasion, and a ninety-minute fireworks display.

"The small towns of Montepertuso and Nocelle are easily reachable by bus from the center of Positano. The buses run approximately every hour. A more picturesque way to return from Montepertuso to Positano is through a seventeen-hundred-step pathway that cuts through terraced olive groves and small gardens. The fantastic journey down toward the sea takes about an hour," he adds as we walk to the van.

But before slipping inside, I stroll closer to the railing. From the hillsides, the panoramic views of Positano and of the coastline are incredibly stunning. Focusing on the SS163, my eyes trace its path as it cuts deep into the Lattari Mountains. Miniature cars and buses in a rainbow of colors disappear and reappear around each bend. Turning my attention straight down to Positano, I aim my camera and snap another series of pictures. So far I have taken close to two hundred photographs of the subject, from many angles, at different times of the day, in the spring and in the fall. With a vivid attention for details I have captured the sun's play on the brightly-painted houses, the multi-colored terraces, the churches and the Marina Grande. Snapshots of the town's unique treasures and hidden corners have also found their way into my album. Positano is without a doubt the most photographed town on the Amalfi Coast.

With regret I step back, still pondering the idea of having caught a severe case of the "Amalfi Fever," and almost laugh at myself for thinking that way.

X

Left to my own devices in the mid-upper part of Positano, and with still another hour remaining before rejoining my group, I decide to wend my way down to the beach. Since it is pleasantly warm I take off my sweater and loop it around my shoulders, then retrieve my water bottle from my bag, sip a couple of times and set out.

The origins of Positano are shrouded in a fascinating mixture of historical theories and mythical stories whose roots must undoubtedly have some connection to real events. One legend relates that Positano was founded by Poseidon in honor of the nymph Pasitea, whom he loved. Another narrates the story of sailors who, while transporting a stolen icon of the Virgin Mary across the stormy sea, heard a voice telling them repeatedly to *"Posa . . . Posa,"* or "Put it down . . . Put it down." As soon as they landed on a nearby small beach and deposited the picture on the sand, the storm subsided.

According to ancient sources the town's name is said to originate from Paestum, whose habitants, fleeing the constant Saracen incursions and disease in 915 A.D., sought refuge in the area. Historians tend to believe that it derives from the Posidii, a group of freed slaves or *liberti* in Latin, who settled here on the largest piece of land during the time of Emperor Claudius. The ruins of a villa, recently discovered under the Chiesa Santa Maria Assunta, testify that Positano was once a Roman colony as well as a popular resort. Before the Romans, Phoenicians and Greeks used to dock their ships in the fishing village on their journeys to the west.

Walking along the Viale Pasitea, it is impossible not to be drawn to the beautiful boutiques. Vendors on both sides of the street are showing off the famous "Positano Fashion Style," which has become increasingly more popular and recognized, by exposing elegant attire outdoors. One has particularly caught my eye. Moving closer, I see that several layers of deep purple velveteen, lace and ribbons have been pieced together to create a unique three-piece outfit. The effect of the design is both original and sophisticated, its intricate pattern revealed only to an observant seamstress.

The production of clothing is not something new in Positano, but a centuries-old tradition. Local artisans have always been busy creating and making garments. In the past silk and linen were more commonly used, as well as tombolo lace, said to have been invented by the nuns of the Chiesa Nuova Convent. The women of Positano were known throughout the area for creating exquisite white wedding dresses, many of which were hand sewn in little shops along Canovaccio street.

Across the street, white and pastel-colored lacy cotton garments are featured in a little shop's windows. The lavender sleeveless blouse with a ruffled neckline and the white sweeping skirt with scalloped hem look very romantic. However, it is the simple white dress with a lace bodice and plain eyelet-cotton skirt that holds my attention. I envision myself wearing it on a hot summer day while walking along the beach with my husband. After a moment of hesitation I enter the shop, trying to remember the last time I bought a dress. This type of garment is not usually found in my closet as I am more comfortable in pants and casual tops. But the opportunity to own something so prettily and uniquely made in Positano is too good to pass up.

Inside, a pretty young woman steps forward to welcome me. I point to the dress in the window and give her my size. After ushering me to a small room, she hands me the white dress and a lemon-yellow version of the same model.

"The yellow dress will be more flattering to your complexion," she says pleasantly; "plus its color will remind you of the lemons growing along the Amalfi Coast," she adds, smiling.

Quickly I remove my clothes and slip into the first dress. For a few seconds, straightening my shoulders, I admire myself in a full length mirror fastened to the door, then change into the yellow dress.

Catching my reflection, I cannot suppress a grin. To my surprise, the delightful saleswoman is right. The yellow dress looks better on me. This is the one. I glance at the price tag and blink twice. This lacy dress will undoubtedly put a dent in my yearly clothing budget, but I feel so beautiful in it. "Oh, why not be impulsive for a change?" I ask myself.

While waiting for my credit card's approval, the young woman wraps the garment in pretty yellow tissue papers, slides it into a lovely white bag with lemons printed on its sides, then pulls the straps together and hands it over to me. I sign the credit card slip, thank her, and walk out of the store. Although not fast enough to avoid overhearing the saleswoman tell another client: "The yellow dress will be more flattering to your complexion . . . " and I laugh.

In front of the Umberto Carro Ceramic Shop I pause and peek through the window. Their rustic-looking dinnerware sets are truly unique. Each piece is handmade and hand-painted with local fruit motifs such as lemons, figs, grapes, pomegranates and olives. The patterns and the warm earthy tones are lovely indeed. At the store entrance a friendly clerk invites me to step inside. Fighting temptation, I politely decline. Maybe later, I say and continue to amble farther down the street.

Nearing the Piazza dei Mulini, the Mills Square, the central hub of Positano, I scan the faces of the women resting on a concrete ledge under the shade of a gigantic tree. I don't recognize anyone from my group. Most likely they are shopping, enjoying a late lunch or relaxing on the beach.

The piazza is always busy in the morning with people arriving by the local orange buses or by taxi. From here, all the streets leading to the center of town and to the beach are for pedestrians only. Generally tourists arriving with the blue Sita buses get off at the Chiesa Nuova and transfer to the local orange bus that loops around Positano every half-hour. Adventurous travelers who instead climb down the flights of 482 steps, or the *scalinatelle,* to the center of town are rewarded with spectacular views of Positano.

As visitors from around the world come to enjoy this beautiful Mediterranean town, the main streets tend to be crowded in the mornings, on weekends and holidays. The majority spend the day, only a small number stay for two or three nights. In late afternoon, after the daytrippers have left, the town regains its quaintness and peacefulness. Those who choose to stay overnight see a different seaside resort, much less touristy but more relaxed and serene. They get a glimpse of what Positano must have been like before the American writer John Steinbeck's article was published in *Harper's Bazaar* in May 1953. His rendition of the Amalfi Coast enticed many American writers, filmmakers, musicians and artists to move here for inspiration.

I cross the piazza, which doesn't really look like a piazza but more like an intersection, and continue along the Via dei Mulini, Mills Street. Close to the front entrance of the Madonna del Rosario Church, a young girl is doing a brisk business selling granitas from a street cart. The refreshing treat, whose name derives from its granular texture, is a mixture of ice and lemon juice, similar to a French sorbet but coarser.

Further down the street I stop at the Banca di Napoli to withdraw another two hundred euros. Italian vendors accept credit cards for large purchases but prefer cash for small items. Technology is amazing when it works. In less than three minutes, the machine spits out ten newly-printed twenty-euro bank notes, which I immediately stow away in my money belt along with my debit card.

Outside an art gallery, exhibited on an easel, is an impressionist oil painting of Positano's stacked houses clinging to the mountainsides and colored by the morning sun. Not only is Positano the most photogenic town along the Amalfi Coast, it is the most painted as well. The small town's unique and impressive layout inspires artists to capture it on canvas. Oil, pastel and watercolor paintings of Positano's multicolored facades and seaside vistas fill several local art galleries.

Across the street a short flight of steps leads to a small grocery store. Open all day, it is always packed with tourists who are buying bread, cold cuts, fruits and drinks for their picnic lunch or dinner. Communication with shop owners and vendors is not a problem in Positano as tourism is their number one industry and almost everyone speaks English. And if they don't, they will find somebody who does.

Tempted by the desserts in the exterior showcase of La Zagara, I walk inside. "The Orange Blossom" tea room is the perfect place for a quick lunch during the day. On my first visit my husband and I ate a couple of *panini,* small sandwiches, on their wooden terrace overlooking the dome of the Chiesa Madre. From our table, under the lovely shaded pergola, we could smell the fragrant scent of the lemon and orange blossoms, hence the name. All the while, we were savoring one of their famous homemade pastries. In the evening, La Zagara is transformed into a popular piano bar with live Neapolitan music and dancing.

"Mamma, vorrei mangiare tutto," says a small dark-haired boy to his mother, his palms on the glass display next to the entrance, his eyes as big as on Christmas morning. I smile, thinking I too

would like to eat it all. Although I am not sure that I could handle all of the calories. For a few minutes I stare at the delectable temptations. Carefully laid out on paper doilies are: *Babà con Panna*–sponge cake soaked in rum and filled with whipped cream, *Torta Caprese*–almond chocolate cake, *Torta Zagara*–tangerine sponge cake and topped with chocolate, *Delizia al Limone*–sponge cake with lemon Chantilly cream and *Tiramisu al Limone.*

Recalling with a certain amount of guilt that I have already enjoyed a pastry, albeit a small one, I decide to treat myself to a smooth Italian ice cream instead and stride across the room. Lined on the two shelves of the display case are two dozen stainless steel tubs filled with gelato. La Zagara's selection of flavors is quite impressive. Among them are *fragola* strawberry, *limone* lemon, *crema* vanilla, *pistacchio, melone, frutti di bosco* forest berries, *cioccolato* chocolate, *banana, cocco* coconut and *bacio* kiss.

The last one sounds interesting. I wonder if it is made with the Perugia Baci. The bite-sized confections that Italians call kisses, are made with chocolate, cream and hazelnuts, and wrapped in a silver paper sprinkled with tiny blue stars. Since they are in my top-ten list of pralines, I order a *coppa,* a cup with two scoops. One pistacchio and one bacio.

The lanky teenager behind the counter chuckles. Now, why is that? Is it because of my choice of ice cream or the fact that I did not say the word bacio correctly. "Ci" is pronounced "Chi" in Italian. Sometimes I get my languages mixed up. I think in French, try to talk to the locals in Italian and converse with my group in English. He hands me the cup and a plastic spoon, then moves on to serve the next person.

While waiting in line at the cash register, I savor for the first time my bacio ice cream. I am not disappointed, it tastes exactly like the baci chocolates. It is absolutely delicious! Out of the corner of my eye, I catch the little tyke walking slowly to a table nearby, careful not to let his tiramisu fall to the ground. Without bothering to sit down, he picks up his spoon and takes a bite. Witnessing the pure look of delight on his face, I cannot resist a smile.

Adjacent to La Zagara is my favorite boutique in Positano, I Sapori di Positano–The Flavors of Positano–which opened more than twenty years ago. This beautiful shop is impossible to miss for on either side of its entrance is a large lemon-scented burning candle on top of a ceramic pedestal. Inside the first room, which is the larger, are hundreds of lemony items. Lemon jams, liqueurs, perfumes, soaps and candles can be seen everywhere. Exquisite Capodimonte porcelain lemon trees and centerpieces as well as hand-painted ceramics with lemon designs are displayed throughout, on shelves and tables. And the second room is filled with elegant lemon-printed linens. A heavenly fragrance welcomes the customers, and the staff is always very friendly.

Strolling along, I pass, on my right, another art gallery and, on my left, the Palazzo Murat—the eighteenth century summer residence of the French King of Naples, Joachim Murat and his wife Caroline Bonaparte. The Palazzo was once a Benedictine Monastery. Now it is a four-star hotel. In the summer, classical music concerts are held on the patio.

The Chiesa Madre is just steps away. I see the church's beautiful dome through the wisteria-covered trellis designed to shade this section of the pedestrian street. Wisteria vines grow rampantly everywhere in Positano. They drape pergolas, private patios, arbors and balconies. They are stunning in the springtime, when they bloom. Leafless canopies filled with clusters of fragrant deep blue and lavender pendulum racemes, similar to grapes, stand out against pastel walls and over entryways and iron bars.

Along the wall of a raised garden, artists are selling lithographs of Positano and the Amalfi Coast to passing tourists. They appear to be doing a fair amount of business. During the last millennium Positano has had its share of ups and downs.

At the dawn of the eleventh century, the people who had been held in servitude by the Benedictine Abbey of St Vito, today Nocelle, for close to a century revolted and established their own community. A century later they were conquered by the Normans. Then as the powerful Maritime Republic of Amalfi started to decline, the Positano naval forces began to grow.

Throughout the next three hundred years, the town was repeatedly attacked by Pisans—the inhabitants of Pisa, their powerful rival from the north, and by the Saracens and Turks. In the sixteenth and the seventeenth centuries, Positano experienced a period of economic growth. Maritime trade with the East flourished, and the population increased. In the eighteenth century, a number of houses and churches were built or restored in the Baroque style. Amongst those restored was the Chiesa Maria Assunta, the Church of Saint Mary of Assumption, often referred to as the Mother Church or the Chiesa Madre. Its imposing dome, originally built in the twelfth century, visible from any part of town, is covered with blue, green, yellow and white Vietri Majolica tiles, laid out in a diamond-shaped pattern, characteristic of many church domes in Southern Italy.

For a moment I stand in the little square in front of the church. The free-standing bell tower is a few feet away behind me. The facade of the Chiesa Madre is quite plain, unlike the facade of other Baroque churches in Campania. In contrast, the inside takes me by surprise. Constructed in the traditional cross design with its nave and two aisles separated by rows of columns, the interior is painted in white and the walls are covered with several gold ornaments.

The most important adornment in the Chiesa is above the altar: the recently-restored Byzantine Icon of the Black Madonna and Child, on which the town's legend is based. The bust of Positano's patron saint San Vito can also be seen. In the left corner of the church, near the entrance, a large nativity scene is hidden in darkness behind glass. It is traditionally lit up during the Christmas Season as are many other nativity displays throughout Positano. After exiting the church, I cross the piazzetta and descend the steps toward the beach.

At the bottom of the steps is Positano's tourist office. A note left on the door indicates that it is closed for lunch until three. On the Amalfi Coast that could mean three-fifteen or three-thirty. I pass more shops and restaurants before arriving at the Marina Spiaggia Grande, which is half marina, half beach. The beach, the longest one in Positano, is divided into two sections. In the private section, sunbathers are required to pay a fee for the use of colorful lounge chairs, umbrellas and showers; drink service is available. In the public section, clearly indicated as *Spiaggia Libera*, sunlovers can lay down their towels for free on a mixture of volcanic gray pebbles and coarse sand.

Scanning the beach, I locate two of my group ladies resting in the free zone while another lady is testing the temperature of the water with her feet. They seem to be enjoying themselves. Two nice-looking men, wearing black pants, white shirts and skipper's hats, approach and try to persuade them to take a boat ride. From a short distance I follow the exchange, ready to intervene and assist with translations if necessary. I see smiles, gestures and heads nodding in agreement—obviously, they have the situation under control. I check my watch. If they want to see Positano from the sea, they'd better hurry.

Positano's unique layout is best viewed from the sea, and the farther out you sail the more spectacular it gets. In the backdrop, rugged limestone cliffs, partially covered with a luxuriant Mediterranean vegetation, dive into an intense blue Tyrrhenian Sea. Close to the shoreline, the Chiesa Madre with its imposing dome is nestled in a small valley between two cliffs covered with brightly painted houses, villas and hotels, virtually on top of each other. The unforgettable panoramic vision just takes your breath away.

Looking at Positano, it is hard to believe that it was once the poorest town along the Amalfi Coast. In the mid-nineteenth century close to seventy-five percent of the male population immigrated to the US, leaving mothers, wives and children behind. These women quickly had to learn to fend for themselves. To survive, they became entrepreneurial. They opened their homes to the English nobility and Romantic writers as they were passing through on their Grand Tour of Europe. They sold them home-cooked meals and handmade garments. Abandoned houses were bought by outsiders and foreign visitors, who hired local craftsmen to restore and repair them. A small number of villas were actually purchased by the European aristocracy, who fell in love with the scenery and the Mediterranean climate.

Slowly, the town's economy turned around. In the first years of the twentieth century, Russian artists came to live for a time in Positano. They were followed by Dutch landscapists and German ceramic painters. In the fifties, it was the turn of Russian composers and dancers, together with American artists. For the last 100 years Positano has been a place of inspiration as well as a place to relax and enjoy the good life. At present close to four thousand people live in Positano.

Each time I visit, I feel the town's magnetic charm. I could quickly get used to living here. I would probably paint all day. Both of my grandfathers were painters. Perhaps I have inherited some of their talents? For now I can only to try to absorb it all, so that on a rainy day back home, I can imagine myself here, relaxing on a concrete bench at the water's edge, enjoying the sea breeze and the warmth of the sun on my face.

Too soon, giggling sounds snap me out of my wishful day-dream. At the end of a ramp six very pretty young girls with long blond hair are taking turns at being photographed. Stepping forward I offer to take a group photograph with one of their cameras. This way, they will have at least one group picture in their albums. As I detect an unfamiliar accent I ask them where they are from. Sweden is the answer. I should have guessed. They all have blue eyes. I wonder how many of them will be coming back here for their honeymoon, as Positano is listed in the top five romantic destinations in Italy.

One of my favorite spots in Positano is the secluded Spaggia del Fornillo. The small beach is just steps away from the western end of the Spiaggia Grande, easily accessible through a beautiful panoramic path that runs along the sea, christened Via Positanesi d'America in memory of the local people that immi-grated to America.

On the waterfront of Fornillo Beach is the wonderful Hotel Restaurant Pupetto. The restaurant is idyllic for a romantic lunch or dinner under a lemon covered pergola. Fornillo Beach, named for the bread-baking ovens that were here during the Roman pe-riod, is tucked between two Saracen watch towers, the Torre Trasita and the Torre di Clavel, or Torre di Fornillo. These towers, includ-ing a third one located at the eastern end of the Marina Grande, the Torre Sponda also called the Torre Pattison, played an impor-tant role in the defense of Positano. All three were totally restored in the last century and are now privately owned.

A quick glance at my watch tells me that I need to get moving.

What a glorious day this has been so far, and I can't think of any better way to end it than with a wine tasting.

Andiamo—Let's go, as the Italians would say!

A Passion for Wine

*M*ention Italy to friends and they'll immediately think of food and wines. Talk about Italian wines and they'll cite you renowned Tuscan names such as Montepulciano, Chianti and Vernaccia. However, in Italy, every region produces great wines and Campania is no exception. They might not be as internationally illustrious as the Tuscan wines, but they deserve recognition nevertheless. And, since we are in Campania, it might be fun to try some of their best wines.

Five minutes ago we regrouped at the Piazza Flavio di Gioia, the small square in front of the Santa Maria Assunta Church. While the women exchange shopping and lunch stories, I try to make up my mind which route to travel to the Conwinum bar. Although the easiest way to reach Positano's most unique wine cellar is from the Marina Grande, I finally decide to lead the group through a more interesting path, behind the church, down a narrow shopping street and a short alley.

Inside the bar, at the bottom of a flight of stairs, two sommeliers greet us with *"Benvenuti."* Around me, the women are whispering, "Mmm, gelatos."

"Sweet Dreams!"

"Italy is certainly a feast for the visual sense."

"Girls, let's not fight, I saw them first." And each comment is met with a flurry of giggles.

Having difficulty keeping a straight face, I somehow manage to introduce myself and my companions. I hope they don't understand our secret code, but I do agree. They are quite attractive. They are both wearing white shirts, red ties and black pants. The younger of the two, who looks to be in his thirties, steps forward. His name is Leonardo. The older one, who appears to be in his mid-forties with a little gray at the temples, is Peppe, short for Giuseppe.

A quick survey confirms that we will have the trendy establishment exclusively to ourselves. This will be an intimate tasting experience. I smile at the thought, for the style of the bar is almost reminiscent of a Moorish harem. The only things missing are puffy silk pillows on the brightly-painted benches in private alcoves. The floor is lined with a combination of terra cotta and blue-gray ceramic tiles and the walls are covered with oil paintings of nude women. It is ironically coincidental that the bar, which functions as a gallery for local artists, currently features a painter of female nude models, as we are a women-only group. I seem to recall that during a previous visit landscapes were exhibited.

In the center of the large multicolored arched room, opposite a semicircular bar fronted with black stools, are eleven small square volcanic tables pushed together in a U shape. On each table are three different size glasses on a rectangular white paper placemat and an informative leaflet on the three wines that we are about to taste, compliments of the Conwinum Bar.

We settle down and study the watercolor designs on the tables. They are stunning. On the table in front of me is the Chiesa Madre. On the one to the left is the garden of the Villa Cimbrone in Ravello and on the right is an aerial view of Positano. I grab my camera and take their pictures. "The tables were hand-painted by the artists of the Ceramiche Sara factory in Vietri," replies Peppe to my question.

Leonardo introduces the first Campania wine, a Greco di Tufo Cutizzi 2007 from the Feudi di San Gregorio Winery. The Cutizzi wine is made from "Greco" white grapes, labeled appropriately for the Greek settlers who planted the first vines on the slopes of Vesuvius in the seventh century B.C. The "Greco" variety was later transplanted near and around the town of Tufo where it thrived. In that part of Campania, the grapes are known as "Greco di Tufo." The small town of Tufo, named for the volcanic rock present in the subsoil, lies in the Province of Avellino not far from its capital, which bears the same name.

Founded in 1986, the Feudi di San Gregorio Winery is just outside the town of Avellino, on top of a lush and gentle hill near the small village of Sorbo Serpico. The state-of-the-art wine facility produces an average of three million bottles a year, seventy-five per cent of which are white wines. The winery is open to the public only through reservations.

Leonardo pours the wine into our glasses while Peppe serves us a unique appetizer of marinated tuna wrapped around fennel. Glancing at my companions I recognize the wine connoisseurs. They are looking at the color of the Cutizzi, slightly twirling their glasses to check its alcohol content or its legs, then smelling its aroma. I flip my attention to the woman at the far end. Ignoring all protocols of fine-wine tasting, she swigs down her wine, then catches my stare. Resisting the urge to teach her the proper etiquette, I raise my glass and say, *"Salute."*

Immediately the room reverberates with its echo. After taking a sip I record my comments in the leaflet. Color: intense yellow.

Bouquet: pleasant. Taste: very nice. "The Greco di Tufo Cutizzi is perfect as an aperitif or to compliment any fish and shellfish dishes. It should be served cold, at a temperature of eight to ten degrees Celsius," recommends Leonardo, refilling our glasses.

Historically known as Irpinia, the Province of Avellino is located some thirty-five miles east of Naples, on the Southern Campania Apennines belt. Its terrain is largely mountainous, and because of the region's volcanic activity, its soil is rich with minerals laced with sulfur, chalk and iron.

The last earthquake that shook the Irpinia Region occurred on November 23, 1980. It measured 6.8 on the Richter scale and centered on the village of Conza. The Irpinia earthquake or Terremoto dell'Irpinia, as it was known in Italy, destroyed entire towns and many medieval buildings in the province, as well as in the sur-rounding areas. It was felt as far away as Salerno and Naples, where a dozen structures were leveled. There were many casualties, in-jured and homeless people. I remember it well for I was working for an Italian tour company in Belgium at the time. Several of our Italian employees drove to the region with goods and money that we had collected. Slowly, the people of Irpinia, passionate about their land as well as their winemaking, rebuilt the villages.

Nowadays the town of Avellino is completely surrounded by vineyards planted at higher elevations. The vines bask in the hot Mediterranean sun during the day and cool down with the up-draft from the sea and the downdraft from mountains during the night. With the combination of volcanic elements in the soil and the ideal climate for wine cultivation, the Avellino Province pro-duces some of the finest wines in Campania, many of which have been rewarded with the *Denominazione di Origine Controllata e Garantita*—Controlled and Guaranteed Denomination of Origin, or DOCG status. Another white grape that thrives very well in the

Province is the "Fiano," also imported by the Greeks more than two millenia ago. Today, the two best white wines of Campania derive from the Greco and Fiano grapes, respectively the Greco di Tufo and the Fiano di Avellino.

Leonardo serves the second wine, a red Vigna Camarato 1999 made with one hundred per cent Aglianico grapes from the Villa Matilde Winery. Peppe places a small dish of *bruschette Capresi*, consisting of cherry tomatoes and little mozzarella balls, in front of us.

Occasionally Leonardo glances in my direction as he tries to find the correct English words to describe the character of the wine and its pedigree. He needs assistance with translation and I gladly oblige. Although I prefer white wines, this red one is wonderful. It has a nice body, a deep ruby color and a beautiful perfume.

"The family-run Villa Matilda winery is located in Cellole, in the province of Caserta, approximately fifty miles north of Naples," informs Leonardo as he fills each glass halfway.

"This wine is recommended with lasagna, baked lamb, good roasts and Neapolitan sauces," he adds, grinning at our joyful mood.

While listening to the murmur of quiet conversations around me and an occasional boisterous laugh, I study the wine. It nourishes my spirit to know that the women are enjoying the experience. They are relaxing and confiding in one another. A few have removed their sweaters and a couple are fanning themselves. I smile. It does feel hot all of a sudden. Once again lifting my glass, I clear my throat and say: "Here's to us," then clink it to the glasses of my closest neighbors and sip.

The third and last wine is a Taurasi 2000 from La Casa dell'Orco Winery. The Taurasi wine is made exclusively with Aglianico grapes grown around the town of Taurasi, in the Avellino Province. It is believed that the name Aglianico derives from a dialect version of the word "Hellenico" and that the red grapes were also introduced to Campania by the Greek colonists. These high quality grapes, round and deep blue in color, are very important as they are chiefly responsible for the only red DOCG in the region. Their clusters are of medium size and ripen very late. Taurasi wines must age for three years before they can be served.

Pulling my Michelin map out of my shoulder bag, I ask Leonardo to pinpoint the location of the town of Taurasi. As he steps closer, he mentions that the medieval town is about ten miles east of Avellino, off the A16 Naples-Bari freeway. "The hill town is well worth a visit," he comments.

In my guide book I read that Taurasi is dominated by a castle built by the Lombards and later enlarged by the Normans. It mentions numerous elegant Baroque buildings with refined stone portals and the Church of the Rosario. I close the book and return it to my bag along with the map.

While we smell the bouquet of the Taurasi 2000, sip from our glasses and savor its fruity qualities, Leonardo delights in pointing out the characteristics of the wine. "It is a wine of distinction and a substantial dinner companion for grilled meat dishes and strong-flavored cheeses, as well as for sweet desserts. The bottle should be previously opened to let the wine breathe and served at room temperature."

The Taurasi is excellent. It is my favorite. Its potency is tingling straight down to my toes. No wonder the Greeks and Romans referred to wines as the nectar of the gods. This afternoon we are all goddesses. After another sip, I glance at the last appetizer plate, a small tray filled with pieces of Provolone del Monaco—a Sorrento cheese—almonds and drops of cherry marmalade and honey.

Leonardo steps in front of me to refill my glass and asks me to translate. "The main wine production area in Campania is centered around Benevento, Avellino and Caserta. There is a modest winemaking industry in the Cilento Valley, on the island of Capri and on the Amalfi Coast. The wine growers of Campania are very proud of their wines. They have been largely ignored in the past; even so, they have been producing excellent wines for more than two thousand years. Quite a feat compared to the production of wines in the other regions of Italy," he says proudly. I quickly interpret.

"But it is changing. There is a dynamic resurgence of sorts. For the last twenty years, wine makers have combined old traditions with modern technologies to produce exceptionally good vintages and wine lovers have started to notice," he concludes, then moves on to refill the other glasses.

Checking my watch moments later I signal to the group that it is time to leave. Leonardo rattles something off in Italian to Peppe that makes me laugh, or is it the wine? We all seem to be feeling a little woozy as we say our goodbyes to the charming sommeliers and walk toward the exit.

The climb back to the van is a challenge, especially after a few glasses of wine, or if you carry wine bottles and heavy ceramics. I chuckle as everyone complains about their fitness. It takes us approximately twenty-five minutes to reconnect with Aronne. Always the gentleman, he steps forward and opens the doors. His eyes are gleaming with laughter as he listens to women describing all the good-looking men, or *gelati,* they have seen in Positano. Earlier today I let him in on our little private joke. When he glances in my direction and shakes his head, I laugh.

On our way out of town, driving through Via Cristoforo Colombo, I indicate the famous Sirenuse Hotel, named for the legendary Sirens. The five-star hotel was featured in the movie *Only You.* La Sirenuse is owned and operated by the Neapolitan Sersale family, who transformed their eighteenth-century summer residence into a magnificent hotel in 1951. The lobby and the public rooms are filled with many wonderful century-old antiques of the sort that I would love to have in my own home. Beautiful Vietri floor tiles in brilliant colors and patterns are seen throughout. Magnificent bougainvillea vines cover the white columns of the terrace surrounding the pool and the outdoor bar with a splash of color. Most of the rooms have a large terrace that overlooks the azure sea, the Li Galli rocks and the gold and green mosaic dome of the Chiesa Maria di Assunta. This hotel is an oasis of tranquility in the center of Positano.

Further up the road, I point to the balcony where Frances had a tryst with the handsome Marcello in the movie *Under the Tuscan Sun*. On the opposite side of the street is an unobstructed view of the western slope of Positano. And at the end of the road, near the Fermata Sponda where a large group of tired-looking people is waiting for the Sita bus, Aronne turns westward.

Positano is a town like no other. You either find it too touristy and walk through it rather quickly, totally detached, or you find it one of the most amazing towns you have ever seen and want to discover all its secrets. I think that by now it is quite obvious where I stand. I believe that Positano is meant to be explored at leisure, to feel its pulse and to savor all its flavors.

Day Four

The Isle of Love

A loud noise shatters the silence of my room, pulling me instantly from a deep, luxurious sleep. I stir, then squint at my alarm clock. With fifteen minutes remaining before the start of my daily morning routine I lay quietly, trying to identify the source of the noise. It did not sound like Sant'Agata's church bells, which I really enjoy. It was more like a ship's horn. Maybe I had been dreaming that I was onboard a cruise ship somewhere in the Mediterranean. Here is that noise again. Louder this time. But then I remember leaving the balcony door open last night for a breeze. Still a little sleepy, I slip from the bed, put on my robe and tiptoe outside.

It is almost light out, my favorite time of the day. I love to watch the sunrise grow and spread. The skyline is a beautiful shade of lavender. Sailing into the bay are two cruise liners. Overhead, a flock of seagulls swoops down on their wake for an early breakfast. The captains are taking turns blasting the horns to apprise their families and those of their officers of their arrival. Many of them are natives of this area and have attended the prestigious Nautical Institute "Nixio Bixio" in Piano di Sorrento. It is one of the oldest maritime schools in Italy. By the size of the cruise ships, I estimate that at least four thousand people will disembark shortly. They will be tendered to the Sorrento Marina Piccola, where many will then board large buses to Pompeii or the Amalfi Coast. Some passengers are likely to take a hydrofoil to Capri or Ischia, while others will simply stroll around the center of Sorrento. They'll enjoy a gorgeous day in Campania as the weatherman has predicted a blue sky, plenty of sunshine and seventy-six degrees.

Our destination today is Capri, the island of Love. Whenever I think of Capri or mention the name, the lyrics of the French song "Capri, c'est fini" cross my mind. "Capri, it's finished" was written and interpreted by a young upcoming artist, Herve Villard. His love song was tremendously popular when I was growing up. The lyrics evoke a breakup between two people who met on the island, fell in love but ultimatly went their separate ways. Villard got the inspiration for the title of the song from a travel poster in the Paris Metro that featured Capri and from another famous French melody "C'est fini," sung by Charles Aznavour.

This will be my sixth visit to Capri, and somehow I have a feeling that it will not be the last one.

Ninety minutes later, our group is traveling in a white minivan toward Sorrento, on the winding Nastro Verde, the Green Ribbon. The road owes its name to the abundance of green seen on both sides, from the lemon and olive groves. To pass the time, I try to converse with the driver, a young man in his early twenties, whose sole job is to transfer tourists back and forth from their hotels to the Marina Piccola. Try is the appropriate verb here, for I don't understand his replies. Intrigued by the fact that garbage containers are always overflowing in this area, I point to one and ask him if the collectors are on strike? *"Bidone,"* he replies. Yes, I know the Italian word for bin so I rephrase my question. Once again my mind attempts to process his answer. Finally, I realize that he speaks Napoletano. No wonder I don't grasp everything. I could almost kick myself.

Napoletano is a rich patois comprising words of Oscan, Greek, French and Spanish origin—basically an amalgam of 2,700 years of history. The dialect, which originated in Naples, is widely spoken throughout Campania, with slight pronunciation variations from one town to another. Napoletano is not taught in school but is kept alive by people who teach it orally from generation to generation.

Traffic is flowing freely as we drive through the historical center of Sorrento and begin to descend the extraordinary Vallone dei Mulini, the Ravine of the Mills. The three-quarters-of-a-mile-long ravine stemmed from a huge volcanic eruption that shook the area about 36,000 years ago. Debris from the eruptive activity filled the entire valley from Punta Scutolo to the Capo di Sorrento, forcing watercourses to find new paths toward the sea. Their progressive carving of the tufa stone cliff on which Sorrento stands resulted in the formation of the gorge.

The name Vallone dei Mulini derives from the existence of a water-mill that ground grain until the beginning of the twentieth century, and from a sawmill that supplied wood to the cabinet-makers of Sorrento. Next to the mills was a public washhouse where local women washed their laundry. The construction of the Piazza Tasso, which began in 1866, blocked the ravine's opening to the sea, causing the humidity level to rise inside, which eventually led to its abandonment. It created the perfect conditions for the growth of the lush vegetation that we see.

At the mouth of the steep ravine, we stop to let the driver of the orange city bus maneuver a tight curve. The two-way hairpin road is so narrow that buses render it impossible to drive it simultaneously. Four minutes later, we arrive at the Marina Piccola and step off the van into the Sorrento Ferry Terminal parking lot.

Scanning the area, I spot Danilo standing in front of one of the ticket booths. I hope that he hasn't been waiting a long time for us. As soon as we make eye contact, he waves and gives me that little flirty smile of his. I met him about six years ago, and each time I see him, I am reminded of how handsome he is. I am sure that he has no problems getting girlfriends. He looks to be in his late twenties, with light brown hair, a suntanned complexion that makes his pale green eyes, with hints of gray, appear even more stunning, and a light beard shadow on his square jaw. He is wearing a silver chain around his neck, which is typical for Italian men. It is part of their macho image.

We greet each other with a couple of kisses on the cheek under the envious stares of my companions. Holding on to one of his arms, I jokingly introduce him as my gelato. They all smile and nod approvingly. One of the women standing in the back joyfully comments, "He is definitely a gelato!" I laugh. Not sure of what is going on, Danilo raises his eyebrows as he hands me the tickets for the 9:45 hydrofoil to Capri, the 5:25 back to Sorrento and the electronic stubs for the island's funicular. He states that the hydrofoil will depart from Pier 4 and recommends that we stand in line, as already there are hundreds of travelers waiting to get on board the ship.

In front of us people are speaking French, English, German, Spanish and what I think is Russian. They must have come off the two cruise ships in the bay. Right behind us is a large group of Chinese people. Tourists of all nationalities come to visit Capri. Most will visit the island just for the day. Only a few plan to stay a little longer, and you can always tell who they are by the suitcases they are lugging. Steps away, an older gentleman, holding a large laminated map of the island, is trying to convince a small group of people to hire him as their tour guide for four hours on Capri. I have seen him doing the same thing before, over and over again, until he finds someone who will accept his proposal. I am sure that it is his way of making a living. He speaks numerous languages, too.

The line is moving now. We are about to board the Linee Marittime Partenopee, or the LMP, jet boat. I say goodbye to Danilo. We kiss each other again, and as he walks away we exchange, *"Ciao, ciao, a domani."* I have noticed that the people in Sorrento and the Amalfi Coast have a habit of saying the word Ciao twice when leaving, so as the expression, "When in Rome, do as the Romans do," applies here too, I do the same. I will see Danilo tomorrow in his office to reconfirm the arrangements he has made for the remainder of the week.

Several men and women are boarding before us. I assume that they live on Capri and are returning from a visit with relatives or from a shopping trip in Sorrento, or maybe they have jobs on the island. Listening to their conversations, I frown as their words keep swirling in my head in search of the English or French translation. They, too, must be speaking Napoletano. Their sentences and expressions are laced with French and Spanish words. When speaking to foreigners, Italian is used. But, when speaking among themselves, locals often revert to their dialect.

Once on board, we scatter to find a vacant seat inside the passenger lounges. The nine-mile crossing, in a straight line from the Sorrento Pier to the Capri Marina Grande, will take about twenty-five minutes. It should be a smooth one, as at first glance the sea appears to be calm.

Through the hydrofoil's left windows I watch the beautiful coastline of the Sorrentine Peninsula, as it comes into view. Geologically, Capri was not always an island. Experts who have studied the rock formation, the fauna and the archeological findings from both the island and the peninsula have determined that Capri was once part of the mainland. It was, in fact, the last strip of the Peninsula until about ten thousand years ago. At the end of the last glaciation, when the ice-caps began to melt, a continental drift caused a fracture in the Lattari Mountains, which resulted in the formation of the island.

Of the three islands in the Gulf of Naples, Capri—which lies at its southern tip—is the second largest after Ischia, covering an area of 2,560 acres (4.3 square miles), approximately 3.8 miles long and 1.7 miles wide, with a beautiful coastline of about ten miles.

There is a big debate over the origin of the name Capri, which is pronounced KApri, with the emphasis on the first syllable. The name was first thought to derive from the Latin word *Caprae* for goats or from *Capriam,* the Phoenician word for two towns. It is more logical to believe that it came from the Greek word *Kapros* for wild boar, as Greek settlers were already living on the island before it became a possession of the Roman Emperors. The Greek derivation is more plausible since numerous fossil remains of wild boars were found on the island.

Augustus was the first Roman Emperor to be *innamorato,* enamored with Capri. The Emperor's great love for Campania began when he stopped in Naples as a young man, on his return journey from modern-day Albania, where he had been studying. After he assumed power, Emperor Augustus would frequently leave the political atmosphere of Rome for long sojourns in one of his villas along the Campania shores and on the islands. The first time he discovered

Capri was in 29 B.C. on his return trip from Egypt after the battle of Antium. While sailing close to the island, he was struck by its natural beauty and its Greek character. The latter appealed to his Hellenic taste so immensely that he asked the authorities of Naples to exchange his private Ischia for the more intimate and exclusive Capri.

Augustus enjoyed a simple and quiet life on Capri, which he adorned with beautiful buildings, sumptuous villas, temples and lovely gardens. He liked to entertain, and we are told that during one of his lavish parties, he jokingly invented a city that he called *Apragopolis*—Greek for the "City of do-nothings." Nineteen hundred years later, the Italian version, which had been changed in the meantime to *Citta di dolce far niente* or "City of do-sweet-nothing," literally, would be used as a slogan to promote the city of Capri. Nowadays, the whole island is promoted as the *Isola del dolce far niente* in several travel magazines.

After cruising by the tip of the Sorrentine Peninsula, I grab my camera and step outside to the rear of the ship. Leaning slightly over the railing, I admire the dramatic slopes of Mount Solaro, Capri's highest peak (1919 ft), which dominates the western landscape of the island. The eastern peak is Mount Tiberio (1114 ft), named for Emperor Augustus' successor, Tiberius. On top of Mount Tiberio are the ruins of the Villa Jovis, the largest of the twelve villas Emperor Tiberius built on the island. He named each one after a Roman god. Villa Jovis was named for Jupiter.

Capri was as much a retreat for Tiberius as for Augustus, except that the former lived on the island permanently for the last ten years of his life, from 27 to 37 A.D. Those years were described by Suetonius and Tacitus, both historians of the Roman Empire, as scandalous. Their slanderous tales, so-called "Orgy of Capri," and their stories of cruelty, gave Capri such a bad name that centuries later it would make the island's fortune. Many historians have since tried to rehabilitate Tiberius' reputation, but ironically, it would be bad for business.

Marina Grande, the commercial port of the island, is becoming more and more visible as we approach. On the eastern side of the island, on the plateau of a deep depression between the two rocky massifs and right above the marina, lies the town of Capri. Anacapri, the island's second town, is concealed behind Mount Solaro. The hillsides are dotted with colorful, modest villas surrounded by lush vegetation. The island is looming now, beckoning us to its shore. What a splendid vision! Each time I gaze at Capri's enchanting beauty, I find myself compelled to discover another one of its sights.

We have just docked along the western side of the Marina Grande where each day, from April to October, thousands of tourists from around the world arrive and depart every few minutes. It is estimated that in peak season alone, July to August, up to 6,000 people a day come to Capri from Naples and the Amalfi Coast.

Capri's main harbor was built in 1928 to accommodate the constantly increasing number of visitors. Prior to its construction, boats used to dock in the center of the small bay, while large vessels dropped anchor farther out at sea. Back then, trade goods and passengers were tendered to the pier by the local fishermen.

Immediately after disembarking, we regroup. As we walk toward the port town, passing several large ferries and hydrofoils along the way, we glance at hundreds of pleasure boats, sailboats, speedboats and luxury yachts moored further afield on the eastern side of the Marina.

At the end of the pier, in the middle of the Marina's nerve center, I stop to let everyone catch up. This is a bustling place, where people rush in one direction to board local buses or to grab one of several convertible taxis to reach the towns of Capri or Anacapri, and in another direction to stand in a long line for the motorboat trip to the Grotta Azzurra.

The Blue Grotto is one of sixty-five grottos on the island. Listed as one of the most famous tourist attractions on Capri, it is best enjoyed if overnighting on the island, early in the morning before the mainland people arrive, or late in the afternoon when they have gone. For the daytrippers, the best way is to hire a private boat to take you directly to the grotto and around the whole island afterward. However, a visit inside the grotto is only possible if the weather conditions are favorable.

It takes about twenty minutes from the Marina Grande to reach the mouth of the Blue Grotto, where a maximum of three persons at a time are transferred into little rowboats. After the people have paid the toll fee to enter the cavern, they are asked to lie down on the bottom of the boat, as the headroom clearance to the grotto's entrance is very low and narrow.

Because of its popularity, the wait time to enter the cave can be a lengthy one, and it might be uncomfortable for people who suffer from seasickness. When the green light has been given, the skillful boatmen set down their oars and pull themselves inside the grotto with the aid of a chain fastened to the entrance wall.

Inside, people delight in seeing the spectacular, intense transparency of the pool and its reflection on the surrounding walls. The neon-blue color is caused by deflected sunrays that penetrate through a large underwater opening located right below the entrance.

Tiberius, the great lover of solitude, had the natural cavern adorned with mosaics and statues of Neptune and Triton, now preserved in the National Archeological Museum of Naples. He used it as a marine nymphaeum, a nymph water pool.

To demonstrate the cave's marvelous acoustics, the sailors serenade sightseers. A gratuity is expected on the way out. Completely ignored for centuries, the Grotta Azzurra was rediscovered in 1826, to the great delight of the Grand Tour travelers. Since then it has been a wonderful source of income for the local people.

The fishing village of the Marina Grande is very old. Its initial appearance can be seen in paintings and old prints sold around the island, and traces of original structures can still be found amongst its renovated buildings. The colorful shops that front the wharf nowadays used to be storerooms where, during the winter months, fishermen would store their boats and nets to protect them against the rough seas. Their families lived on the floor above. The houses had been built right at sea level, close to the water's edge. Too close, in fact, for they were flooded many times.

In the second half of the nineteenth century, the look of the small village was drastically changed. The pebbled beach along the waterfront was widened and covered with concrete, floors were added to a large number of one-story houses, and businesses and outdoor staircases were covered with tunnel vaults. Today it is quite obvious, when walking along the waterfront around the large Piazzale della Vittoria, that the Marina Grande's primary industry is tourism, as the town's multi-colored buildings house several restaurants, bars, little grocery stores, tourist gift shops and hotels.

Hundreds of travelers are coming and going, buzzing around the Piazzale as we try to cross it to reach the entrance to the island's funicular. The cable car was build in 1907 to link the Marina Grande to the center of Capri town. Trains leave roughly every fifteen minutes, more often in peak season and at peak times. The run takes about three to five minutes. To facilitate the flow of people, tickets are sold away from the entrance, at the ticket office around the corner from the harbor headquarters.

After handing out the souvenir stub to each member of my group, we proceed through the electronic gates. A couple are laughing as they fumble while inserting the magnetic strip card into the ticket slot. It is obvious that they have never taken an underground before. Impatient people try to cut them off as I offer to assist them from the other side.

Finally, a grumpy employee steps forward and demonstrates the system. By his annoyed expression, he must be doing this every day and all day long. Another employee is urging the crowd to move forward, pressing us together like sardines in a can. I feel dizzy amongst the squeezed bodies and cannot wait to reach Anacapri to escape.

The funicular is slowly coming down the tracks. Doors first open on the opposite side to let people exit before we are allowed to move in. Within seconds my entire group has successfully managed to find enough room in two adjacent compartments.

The ride up the hill is rather pretty. Looking down, there is a complete view of the harbor, the backside of the Marina Grande and the white-washed bell tower of the Church of San Costanzo. This, the oldest Catholic building on the island, is dedicated to the island's patron saint who came here in the sixth century.

After passing through the exchange tunnel, we glimpse the outer edge of the town of Capri and the multi-level terraces that cover the hillside below, dotted with white houses surrounded by small gardens filled with blooms.

Upon exiting the rail car, we climb a short flight of stairs and step outside onto a large terrace ringed with red bougainvillea-wrapped white columns. The scenic terrace, built on top of an ancient Greek wall, offers a spectacular panoramic vista across the entire Gulf of Naples, from Capo Miseno, where Pliny the Younger witnessed Vesuvio's eruption in 79 A.D., to Punta Campanella, the tip of the Sorrento Peninsula.

In the background are the Campania Apennines and the Lattari Mountains, while center stage in the foreground, the sleeping giant looms over the valley. In the distance, the large city of Naples and its bay are barely visible through the mist, whereas the Bay of Sorrento and the town of Sorrento that lies above the sheer cliffs are clearly viewable as they are closer to the island.

In the morning light, the towering Mount Solaro is both impressive and magnificent; its chiseled limestone cliff wall is reddish gray. Overhead, rays of sunshine brighten a cloudless sky, and down below the familiar seven white sails of Windstar Cruises's luxury five-masted yacht stand out in the Bay of Capri against the intense blue of the Tyrrhenian Sea.

Earlier in the day, I recommended that we travel together as a group to the town of Anacapri to visit the Church of San Michele, then separate and reconnect in front of the Marina Grande harbor's headquarters, in time to take the hydrofoil back to Sorrento. Anacapri is my favorite town on the island. I love its quaintness and remoteness. I could spend a good part of the day getting lost in and around the small town. From Capri, the quickest way to reach Anacapri is by bus.

Leaving the terrace, we stride along Via Roma, dodging sight-seers, baggage-filled trolleys pulled by bellmen and Ape trucks en route to the town's bus terminal. We purchase our *biglietto di ritorno,* round-trip ticket, proceed through the clearly-defined queuing line and board a side-scraped orange minibus.

The construction of the winding, narrow road leading to Anacapri began in 1874 and took three years to complete as it was literally chiseled out of Mount Solaro's limestone cliffs. In 1950, the road was widened to accommodate the increasing traffic on the island. Prior to the road construction, people used to climb the Scala Fenicia, the Phoenician stairs carved out of the solid rock of the mountain by the first Greek settlers.

The unforgettable ride to Anacapri is spectacular if you are not terrified of heights. If you want to avoid looking at the sheer drop off along the edge of the hair-raising mountain road, or if you do not want to see the buses barely passing each other while hugging the sides of the cliffs, hence the reason behind the scrapes, look at your feet, or better yet, smile at a fellow traveler and strike up a conversation. This perilous twisting road is one of the reasons why tourists are not allowed to bring their cars over to the island. It is definitely less stressful to leave the driving to the locals.

Morning in Anacapri

*W*ith the fall of the Roman Empire, the island's sovereignty reverted to the Byzantine Duchy of Naples. In the seventh century the Saracens, whose naval base was located just south of Paestum in Agropolis, began to terrorize the inhabitants living on the Amalfi Coast and on the islands in the Gulf of Naples. The islanders, who feared being kidnapped and sold into slavery, left the Marina to relocate up in the hills, to the *Citta di Capri* and to the *Terra di Anacapri—Ana* means "above."

In 866, Emperor Ludwig II of Naples granted the Maritime Republic of Amalfi dominion over the island of Capri for having defeated the Saracens in 849. Through its close connection with Naples and Amalfi, the island began to experience an economic growth. For the next few hundred years, the two small villages—Capri and Anacapri—lived relatively in peace with the outside world, except for feuding with one another. Maritime relations developed between the people of Naples and the islanders, creating opportunities for many of them, who largely resided in the town of Capri, to become master sailors, shipbuilders and boat owners. Amalfi's finest craftsmen came to the island and introduced the locals to their unique architectural style. Characterized by the use of vaulted roofs on top of main buildings and one-story houses, the "Caprese style," as it is labeled, can still be seen today in both towns.

The inhabitants of Anacapri delight in telling tourists who are interested in the local folklore that their small village was founded a long time ago by a young couple from Capri. Much like Romeo and Juliet, their families were bitter enemies and would not allow them to marry. So the young lovers left their parents behind and eloped to the top of the mountain. From that point on, whenever young people would be forbidden to wed, they would escape to Anacapri, and eventually Anacapri became known as "The Town for Lovers."

The relationship between the two municipalities on the island has not always been a smooth one. While the inhabitants of Capri made their living off the sea, the people of Anacapri made theirs mostly from the land, and there were several times when they actually resented each other and came to blows.

One of their conflicts, recorded in the island's diocesan documents and the Naples archives, happened in the Middle Ages, during a plague epidemic that broke out in Italy. In 1493, the dreadful disease reached the town of Capri, where it quickly took a toll on the population. When the inhabitants of Capri decided to bury their dead at a higher elevation on the island, beyond the city boundaries, they unknowingly spread the infectious disease to the people living in Anacapri. Furious, the Anacapresi then retaliated by throwing stones at the Capresi whenever they would come up. Three years later, to appease the people of Anacapri, Frederick II of Aragon granted equal administration standing to both towns.

The action only temporarily restrained their feud. It did not stop the people of Capri from continuing to terrorize their neighbors.

Nowadays, their rivalry is inconspicuous as they both try to seduce the visitors. Each town has its own mayor and patron saint. San Antonio is the patron saint of Anacapri while San Costanzo is the patron saint of the town of Capri, as well as of the entire island.

)(

The bus is slowly rounding the last corner on the twisting road to Anacapri. The abyss is no longer looming. It is now safe for me to peek through the right window. Emerging onto Via Orlandi, the town's main artery, flanked on both sides by tall European maples, we are greeted by a life-sized statue of Emperor Augustus. The statue is standing a thousand feet above the sea, at the edge of a beautiful garden terrace that belongs to the Hotel Caesar Augustus. The luxury five-star hotel is the perfect place for affluent guests to discover the "Dolce far niente lifestyle" of Anacapri while enjoying front-row seats to a panoramic view of the entire Gulf of Naples.

Unlike Capri, Anacapri is relatively flat, as it lies on a plain on the western side of the island at the foot of Mount Solaro. An estimated eight thousand Capresi live in the town of Capri, while close to seven thousand live in Anacapri. A large number of the people living and working in Capri also have homes in Anacapri.

The town's main tourist hub is the Piazza della Vittoria where we are getting off. This area is always crowded in the morning with hordes of daytrippers who seem to be more interested in the souvenir shops surrounding the piazza than in seeing the sights. We slowly squeeze by and make our way south on Via Orlandi, in the direction of Piazza Diaz, to see the Chiesa San Michele, the Church of Saint Michael, and its exquisite octagonal majolica tiles, before lunch time.

As I glance around, it seems that I have lost a few of my traveling companions. There are only seven of us now. The lure of the charming boutiques along the pedestrian street Via Giuseppe Orlandi was too hard for them to resist. I guess they will catch up with me later. When describing the island, I often compare it to a wonderful theme park for adults, and I believe that visitors should take the time to discover its treasures at their own pace.

The Chiesa di San Michele Archangelo is easily found by just following the ceramic signs posted along Anacapri's main street. Its entrance faces a small square, the Piazza San Nicola, at the end of a side street, right off Via Orlandi. The church, together with the adjoining convent of the Teresian nuns, was built in a Baroque style between 1698 and 1719 over the old church of St Nicola, hence the name of the square and its cloister. Mother Serafina had pledged to the Archangel Michael that if he spared the island from Turkish attacks, she would build him a sanctuary.

We enter the vestibule of the convent, pay the small fee, then step inside the chiesa. Immediately I note with amusement something unusual. To preserve the church's unique feature, which covers the entire floor, visitors have to walk on an elevated thin wooden platform around its perimeter. This will prove to be an interesting exercise.

Touching the white wall for support, I move forward and lead the way. Behind me, the women are giggling. The platform is so narrow that, should anybody want to pass us, we would find ourselves in an awkward position. Suddenly, as if reading my mind, the woman next to me asks in a hushed tone, "Do you see any gelato behind us?" I smile. "If you do, let's move very slowwwwly," she teases. And they all burst into laughter.

"Shush, this a church," I say, trying really hard not to join them.

The magnificent tiled pavement is the work of Leonardo Chiaiese, a master tile artisan from the Abruzzo region who was living in Naples in 1761. For his masterpiece, Chiaiese took inspiration from the Italian Baroque painter Francesco Solimena, who was born in Avellino but spent most of his life in Naples (1674–1747). Several of Solimena's paintings adorn the church.

Walking cautiously around the 2,500 riggiole mosaic, we focus our attention on a large menagerie of domesticated and exotic animals. In the middle of the painting, right above Adam and Eve, is the Devil in the shape of a snake wrapped around a tree trunk. For a complete view of the painting, which depicts the expulsion of Adam and Eve from the Garden of Eden, we step back into the vestibule and climb a narrow steel spiral staircase to the church's second-floor balcony. By narrow, I mean that people who want to ascend have to wait for the passage to totally clear before proceeding and vice versa, as there is just enough room for one person to squeeze by. For obvious reasons, it might be less embarrassing for women if they were wearing slacks instead of dresses or skirts when climbing these steps. Luckily, I am wearing a yellow top, a pair of black jeans and matching flat shoes.

Once above, we stand on a choir platform in front of an organ and stare at the complete tiled floor. After snapping a number of pictures, we wait our turn to descend.

Outside the church I check my watch to happily discover that I still have some time before the stores close. In Anacapri, the few shops that cater to the tourist trade tend to stay open all day. The specialty boutiques, however, take a lunch break. Leaving the women, I walk back to Via Orlandi and continue westward toward the Piazza Diaz.

Anacapri is a delight to stroll through, as cars are not allowed on most streets. It is quite evident that the Anacapresi cherish their town. They keep it absolutely spotless, and several buildings sport fresh coats of paint. The faint smell of brightly-colored bougainvillea permeates the air as I pass clothing, linen, shoe, perfume, purse and ceramics shops.

Just before the Piazza Diaz, I stop in front of a children's clothing boutique. In the window are the cutest outfits I have seen in a long time. As if sensing my admiration, a sweet-looking petite gray-haired lady opens the door and greets me with, *"Buongiorno."* She graciously invites me to step inside.

Her small boutique is filled with romantic little girls' dresses trimmed with knitted lace and ribbons, eyelet summer pinafores, heirloom baby bonnets, precious little booties and christening gowns embroidered with silk threads.

"Ho fatto tutto a mano, I made everything by hand," she says, her voice filled with pride. Her name is Tina, short for Battistina, she replies to my question. She opened her little shop, which she named *Pizzi e Merletti,* Italian for Laces & Embroideries, more than a decade ago.

"I always wanted to own a shop. It was my dream," she confesses. Curious, I ask her what she did before. She grins broadly. "Mamma. My four sons are grown now," she adds, lifting her hands.

My maternal grandmother used to make me pretty dresses like the ones hanging around the room. My mother did, too. Grandma had a passion for knitting, and I am glad that she passed it on to her daughter and then on to me. Nowadays, we buy everything "Made in China," but in the old days, everything was made by hand, with love.

Tina creates many of her darling garments while sitting in her favorite antique chair in the corner of her store. "My hands cannot sit still," she admits—words that echo those of my mother. Next to her chair is a black dresser. Its top is covered with spools of pastel-colored yarn, rolls of silk ribbons, pearly white buttons and a variety of sewing threads. She enjoys meeting people, even though she cannot communicate with most of them as she'd like to, she says, laughing. The majority of her customers are Americans, Germans and Japanese. Several clients have sent her pictures of children modeling her beautiful creations. Tina proudly displays those pictures on the walls. She is delightful. It is hard for me to leave her. But I must, if I want to continue exploring Anacapri. I promise to see her again someday. I sincerely hope so and walk out.

Minutes later, I stand in the middle of the Piazza Diaz, one of the most charming squares on the isle of Capri, with a terra-cotta pavement and beautiful majolica-tiled benches. The parish church dominating the square is the Chiesa di Santa Sofia. It was built in 1510 over a smaller existing square and the ruins of an older church, later enlarged in 1698 when two lateral chapels were added, and again in 1878. There is a three-clock bell tower, adjacent to the church, which can only be seen from a certain angle.

The lovely ceramic benches were designed by Sergio Rubino in 1979 when he was commissioned with the renovation of the little piazza. Born in Anacapri, where he resides most of the year, Signor Rubino, a painter as well as a sculptor, has received numerous international acclaims for his work. The benches' hand-painted panels feature garlands of grapes and bunches of lemons as well as scenes from a bygone era: the harvest of olives and grapes, wine cellars, and women wearing traditional garments in their everyday life. The women of Anacapri were reputed for their graceful beauty, and also for transporting goods on their heads.

After a quick peek inside the church, I resume my leisurely stroll along Via Orlandi, the longest street in Anacapri. An elderly woman holding the hand of a child dressed in a blue school uniform and carrying a knapsack is about to pass me by. The darling little boy is joyfully skipping alongside his grandma, who is taking him home for lunch. Farther down the street, two dozen children, wearing blue and white uniforms, are playing in a grammar school yard. They are laughing and screaming while waiting for their parents to pick them up. Assumably, those children represent the island's future generation of hotel employees, managers, tour guides, teachers, ceramic artisans and bus drivers.

As I retrace my steps, I glance at a lovely outdoor staircase at the corner of Via Orlandi and Via Pagliaro. Each riser of the staircase is covered with a lovely ceramic tile decorated with exotic flowers on either side of a pretty bird and, while the flower pattern is repetitive, the birds are all different.

Exploring the charms of Anacapri is something I thoroughly enjoy. If I had the time, I would amble all the way down to the lighthouse at Punta Carena and back. According to the island's guidebook, the path to the lighthouse is a very pretty one, as from April to October many flowers are in bloom. Built a century ago, the lighthouse stands at the extreme western point of the island. Ironically, the name given to its location is a combination of two words that mean the same thing. *Punta* is the Latin translation for "point" and *Carena* or *Karena* is the Greek word for "head-point." Punta Carena is the perfect place on the island for lovers to watch glorious sunsets.

In the meantime, I am content with meandering through the narrow streets of the Boffe district around the Piazza Diaz. The farther away from the piazza I amble, the more peaceful the atmosphere becomes. The seventeenth-century development owes its name to the houses that were covered with cloister-vault type swellings, which in Napoletano dialect are called *Boffe*. The streets, flanked on both sides with white-washed houses, are practically empty as locals discreetly try to avoid the tourists that are invading their town on a daily basis. Who can blame them? Anacapri had remained pretty isolated from the outside world until the road linking it with the rest of the island was built at the end of the nineteenth century.

The simplicity of the inhabitants' lifestyle is quite obvious when strolling through this neighborhood's picturesque streets. Through wrought-iron gates, I catch glimpses of immaculate private gardens with brightly-blooming flowers, and of small courtyards with ceramic fountains and garden statues. Antique looking mailboxes hang outside each house, marked with a decorative hand-painted ceramic tile number. The main attribute of Anacapri is that it feels more like a village than a town, and I silently pray that it will remain that way for a long time.

Somehow, without purposely meaning to, I have found my way back to the Piazza Diaz. Feeling hungry, I scan the area, hoping to find a quaint little restaurant where I can satisfy my growling stomach. Under a vine-shaded terrace, I spot one of the women sitting in a corner alone, at a small table covered with a yellow linen cloth. I stride across the restaurant and slip into the chair in front of her. But before I have a chance to ask her about her morning, a waiter appears out of nowhere and places a menu in front of me.

Consulting the menu and seeing many of my favorite dishes, I settle for *Spaghetti alle vongole,* spaghetti with clams, and a small beer. My companion seems to be enjoying an *Insalata Caprese,* the classic salad, of tomatoes, buffalo mozzarella and basil leaves, which originated here.

Between bites, she tells me that she took the chair lift from the Piazza della Vittoria to the summit of Mount Solaro and that the experience was fabulous. "The ten-minute ride was a little scary at first, with only a single bar for protection, but once you reach the top, it is well worth it," she says, her face alight with pleasure. I encourage her to continue.

"The lift does not slow down," she warns. "You stand for maybe a minute in a marked spot before a chair scoops you up and away. You slowly move up the mountain, your feet dangling in the air, and when you get to the summit, you have to jump off the chair and get out of the way fast," she adds, laughing. "The view is so spectacular, it takes your breath away. You see the entire Amalfi Coast, the Gulf of Salerno and the Gulf of Naples with Ischia and Procida. It was amazing. I was on top of the island and I wanted to shout." She laughs again.

Her morning adventure will not be soon forgotten. I smile, thinking that it will probably be the highlight of her visit to Capri. She enjoyed it immensely and assures me that she will be coming back with her husband someday.

"Next time walk back to Anacapri. The footpath leading up to and down from the summit is considered to be one of the prettiest walks on the island, and the return journey should only take you about fifty minutes," I recommend. "Better yet, stay on the island and catch the gondola early in the morning or late in the afternoon to marvel at a romantic sunrise or a glorious sunset." I make a mental note to do just that if I overnight here. The waiter arrives, bearing a platter in one hand and a cold beer in the other. Thinking back, I should have ordered a glass of Caprese wine, but during the day I prefer to drink one of Italy's finest beers, the Nastro Azzuro.

After lunch, I set off again. This time in the direction of the Piazza della Vittoria. In front of the Casa Rossa, I stop and glance at my watch. In five minutes the museum will open its door. I decide to wait.

The towering building stands out against the surrounding white structures by its eclectic architectural form and its bright pinkish-red color, referred to as Pompeian red. I glimpsed the Casa Rossa a couple of years ago, when I took shelter from the pouring rain under an archway across the street. While standing there, I noticed a panel next to the entrance. When it stopped raining, I walked over to read it.

The inscription said that the Casa Rossa, which today houses a permanent collection of Italian and foreign artists' watercolor and oil paintings, had been built between 1876 and 1899 by the American Colonel John C. MacKowen, a native of New Orleans, who came to the island at the end of the Civil War and lived here for two decades with a young woman from Anacapri.

Numerous famous individuals traveled to Capri during the nineteenth and twentieth centuries. European noblemen, wealthy entrepreneurs, writers, poets, painters, physicians and other intellectuals were drawn to the island by its unique natural beauty and mild climate and seduced by the gracious hospitality of the islanders. Some chose to reside on Capri for a short time while others remained here permanently, as about two hundred foreigners are buried in the island's non-Catholic cemetery.

Strangely, none of the guide books mention him. Still, the panel's first couple of lines teased my curiosity. The story sounded romantic. I wanted to get more information. Unfortunately, I could not ask anyone, as the museum's iron-gated door was locked. Who was this Civil War colonel that resided on Anacapri for twenty years? Completely intrigued, I could not wait to begin researching his biography when I returned to the States.

What I found was so interesting that I have since become totally fascinated by his life story. Different sources revealed alternative spellings of his name. In America, he is was known as McKowen, while in Europe as MacKowen.

John Clay McKowen was born in Jackson, Louisiana in 1842. His father, John McKowen, who immigrated from Ireland to the United States as a young man, was a general merchant and a plantation owner in Jackson, East Feliciana Parish. John Jr. entered Dartmouth College in 1859, which he left in the summer of 1861, at the beginning of the Civil War, to enlist in the Confederate Army. In 1863, then Captain McKowen distinguished himself by crossing the enemy lines and capturing Federal General Neal Dow in his headquarters. And for his heroic action he was promoted to Lieutenant Colonel. General Dow was to be later exchanged for General Robert E. Lee's son.

At the end of the war, he returned to Dartmouth and graduated with the class of 1866. He went to Paris to study medicine for a couple of years, then sailed back to New Orleans where he interned before moving to California in 1869. There, he bought a ranch near Los Angeles, which he sold in 1870 to relocate to

San Francisco, where he held the position of Vice Principal of the public schools for two years. Between 1872 and 1876, he was a student of medicine in Vienna, Austria, getting his degree of M.D. in Munich, Bavaria. He engaged in the practice of medicine in Rome from 1876 to 1878, when he was taken with malarial fever and went to Capri to recover. In Anacapri he fell in love with a local beauty named Maria, with whom he had a daughter, Giulia.

Lt. Colonel McKowen built his residence around an existing Aragonese tower that had been erected in the sixteenth century by the people of Anacapri to defend their town. While living on Capri for the next twenty years, Dr. John C. McKowen devoted himself to his greatest passions: history and archeology. He explored the depths of the Blue Grotto, exposing several marble pieces and statues and affirming its significance as a nymphaeum in Roman times. He traveled to Egypt, Greece, Tunis and Southern Spain, and from each trip he brought back artifacts that he incorporated into the architectural design of his house.

Before entering the house, I glance up. Right above the museum's entrance door is a long and narrow marble fragment that has been chiseled with Emperor Augustus' Greek epigraph "Welcome people—to the land of leisure." The paved courtyard is filled with odd antiquities collected by the Colonel. The most impressive is a large priestess statue dating from the first century A.D.

As I mount the stairway leading to the upper floors and wander slowly through Moorish archways into empty rooms, my sentimental nature is trying to imagine how John and Maria lived here. Between his many travels, he ministered to the poor, cultivated olives and grapes, and wrote several articles that were published in medical journals and magazines.

McKowen wrote a book on Capri, of which unfortunately only a few copies still remain. However, some of its content can be found in several books written after his death. I could not find any records showing that Maria accompanied him abroad. I assume she occupied herself with raising their child and managing his house and estate while he was away.

Going up the last flight of stairs, I reach a small outdoor landing where a handful of steps brings me to the old fortified tower's battlement. Standing on the crenellated terrace, glancing at the landscape, it occurs to me that since the original tower was built outside the ancient nucleus of Anacapri, the Casa Rossa must have stood alone a century ago amidst hundreds of acres of vineyards and olives groves. Today, it is largely surrounded by shops and houses.

The 360-degree view is lovely and well worth the price of admission. From one side of the tower's rooftop I gaze over the Gulf of Naples and at the looming Vesuvio in the far distance, close to the edge of the deep blue sea. I move to another side to view interesting rooftops with multiple TV antennas, small garden patios, and the dome and church bells of the Chiesa San Michele. Finally, I step to the opposite side of the terrace to look at a multilevel cultivated garden at the foot of a beautiful villa built on the side of a hill, and down below, at people walking along Via Orlandi and Via Timpone.

While I descend the stairs, ready to exit the house, I recall reading that Doctor McKowen had expressed a desire to return to the United States to offer his services in the Spanish-American War, but he had been advised against it by his friends as he had taken ill during a trip to the Orient in 1897. He did return to New Orleans in 1898 and wrote an exposé titled "Murder—a money making art," in which he denounced city health officials for not taking the right steps to protect the local population from a yellow fever epidemic. On September 18, 1901, McKowen was shot in Clinton, Louisiana, where he resided at the time, over a land dispute, by his neighbor Robert Thompson. He was only fifty-nine years old. On his death, his daughter inherited the house, and after her death, the Casa Rossa passed to several owners until the city of Anacapri acquired it more than two decades ago.

My leather shoes are starting to pinch my feet. While they are practical for walking around Capri, they tend to confine my toes whenever the weather gets warmer. I remember glancing briefly at a pair of darling sandals earlier. Maybe I should pay them a closer look. After all, I have the perfect excuse: I need to buy a new pair of shoes to match my yellow Positano dress.

Sandals have been around since Roman times. They were mostly worn inside the house back then, unlike today. Since modern sandals have become more comfortable and more fashionable, we seem to wear them everywhere, for any occasion and with any outfit.

Lost in my thoughts, I nearly miss the small sandal shop nestled between two large souvenir stores along Via Orlandi. In the center of the shop is a double-shelved square workbench littered with tools and several pairs of eyeglasses. The walls are covered with at least five dozen pairs of sandals in different styles, all made of leather. Some of the models are quite simple, while others are more sophisticated, as their patterns include a rich assortment of colorful beads, pearls, rhinestones, and other stones.

The cobbler greets me with a smile. His name is Signor Antonio and he has been making sandals for close to fifty years. He is a little bit of a celebrity. Articles have been written about him and published in several magazines around the world. His long list of clients includes famous international movie stars and singers.

Pointing to a pretty pair of sandals, with narrow white straps and turquoise stones, hanging on the wall behind him, I ask him if he can make me a similar set, but with yellow and black beads. "No problem, " he replies as I quickly remove my shoes and socks so that he can measure my feet. When he comments that my feet are the prettiest he has seen in a long time, I laugh. I am sure that he says that to all the ladies he makes sandals for, but it is nice to receive a compliment once in a while. It is good for the ego.

From shoe boxes stacked in a corner of the shop Signor Antonio grabs an already-made pair of soles and a few beads, then settles down on his black leather chair. His hands move with skilled efficiency. He probably can assemble them with his eyes closed. Smiling, I ask him to name some of the famous people he has made sandals for. His eyes light up as he cites a few: Jacqueline Onassis, Julia Roberts and Sophia Loren, among many others.

As the shop is devoid of customers at the moment, I have the chance to ask him more questions. He has two sons. "They will continue the business," he boasts. "You always need shoes, so their jobs are secured," he adds, chuckling.

"What about China?" I counter. He glances up, spreads his hands apart palms up, and shrugs at the same time in a uniquely familiar Italian fashion, and quickly comments that his sandals are made a thousand times better than the ones made in China. The leather he uses is of the best quality plus—he emphasizes the plus—they are made by hand with tender loving care, and he chuckles.

My gorgeous sandals are ready. I try them on. They fit perfectly.

Signor Antonio wraps them in a small bag while I pull euros from my money belt. I don't need to wear them, since my bare feet have had a few minutes to cool off. I quickly slip back into my socks and shoes, thank him, step outside and enter the adjacent souvenir shop to purchase a kitchen towel with the limoncello recipe printed on it for a friend back home before continuing to the bus stop.

※

The Piazza della Vittoria is not as crowded as it was this morning. Most of the tourists have moved on to Capri. At the heart of the piazza is the fabulous five-star Hotel Capri Palace and Spa. Coming from Via Orlandi, the ruins of the Barbarossa Castle are quite visible on the top of the cliffs, right behind the hotel.

The castle was built in the late tenth century, when the ancient Maritime Republic of Amalfi ruled Capri, with material taken from Roman structures, to defend the gate of Anacapri, which stood below. The structure owes its name to the notorious Turkish raider Kheir-ed-Din, otherwise known as Barbarossa, who landed on the island in 1534 and destroyed it. Crumbling walls and two towers are all that remain of the castle, and today they belong to the Axel Munthe Foundation.

The "must see" in Anacapri is the Villa San Michele, the famous Swedish Doctor Axel Munthe's residence on the island, which sits on a ridge at the top of the Phoenician Steps. Years ago, in the springtime, I visited the villa and truly enjoyed it. The San Michele is reached by following the ceramic-tiled signs when ambling from the Piazza della Vittoria onto the narrow Via Capodimonte.

Axel Munthe discovered Capri for the first time in 1875 at the age of eighteen. During his visit he climbed the Phoenician Steps to Anacapri. At the top, he stumbled onto the ruins of an imperial villa and the remains of a small medieval chapel dedicated to San Michele.

In his book *The Story of San Michele,* published in 1929 and translated into more than forty languages, Munthe described how captivated he had been by his discovery and his desire to rebuild the ruins into a home. Munthe gave us a loving account of his life on Capri, where he moved in 1887. That same year, he managed to purchase the ruins, and he began the restoration process a year later.

He not only designed the plans for his estate but he also did most of the work himself. In 1890, low on funds, he opened a practice in Rome where he could doctor to a wealthy clientele as well as the local population. From that moment on, Munthe divided his time between the capital and the island. Two years later, he was appointed physician to the future queen of Sweden, who was suffering from severe bronchitis. Following the advice of her doctor, Queen Victoria spent several months a year on Capri. She lent Munthe her support in his efforts to acquire Mount Barbarossa, where he established a sanctuary for the study and protection of migratory birds.

Dr. Munthe, like his American colleague Dr. McKowen, graciously administered to the poor of Capri. But when it came to excavating antiquities on the island, the two men were bitter rivals. And while McKowen's house bears resemblance to a fortress, Munthe's home layout reminds us of a Roman villa with its white walls surrounded by a gorgeous manicured garden. Although the Villa has some Moorish and Norman features, they do not overshadow the simplicity of its design. The main building contains an impressive collection of Roman, Etruscan and Egyptian artifacts. Only a small number of the Roman pieces were actually found on the island. Most were excavated somewhere else by Munthe himself, purchased, or donated to him by his friends. Dr. Axel Munthe lived until 1942 in his beloved house before returning to his native country. He died seven years later in Stockholm. At his death, the State inherited the house.

From the house, visitors gaze over a beautiful panoramic view of the Gulf of Naples as they stroll under a long bougainvillea-covered pergola to the Chapel San Michele. In a little gallery next to the chapel, on a ledge overlooking the Marina Grande and Capri, a granite Egyptian Sphinx stands guard. According to legend, if you pat the animal's left lower back and make a wish, your wish will come true.

The legend is really a clever invention by Axel Munthe's friend Joseph Oliv, who visited him frequently in Capri. Oliv also named the lovely cypress avenue, which separates the lower garden from the upper garden and where summer concerts are hosted every year, "Friendship Alley." Munthe brought the cypress trees to his house from Villa d'Este in Northern Italy and planted them in two straight rows, under a full moon.

It is not unusual, when strolling to the end of Via Capodimonte, past the Villa San Michele, to see hikers tackling the Scala Fenice, the Phoenician Steps. Those steps provided the only access between Anacapri, Capri and the Marina Grande before the road was built. The Scala Fenice starts below the Chapel of San Michele at the Puerta della Differenza, which marks the entrance to the town of Anacapri. It is called "The Door of the Difference" to indicate the border between the two territories on the island. The road of the ancient sailors is about a mile long with 921 steps. It takes on average an hour and a half to reach Anacapri from the Marina Grande.

The return journey should only take about forty minutes. If I had the time and was dressed appropriately, I would descend the Scala to Capri just to admire the spectacular views.

The orange island bus is slowly coming to a stop. Only four people besides myself climb on board, where we have no problem finding seats. Seconds later, we are heading down toward Capri.

Afternoon in Capri

$\mathcal{T}$he drive down the steep, narrow, twisting road is as scary as the drive up to Anacapri. This time, I manage to find the courage to keep my eyes open and to snatch pictures of the sweeping view of Capri and the Marina Grande. Twenty minutes later, the bus pulls to a stop along the curb of Via Roma where I alight, happy to have made it back safely.

Lined on both sides with a variety of boutiques, Via Roma is part of Capri's shopping scene. During the tourist season, this street swarms with visitors and this afternoon is no exception. Side-stepping dozens of dazed travelers along the way, I stroll toward the Piazza Umberto I, nicknamed the *Piazzetta* by the Capresi. Here and there I peek at gorgeous leather bags, gigantic rose candle holders, hand-painted tiles, leather sandals, island souvenirs and beautiful jewelry. In Capri jewelry stores are absolutely everywhere.

Nearing Capri's main square, I squeeze my way through a sea of Belgian retirees assembled in front of a gelateria. By the look on their faces they are thoroughly enjoying their three scoops of Italian ice cream. Their comments make me smile. When I was growing up in Brussels, there was a string of ice cream push carts named "Capri." Seen everywhere—in parks, at special events, at country fairs, in school yards even in neighborhood streets—these small vending machines were owned and operated by Italians who had immigrated to Belgium in the sixties in the hope of finding work in the coal mines. I still treasure the memory of my grand-mother treating my sister and me to waffle cones filled with deli-cious chocolate and strawberry-flavored ice cream.

At the Piazzetta, Capri's open-air drawing room, people relax and socialize while watching the world go by. I pause for a moment and glance around. Sitting lazily at one of the umbrellaed tables in an outdoor café, two of my traveling companions are waving at me to join them. I feel the need to grant my feet some rest and gladly accept their invitation.

As soon as I sit down in a chair next to them, a waiter comes by to take my order. I know that I am not supposed to drink a cappuc-cino after ten in the morning—no Italian would be caught doing so. But what the heck. I am a tourist, after all, and I do enjoy the way Italians brew them. I order one. A heartbeat later, the waiter reappears, serves me a nice steaming hot cappuccino with a heart-shaped design in the foam, sets the bill on the table and leaves after muttering *"Prego."* I grab the bill and look. "Wow, eight dollars! That's the most I ever have paid for a cappuccino in my life."

Suddenly, I realize that I must have expressed my remark in a louder tone that I intended for there is odd silence around me. Feeling the regard of several onlookers, I return their stares and offer them a rueful grin. I could almost kick myself, knowing that Capri is expensive, but it seems to me that this price is a little excessive for a drink consisting of about one-third expresso, one-third steamed milk and one-third froth. I am pretty sure that the

Cappuccini monks, who invented this concoction, could not have predicted that it would become such a luxurious beverage.

Leaning back into my chair, I slowly survey my surroundings. From our table I have a perfect view of the sculpted dome of the Baroque Chiesa di San Stefano, on the western side of the Piazza Umberto I, built in 1685 in the same location where a sixth century Benedictine monastery once stood. I read in one of the travel guides that there are three features worth seeing inside the church: the well-preserved marble floor around the high altar, taken from the Villa Jovis, a statue of San Costanzo, Capri's patron saint, and the tomb of Mother Serafina.

Standing tall in front of me is the Clock Tower or the Campanile, topped with a hemispherical dome reminiscent of Amalfi's Moorish influence on Capri's architecture. The bell tower is the only remnant of a modest church that once stood at the entrance of the village before being demolished in the seventeenth century. Today it houses Capri's tourist office. Adjacent is a newspaper stand where tourists can buy postcards, Italian magazines and international newspapers. On the opposite side of the Chiesa is the municipio, Capri's town hall, formally known as the Bishop's Palace.

The piazza has gone through quite a few transformations over the centuries and even more so in the last fifty years, when visitors started to come in large numbers. It is speculated that the square probably existed as a natural meeting point of access roads in Tiberius' time. Then in the Middle Ages, it became a courtyard in a religious complex surrounded by a continuous wall.

In the first half of the nineteenth century, foreigners began to visit the island, and several shops and a small *albergo* opened up on the piazza. In the second half of the nineteenth century, the wall was demolished and the square reverted to an open space. In the last twenty-some years, small cosmetic touches were added to the Piazzetta, thanks largely to a growing influx of wealthier visitors. The square, along with a few connecting streets, grew increasingly ritzier and more glamorous as several famous clothing designers decided to open boutiques in Capri. This spurred restaurant owners, who wished to cater to a more upscale clientele, to line the little piazza with fancy outdoor cafés.

In the daytime the four cafés of the Piazzetta are crowded with tourists who watch scores of dazed sightseers walk by while they enjoy a meal or a drink. In the early morning and late afternoon, after thousands of daytrippers have blissfully moved on, the outdoor tables are occupied by local residents and hotel guests, celebrities, politicians, writers and international jet setters who come to the island in search of anonymity.

Tilting my head, I stare at the blue sky above. The sun is shining and there is not a cloud in sight. One of my companions nudges me and points with her chin. "Just look what's coming our way," she says, smiling. Pulled from my contemplation, I watch a tall, handsome, nicely dressed man, with dark hair neatly trimmed, slide into a chair nearby. With an air of confidence, he casually removes his dark sunglasses, slipping them into the front pocket of his shirt. He is well built with broad shoulders and in his mid-forties, I would guess. He reminds me of the Scottish actor Gerard Butler, except that this man has a tanned face, and brown eyes instead of blue.

Ironically, this morning I asked Amelia, back at the hotel, the Italian translation for the word "hunk," as that word describes him completely. He is definitely a *fusto*. He is even more sexy when he smiles disarmingly at the cute little waitress who stepped forward to take his order. He is a *Bacio gelato* with lots of whipped cream and a little red cherry on top. As if he were able to read my thoughts, he turns his head, looks straight at me and smiles broadly. Unconsciously, I quickly close my mouth. I didn't even know I had it open. I smile back a little embarrassed. Hopefully, it did not appear that I was drooling.

A beautiful young woman with a supermodel figure, dressed in the latest fashion, takes a seat next to him. Oblivious to the people around them, they embrace and kiss each other passionately. "Mamma mia! That's *amore* as the Italians would say," I exclaim, laughing. The women quickly join me.

"They are likely on their honeymoon," one of them comments. Which would not surprise me since the island of Capri still holds the number one spot on the list of the most romantic honeymoon destinations in Europe. I shift my focus to my companions and, for a moment, we chat and joke. It is amazing how we women think alike. Unable to resist, my gaze meanders back to the fusto. He turns, smiles and winks. Laughing again, I grab my bag and escape.

Leaving the Piazzetta behind, I pass the entrance to a small arcade between the town hall and La Parisienne Boutique, where a lovely ceramic sign for the Villa Jovis is posted. The sign reminds me of the time I visited the Villa with my husband, who loves to see any vestige of Ancient Rome.

Early one morning, we began our journey by walking through the arcade, down the narrow passageway of Via Le Botteghe, which runs between two rows of tall white buildings that are connected at the top by buttressed arches, to the Via Fuorlovado. This area of Capri, which dates back to the fourteenth century, is intertwined with many narrow alleyways full of small boutiques, hotels and restaurants.

After we walked through Via Fuorlovado, we climbed the steep Via Croce to the Via Tiberio. Incidentally, *fuorlovado* literally means "I go out," for, in the past, this road was located at the edge of the medieval city, where the countryside began. We ascended the slope of Mount Tiberio for a little more than an hour, and the higher we climbed, the more scenic the pathway became.

Along the way we admired beautiful houses amid gardened terraces, small lemon groves, and vineyards. We glanced at lovely front yards shaded by wisteria-covered trellises and at white column-lined alleys adorned with blooming bougainvillea vines in every shade of red and magenta. We saw lush Mediterranean vegetation and wild flowers in every color of the rainbow. I remember that it was quite warm that day and that we were grateful for having brought a bottle of water with us. We continued up the steep incline of Via Tiberio, resting now and then to catch our breath, until we reached the flat-leveled Via Maiuri that led us to villa's entrance.

The original structure of the Villa actually dates back to Emperor Augustus. At Augustus' death, his successor Tiberius had it redesigned to meet his needs and named it "The Villa Jove" in honor of Jupiter. Often referred to as the Palazzo Tiberio, it was one of Emperor Tiberius' twelve villas on Capri, where he lived in a self-imposed exile for the last ten years of his life.

From this villa Tiberius ruled the vast Roman Empire. His orders were communicated to the mainland and to his naval fleet, based at Misenum, by way of a lighthouse that stood nearby. According to Suetonius, the Roman historian, the lighthouse was destroyed by an earthquake a few days before Tiberius' death. Although it was later rebuilt to guide ships around the bay, it was ultimately demolished in the seventeenth century.

By the size of the ruins, their layout and location, archeologists have determined that the Palazzo looked more like a fortress and that it was the largest and the most sumptuous amongst Tiberius' imperial villas. At the gate we were given an informative pamphlet that included an architectural plan of the villa and several drawings. The pamphlet helped us envision how spectacular this Palazzo must have been. Throughout our exploration of the ruins, I kept thinking it was a shame that it no longer existed. It is sadly ironic that we might never have known what a beautiful Roman villa would have looked like if Vesuvio had not erupted in 79 A.D., burying Pompeii and other towns in its vicinity.

After the fall of the Roman Empire, the islanders began to help themselves to the villa's beautiful artifacts. This went on for several centuries. Eventually the villa was abandoned and, over the years, buried under encroaching Mediterranean vegetation. In the eighteenth century, serious excavations were undertaken at the request of Bourbon King Charles VII. Those excavations had a devastating effect on the villa. What had been left standing in the past was totally stripped away. An African marble pavement was uncovered and moved to the Church of San Costanzo. Marble columns, gold and bronze statues, precious objects and decorations were looted or transferred to royal palaces and religious buildings. By some miracle, a few valuable art pieces found their way to the National Archeological Museum of Naples. Building materials were taken away from the Palazzo and incorporated into new constructions around the island. In fact, many structures on Capri can claim ownership to a piece of the villa.

In 1932, the chief archeologist of Pompeii, Amedeo Maiuri, came to Capri and ordered organized excavations of Villa Jovis.

Layers of debris were removed from the site in order to reveal its complete layout and also to preserve it. The archeological complex of the Villa Jovis, which turned out to be much larger than had been previously thought, opened to the public in 1937.

I recall that, for over an hour, my husband and I stepped through the different sections of the villa and its multileveled terraces. At the villa's highest point, we walked around the restored Chapel of Santa Maria del Soccorso, Saint Mary of Salvation, and glanced at a tall, towering statue of the Virgin Mary. When I stood close to the edge of Mount Tiberio and gazed at the deepest blue of the sky and the sea, I understood why Capri had been labeled the "Blue Island."

For a while, I stared at the Gulfs of Naples and Salerno and the Sorrento Peninsula with the Punta Campanella lighthouse at its tip. In the far distance, a partial view of the Amalfi Coast was visible behind the Peninsula. After I finally managed to extract my gaze from that incredible panoramic vista, I turned around to look at a spectacular view of Mount Solaro and at the Marina Grande below.

What makes the visit to the Villa Jovis so thrilling, however, is not the fact that we can look at the ruins of Tiberius' house but rather the visual experience of seeing the magnificent beauty around it—a beauty that is bound to stir your emotions.

When we retraced our steps back to Capri, we passed the sign for the Villa Lysis at the intersection with Via Lo Capo. Unfortunately, we did not have enough time to see it back then, but I hope to do so in the future. The recently restored Villa Lysis was built in 1905 by the Baron Jacques d'Adelsward Fersen, whose ancestors include Axel von Fersen, Queen Marie Antoinette's Swedish admirer. Baron Fersen came to the island at the age of twenty-five in order to rebuild his life after he got involved in a nasty scandal in Paris.

The young French aristocrat, having received an inheritance from his industrialist grandfather, was exceedingly wealthy when he settled in Capri. A novelist and a poet, he resided in the villa with his longtime boyfriend Nino Cesarini, until his untimely death in 1923, allegedly a suicide by overdose. His ashes are buried in the non-Catholic cemetery of Capri.

The villa was first christened La Gloriette, or "The Glory," then later Fersen renamed it Villa Lysis in reference to one of Plato's dialogues about the nature of friendship. After his death, the villa changed hands several times and eventually fell into disrepair. The mansion, which is now owned and operated by the Capri Local Authorities, is used as a concert hall and opened to the public during the tourist season every day except Sunday.

$$\mathbb{X}$$

Suddenly, as I turn onto Via Emanuele, I am beset by a surge of shoppers. Ambling along Via Emanuele and Via Camerelle is like walking through a miniature Rodeo Drive, for this part of Capri reminds me of the glamorous shopping streets of Beverly Hills, California, with their exclusive boutiques, designer labels, high-end jewelry shops and luxury hotels. Capri's upscale shopping area is a haven for Europe's high-class society and the international jetsetters that visit the island.

In spite of being a busy shopping area, it is a beautiful and colorful neighborhood to stroll through, as several of its building facades have been painted in bright and pastel colors such as reds, pinks and yellows. Those facades, partially covered with flowering trellises, are adorned in the upper floors with wrought-iron balconies where the Capresi proudly exhibit their passion for geraniums, verbenas and fuscias.

In this part of town, I particularly enjoy watching the pedestrian traffic go by, as it, too, contributes to its atmosphere. Only a handful of people enter the elegant shops. Most of them are dressed in the highest of fashion, while the majority of people, who are sporting casual clothing, just peek through windows as they wander by. Several women are wearing Capri pants.

"Capris," those sexy three-quarter length pants with a stylish short slit on their outer seams, were created in 1948 by European Designer Sonja de Lennart, as an addition to her 1945 Capri collection, which included a wide-swinging skirt, a blouse and a hat. Lennart, who had chosen to name her collection after the island she was so deeply fond of, was one of the most influential designers of her generation.

Her Capri pants became very popular in Europe in the fifties, especially after Audrey Hepburn wore a pair in the movie *Roman Holiday,* and in the sixties when many American stars modeled them in their weekly television shows. Somewhat disregarded during the seventies all the way through the nineties, they seem to have regained a place in today's new fashions.

Distracted by a beeping sound that seems to be coming from behind me, I interrupt my perusal of an exquisite Valentino dress and look around to find its provenance. Coming down the street is a golf cart laden with suitcases. As car access is restricted in Capri, many hotels offer their overnight guests a luggage transfer service. It is not unusual to see, throughout the day, those small carts whizzing through the narrow cobbled streets of the town.

In the midst of Capri's trendy open-air shopping mall is the five-star deluxe Grand Hotel Quisisana. The sumptuous hotel was originally built as a clinic in the mid-nineteenth century by the Scottish physician George Clark, who believed that the island's mild Mediterranean climate might benefit Northern European patients with tuberculosis. In fact, the name Quisisana literally means "Here one heals."

With the increasing popularity of the island, the sanatorium gradually took on the role of a pension where tourists could stay overnight. By the time of Clark's death the building had been completely redesigned into a hotel. But the management of the Quisisana proved to be too much for his family. The property was sold off to a young butler, Frederico Serena, who did not waste any time expanding it.

During the expansion, elephant bones were found together with stone weapons. Those relics attest to the existence of large animals on the island and to its former connection to the mainland. After Serena's death, the hotel changed hands several times, until it was finally purchased in 1981 by authentic natives of Capri, the Morgano family.

Amid the hotel's guest list are the illustrious names of monarchs, heads of state, actors, writers, industrialists and singers. Their ranks include the Savoy family, the Hohenzollerns, Gerald Ford, Claudette Colbert, Tom Cruise, Jean Paul Sartre, Ernest Hemingway, Friedrich Krupp and Sting. Not only is the Grand Hotel Quisisana designed to impress its exclusive clientele with spacious and elegantly decorated rooms and suites, it also offers a world-class spa for those who wish to be pampered in complete luxury. Celebrity guests who prefer to remain incognito are transferred by helicopter to the private landing pad on the property.

Staring at the pink and white facade of the Quisisana, I smile to myself. How excitingly romantic it would be to arrive on Capri by air instead of by sea. The view of the island from the sky must be unforgettably beautiful.

Lost in thoughts, I twirl away, ready to descend the less crowded Via Serena. While rummaging through my shoulder bag for a tissue, I accidentally collide with a hard body. Just as I am about to open my mouth to apologize with "I am sorry," I hear a rich baritone voice saying *"Scusi."* Startled, I glance up.

The man in front of me is tall, definitely Italian, with thick dark hair tinged with gray, dark eyes and a flirtatious smile on his tanned face. I notice a faint scent of cologne. Probably in his late forties, he is dressed entirely in black, an indication that he must be from Southern Italy, since people prefer darker clothing in the South. He looks absolutely stunning. By his widening smile, I presume that this lady-killer gelato must make every woman's heart flutter, just as mine is doing right now. It is amazing how the mind and heart stay forever young. At least mine do.

Amused by the thought, I finally manage to say, "I am sorry, too." And we both laugh.

"Signora, are you okay?" he asks in English, his hand on my elbow.

"Si, grazie. I am looking for the Carthusia Perfumery," I reply in Italian, even though I know perfectly well its location—having seen it before. But when in the company of George Clooney, one is tempted to lie.

"Oh, you speak Italian," he answers, surprised.

"A little. I am afraid my Italian is not that good," I explain.

"Well, we will practice while I walk you to the perfume shop," he offers.

Smiling, I accept, thinking that the only way I will improve my Italian is to speak with the locals. Besides, this gelato is so good-looking, I am happy to drool over him a little longer. As we stroll down the narrow street, he introduces himself. His name is Marcello. He is from Naples, and today he is guiding a group of Irish tourists to the island. Laughing at the fact that we both have similar jobs, I reveal my name and that I am escorting a small group of American women for a week on the Amalfi Coast.

"Do you like Capri?" he asks.

"Yes, I do. It is such a beautiful island," I reply.

"Ah, I hear by your enthusiasm that you too have fallen under its spell," he answers, smiling.

"What is there not to like?"

"Do you know the story of the perfume of Capri?" he continues. When I shake my head, he proceeds to enlighten me.

"The origin of Capri's famous perfume is a mixture of history and legend. According to the legend, Queen Joanna of Anjou, who, in 1380, was paying an unexpected visit to Capri, was presented with a bouquet of wild flowers gathered in her honor, and in great haste, by the father prior of the Carthusian Monastery of San Giacomo. When, three days later, the prior went to throw the flowers away, he noticed that the water had not been changed and that it had acquired a very pleasant fragrance. He then took the water to the priory's chemist, who traced its source to the "Garofilum silvestre caprense," known today as the Dianthus sylvestris. Thus was born the first perfume of Capri. The rock carnation, as it is often referred to, is still found abundantly between cracks of stony places. The pink, scented flowers bloom in July and August.

"History has it that, in 1948, the prior of the Monastery discovered the old formulas for the perfumes. With the Pope's permission, he revealed them to a chemist from Torino who subsequently opened a small laboratory, which he named Carthusia."

After we round the corner of Via Matteotti, Marcello stops. "The Carthusian Monastery is just in front of you and the Carthusia perfume factory is just a little further, on your right," he informs me. As we are about to part ways, I smile and extend my hand to thank him, but instead of shaking it, Marcello gallantly kisses it. Wow! It is a good thing that he cannot read my mind, as right now I am thinking that this gelato is a smooth operator. I wish I could snap a picture of him, but that might be a little obvious, right?

"It has been a pleasure." He smiles. "I hope that we will meet again someday. If you return to Capri, email me so that I can give you a private tour of the island. Here is my address," he adds, grinning broadly as he hands me his business card.

"*Grazie,* I definitely will," I assure him. Sadly, he turns away, waving goodbye with a lift of his hand, and shouts, "*Ciao Bella.*" I sigh and watch him leave, lifting my hand in return. He even looks gorgeous from behind. The meaning of the phrase "In Italy, you are either seduced or being seduced," could not be truer than when you visit Capri.

Before entering the perfume factory, I pause to admire the building's stone facade, partially draped with magenta bougainvillea. Behind me is the Carthusian Monastery of San Giacomo. Its image is reflected in the factory's three large windows and glass door, which are shaded by a white domed awning with "I profumi di Capri" printed on it. The young couple that just exited the store seems to be on the verge of a spat. Trouble in paradise, what a shame!

Once inside, I step up to a long counter where several young women in white overalls are eager to serve. In the background, a myriad of silver cylinders line the shelves on either side of a large window, through which the Carthusia laboratory is visible. On the counter, dozens of small perfume bottles are perfectly displayed. Traditional craft methods are still being used to create a limited production of about a dozen different perfumes. The main component for those perfumes is readily available locally, as the island of Capri is a veritable Garden of Eden.

Everywhere you turn, there is an explosion of blossoms. Flowers in all colors of the spectrum grow in the wild, in private gardens and in the towns where they adorn facades, walls, pergolas, trellises and columns. Mediterranean orchids, anemones and yellow buttercups are just a few among countless varieties found on the slopes of Mount Solaro and Mount Tiberio. The island's flower, blue as the sea and the sky, which resembles a myosotis, grows on the sea cliffs. Called the "Blu di Capri," it only blooms in the Mediterranean winter, from December to April.

In the olive groves of Anacapri, narcissus are at their best in February and March. Wild crocus, which are cream colored when closed and lilac when opened, peek through the dead oak leaves and winter grasses. In the spring, the fragrance of the citrus flowers fills the air, and red poppies cover the soil of vineyards. But the most spectacular time to see Capri is from April to October when the majority of the floral vegetation blooms. Lavender-blue wisteria and jasmine scents lace the April-May sea breeze, while roses, which are mostly cultivated in gardens—public and private—and on terraces, mingle their fragrance with the summer heat. In the fall, an intoxicating blend of flowery perfumes permeates the air.

The island of Capri not only rewards those addicted to hiking with incredible views of the sea, it also dazzles them with spectacular landscapes covered by an abundance of flowers.

Approaching the counter, a lovely young woman hands me a little strip of paper that she has just spritzed, then waved to let the alcohol dissipate. "This is our most famous perfume, the Fiori di Capri, the Flowers of Capri," she says, smiling. "Wild carnations and lilies of the Valley have been blended together with sandalwood." I sniff it. It smells divine. She continues to present me with additional strips, each time describing the essence she sprays. With a cloud of fragrances hovering around me, I am beginning to feel overwhelmed. Suddenly it occurs to me that I might prefer a lemony scent. At my request, the young woman hands me another strip.

"Lemon and green tea leaves were used to create this perfume that we call Mediterraneo," she informs. Yes, that is the one for me! The lemon blend reminds me of dreamy moments spent under lemon-covered pergolas along the Amalfi Coast.

"I will take this one. Do you have a perfume for men? " I ask.

"We have the Carthusia Uomo. The essence of balance and strength will amaze you," she says, laughing. "Wild raspberry, rosewood and kelp were blended together to create this one," she continues. I bring the strip to my nose. It smells exactly like the perfume Marcello was wearing, and I burst into laughter. I order a couple of soaps and body lotions to go along with the perfumes. While she is wrapping my order, I pick up a perfume bottle from the counter to look at the interesting Carthusia logo. The logo, representing a flowery seductive mythical siren, was beautifully designed by Sergio Rubino, the talented ceramic artist from Anacapri.

Leaving Carthusia, I cross the street, walk down a short flight of steps and stroll along the path that leads to the Hotel Luna. In the fall, the path is shaded by trellises covered with blooming vivid red bougainvillea, while in the spring, blue and lavender clusters of wisteria cascade from the same trellises. In my opinion this is the most romantic, if not the most fragrant, walkway in Capri.

Nearby is the imposing Carthusian Monastery of San Giacomo. The Certosa of San Giacomo, or the Charterhouse of Saint Jacques, was founded as a monastery between 1363 and 1374 by Count Giacomo Arcucci, a nobleman of Capri and Grand Chamberlain to the Queen of Naples, Joanna I of Anjou. To ensure its survival and prosperity, the Certosa was endowed by the Queen with large sums of money, lands and ecclesiastical privileges. In the years that followed, the Certosa increased its wealth by acquiring additional land on the island and on the mainland, and with the tax revenues exacted from those properties. For the next four centuries, the monastery controlled the economic activities of the island as well as the spirituality of its people and their poor living conditions. Its archives contain reports of many quarrels between Anacapri and Capri in which it played an active role.

In the sixteenth century, the island of Capri was continuously attacked by the Turks. Admiral Barbarossa destroyed its castle in 1534, and in 1553, his successor Dragut sacked the Charterhouse, then set it on fire. Ten years later, the Certosa was restored and enlarged to include a cloister and a defensive tower. Less than a hundred years later, the plague broke out in Naples. The deadly disease, which had been introduced to the town by an infected ship from Sardinia quickly spread to the neighboring towns along the coast of Campania and to the adjacent provinces. An estimated

300,000 persons died of the plague during a period of six months.

Capri was not spared. It is believed that the island was exposed by the ignorance and carelessness of guards who allowed the disembarkation of a trunk. In that trunk were the contaminated belongings of a noble young lady who had died from the disease in Naples. Unaware of the consequences, her family had sent articles of her clothing and a tress of her hair to relatives in Capri. As a result, more than half of the island's population died.

Among the victims were many clergymen who had cared for and administered to the dying. When the last priest died, Monsignor Pelligrino begged the prior for the assistance of the Carthusian monks who had cowardly retreated for fear of contagion. His evasive response angered the people of Capri. Siding with their bishop, they began to throw the bodies of the plague victims over the Certosa walls.

The Charterhouse was further enriched land-wise by this human tragedy, as according to an ancient privilege, it was entitled to inherit the possessions of the families that were extinct. Such was the contrast between the wealthy monastery and the poor clergy that the people of Capri did not blink an eye upon learning that the Certosa had been suppressed and its possessions seized in 1807 by the King of Naples Joachim Murat, Napoleon's brother-in-law.

The tower, which had been erected to warn of Turkish attacks, crumbled a few days before the monks left the island in 1808, and after their departure the Certosa served as a prison, military barracks, hospice, and school, until it was totally abandoned by the authorities in 1901.

Efforts to salvage the priceless architectural treasure were undertaken in the last century by intellectuals, government officials and the Mayors of Capri. These efforts were not in vain, as exciting restoration plans are in place to develop the Certosa, now a property of the Italian State, as a world-class museum, a conference center and heritage gardens. Presently displayed at the Charterhouse are the canvases of the German painter Karl Diefenbach, who sought refuge in Capri at the beginning of the twentieth century. He lived on the island until his death in 1913.

※

Lingering under the bougainvillea-covered trellis and enjoying a vision of the reddish clusters against the blue sky overhead while the sun shadows a unique flowery web-like pattern on the stone pavement beneath, I imagine a beautiful bride in a ravishing white gown and her handsome groom walking lovingly down this aisle on their way to their honeymoon suite at the Hotel Luna.

Surrounded by lush Mediterranean vegetation, the hotel is a haven of tranquility perched on the cliffs overlooking a shimmering sea. From the open-air terrace near the hotel's entrance, guests savor an unsurpassed panoramic vista. Beyond the terrace, amid a subtropical garden and with the Charterhouse in the background, is a large swimming pool. The reception area and lounges are charmingly decorated in a simple color scheme of white, yellow and blue. From the balcony of their elegant bedrooms, hotel guests enjoy glorious sunrises and red-flaming sunsets.

At the end of Via Matteotti, a ceramic-tiled sign announces the Giardini Augusto, the lovely manicured "Gardens of Augustus" that were established as a public garden by the German magnate Friedrich Alfred Krupp, owner of the Krupp steel company. Born in Essen, Germany, in 1854, he was believed be the richest man of his time.

Krupp came to Capri to recover from various ailments. He was so enchanted by the island that he would reside each year for a considerable length of time at the Quisisana. Here with his two yachts, the Maya and the Puritan, he nurtured his hobby of Oceanography and financed two major marine expeditions in the waters of Capri. Krupp died in Germany at the beginning of the 20th century.

Following the gravel pathway through the lower section of the gardens, I pass lush evergreen Mediterranean shrubs of various shapes, pleasingly designed flower beds and lovely garden statues, on my way to the upper terraces. At present, the top terrace is quite crowded. Guides love to bring their tour groups to the gardens to show them the Tyrrhenian side of the island and the Faraglioni rocks.

Looking around, I spot an empty seat near the edge of the terrace, on a concrete bench next to two elderly gentlemen. Dressed in short-sleeved shirts and shorts, they are without a doubt tourists, and by the lilt in their accent, Irish to boot. At the other end of the terrace, couples take turns being photographed against the scenic backdrop. They seem to be enjoying the warmth of the sun. I have a feeling that tonight many will have to deal with a sunburned face. Could this be Marcello's group?

My two companions are laughing. I wonder what is so funny? I lean a little closer to eavesdrop on their conversation. "Did you see my Peggy drool over the maitre d' last night? I don't know what came over her. I have never seen her acting that way," the nearer to me comments. He is sporting a plaid shirt.

"And what about my Meg? She kept cooing with Marcello this morning," his friend replies. I presumed correctly, it is Marcello's group.

"What's with our women going gaga over these Italian men?"

"What do they have that we don't have?"

Resisting the temptation to give them my opinion, I turn my head to hide a smile. Silently, the men ponder the matter, then all of sudden I hear, "I think that it is the gleam in their eyes that makes women throw themselves at them," the plaid-shirted man announces proudly, as if by some insight he has found the key to the charm of Italian men.

"You know the one you get in your eyes when you gaze at your first pint of beer after a hard day's work," he continues, chuckling.

"Do you mean to tell me that I need to look at my wife as if she is pint of beer?" the other one asks, incredulous.

"Yes, grant her the same gleaming look you have from seeing your FIRST pint, mind you, not the cross-eyed one you have from drinking your third or fourth," he confirms.

Envisioning that last look, I just burst into laughter. Seconds later, the two Irishmen join me. They are laughing so hard their whole bodies are shaking.

Within a few blinks of the eye, the group is gone, leaving only a handful of people on the terrace. I get up, cross the terrace, lean over the railing and glance down at the Faraglioni emerging from the crystal blue water. The three Faraglioni rocks, often referred to as the island Guardians, are the result of a limestone promontory eroded by the sea. The giant rock formations change color with the play of the sunlight, and right now their ivory hue contrasts dramatically against the turquoise blue of the sea.

Each of the geological formations has been given a name. The first, still attached to the land, is Stella, Star. The second one, Mezzo or Half, separated from the first one by a stretch of the sea, is famous throughout the world for the natural arch at its base, which is large enough for a small boat to pass through. The third rock, the Faraglione di Fuori, or Scopolo, which means "at the outer edge" or "outside," is home to a rare blue-tinted lizard species, appropriately named the Blue Lizard of the Faraglioni. To camouflage themselves, the small reptiles assume the blue tones of the sea and the sky.

To get a better view of the Marina Piccola, Capri's trendiest beach, and the famous Via Krupp, I step over to the opposite side of the terrace. The island of Capri does not have many beaches. There is a small beach a short distance away from the Marina Grande, but even though the locals call it that, I would not, as it is only a narrow stretch of pebble sand.

Set in a picturesque inlet at the foot of Mount Solaro, the Marina Piccola was until the late nineteenth century a fishing village with a few houses overlooking two small bays, and a little church dedicated to St Andrew, the fishermen's patron saint. The mythical Scoglio delle Sirene, "Rock of the Sirens," dedicated to the legendary enchantresses, separates the two bays: the Marina di Pennaulo to the east and the Marina di Mulo to the west.

The Marina Piccola has developed considerably in the last fifty years, thanks mainly to the growing number of tourists overnighting on the island. It is now the home of several restaurants where sunbathers can enjoy fresh seafood. Two restaurants control the access to the beaches: La Fontellina, which is very upscale, and Da Luigi, which is less pretentious, with a natural pool. The beaches tend to be very crowded in July and August. Those are the most expensive months on the isle of Capri. Many of the hotels require a minimum stay of three nights.

The Marina Piccola is reached from the center of town by bus or taxi. It is a twenty-minute walk from the funicular along Via Roma and Via Mulo to the beach. Alternatively, visitors can descend the Via Krupp that begins at the end of Via Matteotti. The winding road was commissioned in 1902 by the German industrialist Friedrich Krupp to connect the Hotel Quisisana to the small marina.

Capri boasts many magnificent vistas that can be enjoyed from different parts of the island. One of my favorites is right here, from the Gardens of Augustus' top terrace. The view of the green hills dropping straight down into the sea and the crystal waters of the Mediterranean sea lapping against the limestone cliffs is without a doubt spectacular.

From my vantage point, I gaze down at the intricate pattern of the pathway with a series of hairpin bends descending 150 feet vertically. They are so close together that they seem to overlap. Krupp designed the forty-five hundred foot road, but it was the engineer Emilio Mayer who created it by cutting through the rock until reaching the sea and by using the local materials for its construction. The zigzagging Via Krupp, which also leads to a favorite nudist spot, has been recently restored. Visitors should be aware of the possibility of falling rocks, especially on a very windy day. Via Krupp was nicknamed the "Road of Love" by the locals, as couples often smooch as they stroll down.

Conscious of the passing time, I check my watch and hurriedly retrace my steps to the center of Capri and the funicular. Passing through the Piazzetta, I notice that it has temporarily emptied out. At the entrance of the cable car, I hesitate. With twenty minutes left to reach the pier on foot I turn around, pass through Capri's old medieval gate, where the town's public restrooms are now located, and start to follow the signs down to the Marina Grande. I descend the large steps of Via Aquaviva, which was used in the old days by the mules and donkeys that were transporting goods and people to the town center, and continue to follow the small ceramic signs to the Marina.

Stepping down a deluge of stairs, I envision the heroic women of Anacapri on the same pathway, with weights gracefully balanced on their heads. Every day they would walk down to the Marina to sell their produce and return with other supplies. They often carried heavy loads of building materials and wood piles, as well as fresh water, up to their town. The soles of their shoes were made of rope to prevent them from slipping on the rocky steps. Foreign artists who came to the island in search of inspiration in the nineteenth century were seduced by those women and captured their beauty on canvas. One of those artists was the American-born Charles Caryl Coleman, who spent most of his life on the island.

From 1806 until 1815, the island of Capri was occupied by French troops, briefly ousted by the English, who called it their "Little Gibraltar." Many of the island's archeological sites that had manage to survive until then were damaged during that decade. At the end of the Napoleonic Era, Capri was ruled once again by the Bourbons of Naples; and the island began to emerge from its magical solitude and rustic lifestyle.

The islanders were freed from military occupation and ecclesiastic oppression. They could finally dance the Tarantella: the courtship dance of Southern Italy, which is thought to have originated in the town of Taranto in today's region of Puglia. Performed by couples, this dance features a fast, cheerful music. Nowadays, the people of Capri and Anacapri celebrate the coming of each New Year by dancing the Tarantella in their town squares.

In the second half of the nineteenth century, Capri was the most popular destination for European writers, such as Alexander Dumas and Oscar Wilde, and for painters like John Singer Sargent and Frank Hyde. In the early twentieth century, Norman Douglas came to the island where he wrote his books: *South Wind, Capri* and *A Footnote on Capri*. All dealt with his life on the island and with its inhabitants. Douglas is buried in the island's non-Catholic cemetery not far from the painter Coleman. Capri welcomes anyone in search of inspiration or self-expression. Graham Greene sought refuge here, too. He spent many holidays on the island; his last visit was in 1988, three years before he died.

During my descent I stop numerous times to take pictures of lovely small backyards and interesting tiled signs. I particularly like the one with the bulldog and the gun that says *Attenti al cane...e al Padrone*, which means "Beware of the dog...and its owner." The islanders have an intriguing sense of humor.

Reaching the oldest part of the Marina Grande, I stride over to the Pier's office, where my group is waiting. As we walk along the dock, the women share their gelato stories. They have encountered quite a few on the island. I try to resist the urge to laugh. I want to tell them about Marcello, but I need to concentrate and make sure that we board the right jet-boat back to Sorrento. What is it with Capri that it has such a concentration of good-looking men? And I didn't even take the time to buy an ice cream today. Too much to see and do on Capri.

Boatmen are standing at the bottom of the gangway, waiting to check our tickets before we board. Once inside the catamaran, we search to find empty seats in the main cabin. As we are leaving, it occurs to me—regretfully—that I have never in fact spent a night on Capri. Maybe someday I will remedy that situation, but for now, I can only sing "Capri c'est fini . . ."

In contrast with the morning crossing, the afternoon crossing is a lot quieter. Earlier in the day the passenger cabin was very noisy. People were chatting away as they waited with trepidation to see Capri. Now they are just tired, and most of them are dozing off. I peer through the window. We are navigating close to the shoreline of the Sorrento Peninsula and passing by the ruins of the famous Villa di Pollio Felice. In Imperial times, the town of Sorrento was the favorite getaway of the Roman patricians. Its entire bay was adorned by a succession of remarkable residences and exquisite gardens. Among those residences was the Villa of Emperor Augustus, which stood on the small promontory between the Marina Grande and the Marina Piccola and where he exiled his nephew Agrippa Postumus in 7 A.D.

According to the Latin poet Publius Papinius Statius, the most splendid of the coastal villas was the one owned by Pollius Felix, his powerful patron. Statius, who was a native of Naples, celebrated the beauty of the villa in his poem "The Silvae." The private estate was composed of several pavilions that extended inland, and which included reception rooms, owner and guests accommodation, thermal baths, servant lodgings, kitchens and warehouses. It even had its own private docking place, a *calidarium* (Roman bath complex) and a nymphaeum whose foundations can still be seen. A model reconstruction of the villa is displayed in the Archeological Museum of Piano di Sorrento, and several of the Sorrento guide books include a drawing representation.

We are fast approaching Sorrento, and the straight-edged cliffs are getting grander by the minute. After stepping off, I will search for the van that will take us back to our hotel. I am so looking forward to a steaming hot bath, after which I'll kick back on my lovely terrace, enjoy a glass of the Capresi wine purchased earlier today in an *alimentari,* small grocery, and gaze at the Gulf of Naples and the town down below.

Day Five

Sant'Agata sui Due Golfi

*O*ne of the benefits of traveling abroad is to taste something truly local, so in lieu of my usual breakfast fare at the hotel, I decide to walk to the center of Sant'Agata.

Wonderful aromas of freshly-brewed coffee and newly-baked pastries are stirring my appetite as I cast a quick glance at the display case in the Bar Fiorentino before placing my order with a pretty brunette. Behind me, mothers with children wait their turn. Another five minutes and the pastry trays will be empty.

Italian conversations are humming in the air as I move past crowded tables, a steamy cappuccino in one hand and a Santa Rosa in the other, to an empty chair near the entrance and settle down. At the first bite of the shell-shaped puff pastry filled with vanilla cream and topped with a sour black cherry, I congratulate myself for making the right decision. The bakers at Fiorentino produce by far the creamiest Santa Rosa in the area. The luscious delicacy, actually a sweeter version of another local specialty, the Sfogliatelle, was invented in the eighteenth century by the Augustine nuns of the Convent of Santa Rosa, in the small town of Conca dei Marini. Each year on August 30th the nuns celebrated their patron saint by preparing the small treats and offering them to the population.

Taking another sip of cappuccino I look around. Standing at the bar, three men in dark suits are vehemently discussing an upcoming soccer game—a national topic in Italy—while drinking their morning coffee. Beside each tiny espresso cup is a small glass of water to help them digest the strong brew.

There are many ways to order a cup of coffee in Italy. Tourists are often confused. The simple word caffè will get you an espresso. *Caffè doppio* means a double espresso. *Caffè Americano* is similar to what we are used to in the States—a big cup of coffee. It is easy to remember.

Caffè latte is hot milk mixed with coffee, usually served in a glass. *Cappuccino* is an espresso infused with steamed milk and drunk only at breakfast. Then you have *caffè Marocchino*—Moroccan coffee—an espresso served with a dash of hot milk and cocoa powder. During our tour of Ancient Rome with Sara, I ordered a Marocchino in the cafeteria of the Capitoline Museums, and to my surprise, I actually liked it.

The last two are *caffè macchiato*—an espresso tinged with a drop of steamed milk and *caffè ristretto*—a coffee with less water, even stronger than an espresso. If I had drunk one of those last night, I could have followed my group to the restaurant Il Quattro Venti, "The Four Winds" and enjoyed a pizza.

Instead, I watched the cruise ships depart with farewell blasts, in opposite directions, north to Rome and south to Sicily, until they became mere dots on the horizon. Afterward, I crawled into bed, totally exhausted from a full day in Capri. Still sound asleep when the phone rang at six a.m., I slowly picked up the receiver and said *"pronto,"* the Italian version of "hello." It took me a couple seconds to recognize my husband's familiar voice. He was eager to talk to me. Without many details, I described our marvelous time on the island, wished he had been there, then told him the women were looking forward to a free day. A handful planned to hop on the Sita bus to Sorrento, others were going back to Positano, and three had decided to simply stay close to the hotel and visit Sant'Agata.

Meanwhile, on my schedule was a morning meeting with Danilo in his office and an afternoon stroll through the town, with a visit to the tourist office for some maps and brochures. Fifteen minutes later I bid my husband goodnight, since home was nine hours behind, hung up, climbed out of bed and went about my daily morning routine.

Now stepping outside the Bar Fiorentino, I turn right; peek at an elegant clothing boutique, round the corner of Corso Sant'Agata, the town's main street, pass a small grocery, a gift shop and a shoe store and head for the church square.

Sant'Agata is a typical medium-size hill town with a population of approximately three thousand. It has a church, a post office, an elementary school, and two banks, each with an automated teller machine. Of course, we should not forget a small pharmacy with a handsome pharmacist. There are no less than a dozen hotels near ours and about the same number of restaurants in and around town. In Sant'Agata I feel right at home. The town is simply delightful: not too big, not too small, just the right size and not many tourists wandering around.

At the tabacchi, I enter to purchase an international phone card and a bag of candy. The tobacco shop is buzzing this morning. Around me there is a continuous flow of men grabbing the daily newspaper and dropping coins into a little tray on the counter on their way out. A few are also buying cigarettes. Unfortunately, many Italians still smoke, even though nowadays in Italy it is forbidden to smoke in public places. I try to skirt around teenagers who can't quite make up their minds which magazines to buy and a delivery man who has just unloaded three large boxes in the main aisle. A moment later I finally manage to exit the store.

Farther down the street, I glance at the famous Don Alfonso, considered to be the best culinary gem in Southern Italy. Alfonso Costanzo Iaccarino opened the restaurant in 1890 after his return from America, where he had been living for several years. More than a century later, his grandson is running the business with the assistance of his wife Livia and their two sons, Ernesto and Mario.

The success of the restaurant is entirely due to Alfonso's passion for food. He loves to create unique dishes with the freshest organic ingredients available. Many ingredients are cultivated locally on the family farm, Le Peracciole, in nearby Punta Campanella. Don Alfonso bought the hillside property from his wife's family in 1990.

On his certified organic farm, Alfonso Iaccarino grows dark purple eggplants, large peppers, carrots, delicious tomatoes, potatoes, lettuce, zucchini, artichokes and a variety of herbs. Each year the large groves of the domain yield an abundance of delicious nectarines, pears, lemons and figs. There are more than two thousand olive trees on the property. Each fall the ripened olives are hand picked and pressed to produce the famous Don Alfonso extra virgin olive oil.

Don Alfonso's wine cellar, dug right out of the Tufo rock, is spectacular. At the bottom of the two-level cellar is a tunnel dating from the Roman era. Through the ancient passageway people could reach Sorrento in fifteen minutes. The most prestigious wines are stored there, including thirteen hundred different labels of great wines from the Campania region and from all the other regions of Italy, as well as famous French wines and a wide selection from around the world.

Italians and foreigners alike come to Sant'Agata to dine at Don Alfonso's restaurant. Surrounded by an elegant decor, they are served exquisite dishes by a professional and friendly staff who seem to anticipate their every need. Patrons who have eaten at Don Alfonso's have described their gourmet experience as "simply divine."

Nowadays, it is possible to overnight at Don Alfonso's in one of several beautifully-designed suites. Guests enjoy an extensive library and an outdoor swimming pool set in a lush Mediterranean garden.

The pride of Sant'Agata's inhabitants is their beautiful church, founded in 1745 by the Casafestina family. The Chiesa di Santa Maria delle Grazie, the Church of Saint Mary of Grace, was built in the shape of a Latin cross. Inside, the marble high altar inlaid with mother-of-pearl, dating from the seventeenth century, is one of the most beautiful pieces of artwork on the Sorrento Peninsula. A large organ above the entrance and notable paintings adorn the interior.

As I continue to stroll, the church bells ring out the nine o'clock hour. The bells are rung every half hour, every day of the week, from six in the morning until midnight. On Saturdays, they also announce weddings, and on Sundays, the beginning of worship services. I love the sound of the carillons. It reminds me of my childhood and I sometimes miss it.

At the intersection with Via Olivella, I veer left onto Via Deserto and ascend the pathway to the Convent of Il Deserto. During my first tour Angelo mentioned that the panoramic view from the summit of Deserto Hill, the second-highest elevation on the western end of the Sorrento Peninsula (at 1,495 feet above sea level) —with Mount Costanzo being the first (at 1,631 feet)—was well worth the hike. He was right. The vista from my vantage point is breathtaking. Words cannot begin to describe what I feel as I finally reach the mountaintop. Amazingly, I have the area entirely to myself.

The air is clear and bright. The sun, high in the sky, shines over the Gulf of Naples, Vesuvio and the towns below. Across the deep blue waters, a hydrofoil jets from Sorrento to Capri, and in the distance a large ship cruises closer to Naples. At the end of the gulf, the islands of Ischia and Procida are clearly visible; while Misenum, at its tip, is shaded by a lonely white puffy cloud.

Turning toward Capri, I am instantly captivated by the stunning view. The island appears so close I can almost touch it. For a brief moment, I study its saddle landscape. Clearly visible are Mount Solaro, Mount Tiberio and Marina Grande at the water's edge. Anacapri and Capri are hidden. I wonder what Ulysses thought when he sailed along the coastline and glanced for the first time at the island. Undoubtedly Capri bears little resemblance to what he might have seen back then. It amazes me that after everything the island has endured it has somehow managed to retain its mystical aura. Capri still lures people to its shore. I snap several pictures, then transfer my attention to the large medieval structure behind me.

With the discovery of a Greek cemetery and another necropolis on this hillside, historians learned that the site was once one of the most important sanctuaries of the ancient world: the Temple of the Sirens. In 1679, the barefooted Carmelite nuns chose this spiritual place to build their convent, next to the Chapel of Monte Calvario.

In 1867, it passed to the order of the Grey Friars of Father Ludovico of Casoria. In 1980, after being abandoned for several years, the building was acquired by the Benedictine Sisters of San Paolo, who relocated from Sorrento.

Angelo had told me that the best views are seen from the roof terrace of the convent, which unfortunately is closed at the present. I will have to come back another time to stare simultaneously at the entire Amalfi coastline, the Gulf of Salerno, the isle of Capri, the Sorrento Peninsula and the Gulf of Naples.

On the bell tower of the convent, the inscription *Tempus breve est* reminds us all that "Time is short," and I glance at my watch. After one last glimpse at Capri, I retrace my steps to Sant'Agata.

During my first stay I discovered that in the morning the town is fairly busy, at least until one in the afternoon, when the majority of the shops close for lunch and siesta. Late in the afternoon, around four, the shops reopen and Sant'Agata comes alive again with the locals congregating for a drink and a chat.

Eating, drinking and talking are the favorite pastimes of the people of Southern Italy and they do all three with *"Fervore."* They will tell you that they take the time to enjoy life, family, and friends, because without the last two they would not have the first.

Walking leisurely down the street on my way to the Sita bus stop, I notice a most unusual sign hanging on the facade of a building next to the entrance of a bar. It's a large ceramic-tiled sign of a cat smoking a cigarette. On the bottom left corner of the artwork is the inscription:

Vedermi per credere, which translates as "See me to believe."

Curious, I step inside the Bar Orlando to investigate. On the wall are several pictures of a black and white cat. In each one, he is holding a cigarette in his mouth. "This is Jolly," says a friendly-looking man in his late fifties, from behind a counter. "He died more that forty years ago. Would you like to hear his story? " he asks, smiling. I nod and order a cappuccino.

Since this might take a while, I sit down at one of the small tables along the wall and wait for him to join me. While he introduces himself, a waiter brings us two coffees, one cappuccino for me and one espresso for him. He is Orlando, the owner of the bar. "This is a true story, not a legend," he begins. From my shoulder bag I extract the spiral notepad and pen I always carry and begin to take notes.

Orlando's father Alfredo befriended a wild cat in 1960 and named him Jolly. Jolly would drop by the bar every night around seven and entertain the patrons with his acrobatics. He was the star attraction. He would sit, jump and stand up like a dog, as well as sit on people's shoulders, all this while smoking a cigarette. Customers enjoyed the show so much that they quickly spread the word of the smoking cat.

Soon everybody in Sant'Agata knew Jolly. In a matter of a few weeks, Jolly had become the mascot of the bar and the town. The show lasted eight years. Jolly died in 1968, but people still remember him.

"It is the best thing my father left me!" Orlando says. "Jolly has put food on our table for more than forty years." He grins broadly.

The beautiful black and white cat named Jolly may have run out of lives, but he is definitely not forgotten. His star is still shining brightly in Sant'Agata. If you visit the area, be sure you pop in to the Bar Orlando to hear Jolly's story and to see his pictures.

Closing my notepad, I get up and offer Orlando my hand. He

grabs it, pulls me gently toward him and joyfully kisses me on the cheeks. "I love kissing a pretty woman. Handshakes are for men," he says, chuckling. Laughing, I express my gratitude for the information and for the two items he would not accept payment for—a postcard of the smoking cat and the cappuccino—and leave. What a charmer.

Once outside, a quick check at my watch warns me that I have a scant five minutes before the next Sita bus to Sorrento stops in Sant'Agata.

Massa Lubrense

*T*wo minutes after reaching the fermata in front of Sant'Agata's gas station, the blue bus pulls to a stop. Still a little out of breath from running—I have not sprinted in years—I climb on board, validate my ticket and grab the front seat near the window. I retrieve the bus schedule that Amelia handed me this morning while I was purchasing my ticket and check the return time from Sorrento.

At the corner of Via Reolo, the driver stops to let three residents step inside: a man in his late seventies and an attractive young woman with an angel-faced, blond toddler. The gentleman takes the seat next to me while the woman and the toddler settle across the aisle.

A short distance down the road, the bus driver reduces his speed in anticipation of a road bump. Almost simultaneously, out of the corner of my eye I see Grandpa slowly lifting himself up with the help of the bar in front of him. After the driver reaches the other side of the bump, the old man slowly sits down again. Each time the bus driver encounters a speed bump, the old man repeats his up and down dance moves. I glance at him with raised eyebrows.

Grinning with his dentures askew, he states that bumps are hard on his butt. I smile in sympathy, then turn my head and stare out the window, trying my best to keep from laughing. When the bus stops again, the old gentleman alights, and hiding behind one hand, I burst into laughter.

Seconds later, my giggles finally subsiding, I concentrate on the scenery. We are driving through the territory of Massa Lubrense along the Nastro d'Oro—the Golden Ribbon. Linking Sant'Agata to the towns of Termini and Massa Lubrense, the winding road is bathed from sunrise to sunset by golden rays virtually every day from March to November.

The territory of Massa Lubrense, with its triangular shape, covers the western section of the Sorrento Peninsula. Its northeastern side borders on the municipality of Sorrento, while the other two border on the sea.

For those addicted to hiking, the unspoiled territory is a natural oasis with walking trails, archeological sites, Mediterranean vegetation, picturesque hamlets and beautiful beaches. Local tourist offices gladly provide detailed maps of the network of paths, mule tracks and lanes, as well as the main roads linking the seventeen villages on the Sorrentine Peninsula and its 13,700 inhabitants.

Through the windows, I admire the lush scenery unfurling on both sides of the Nastro d'Oro. There are fewer villages on this side of the Massa Lubrense territory due to the wild and dramatic vertical terrain—a topography that has the advantage of offering the traveler unobstructed vistas of the landscape and the Gulf of Salerno. Can anyone ever get tired of these breathtaking views?

Seeing the sign for Marina del Cantone, I remember my last visit to the lovely seaside village. At the time, I was escorting my second group to the Amalfi Coast and we were staying in a gorgeous villa on Via Pontone on the outskirts of Sant'Agata. In the middle of the week, after a return trip from Sorrento, I asked the members if they were interested in seeing Marina del Cantone. It was a beautiful sunny day, and I thought they might enjoy a boat ride. Surprisingly, they all elected to stay at the villa to relax and to enjoy the pool. Never missing an opportunity to explore, I asked Aronne if he would not mind driving me to the Marina, and he readily accepted.

Driving down the long winding road to the small harbor, we passed the villages of Metrano, Termini and Nerano. Termini is well known to avid hikers as the starting point of some spectacular walks around the region. The trail to the tip of the Sorrentine Peninsula and the path to Mount Costanzo both start from the little square in the center of the village.

Mount Costanzo, the highest elevation of the Peninsula, has two summits. On one summit is a radio station for air traffic control and on the other is the little white fifteenth-century church of San Costanzo. Each year, on the Sunday following the 15th of May, a small procession travels along the path from Termini to the church to celebrate ancient sacred rites.

The name *Nerano* derives from Emperor Tiberius, whose full name was Tiberius Claudius Nero. During one of his boat trips from Capri to the mainland, Tiberius landed in Marina del Cantone. Charmed by its beauty, the emperor decided to build a villa in the area and named the surrounding village Neronianum.

At Marina del Cantone Aronne parked in front of the pebbled beach, across the street from the village's largest hotel, the Residence. After exiting from the van, I stood for a moment staring dreamily at the shimmering sea. On the beach, sunbathers were lounging under red umbrellas. I wished I'd had the foresight to wear a bathing suit.

The sea was so beckoning that I asked Aronne if we could go on a boat ride. He told me he was afraid of the water. "You are kidding, right?" I asked, truly surprised. He shook his head. "But you grew up here," I commented.

"I can't swim," he revealed. A grin flashed across his face, a glitter of humor in his brown eyes. Again I glanced at the sea. It was pretty calm so I was certain that we would be safe. Sighing, I told him that I needed his help with translation. He laughed, for he was sure I did not really need his assistance. Still he agreed. *"Andiamo,"* he said.

We went down to the beach and spoke with one of the locals. Within minutes, a twenty-five-foot boat pulled alongside the marina's small pier, and at its helm was a white-haired man. His skin was weathered almost black by the elements. We stepped into the boat, which could have easily accommodated my entire group, and sat at the bow near the skipper.

As we motored out to sea, my gaze swept over the small seaside town and the surrounding scenery. At the water's edge, against a background of limestone cliffs covered in lush Mediterranean vegetation, stood a handful of white-painted houses. Fishing boats, sailboats and speedboats were moored in the small bay in front of a long, narrow beach lined with restaurant terraces. Nestled between olive groves, above Marina del Cantone, was the village of Nerano.

Enchanted, I captured a series of pictures before our skipper turned west. We passed the best preserved watchtower on the coastal belt, the Tower of Montalto, and headed toward the tip of the Peninsula.

Following the southern coastline, we marveled at the beauty of the rocky barren cliffs plunging steeply down to the cobalt sea. At the bay of Jeranto with its little beach hidden at the base of a gorge, topless tourists were basking in the sun. Inside a grotto we peered at an underwater natural stone formation, resembling a nativity scene.

We stopped for several minutes at Punta Campanella, the tip of the most extreme promontory of the Sorrentine Peninsula. Our skipper stated that the ancients called it the Athenian Promontory for, according to the Roman historians Pliny and Strabo, a temple dedicated to Athena had once been erected here by the first Greek colonists.

"The remains of a Roman villa are still visible," he informed us. "As for the restored tower, it dates back to the fourteenth century. The Torre Minerva, built as a watchtower under the order of Robert d'Anjou, served to alert the residents of the peninsula of the impending arrival of Saracen and Turkish raiders until the seventeenth century. From the tower, the alarm was sounded with a little bell, or *campanella,* which gave the Punta its name."

The Punta Campanella area has been protected since 1997 by a decree of the Italian Ministry for the Environment. Swimming, scuba diving, fishing and mooring are forbidden in certain zones, while allowed in others with special permits.

Pointing to a rock face on the craggy cliff below the tower, our skipper told us that it was the location of the huge "Cave of Sirens."

"We are in the sea of Ulysses and the land of the Sirens. At nighttime, Sirens can be seen swimming in the enchanted cave." He smiled. Intrigued, I asked him if he had seen them. "When I was a young man," he replied, with a sparkle in his eyes.

Amused, I glanced at Aronne who was testing the water's temperature with his left hand. "Remember, I can't swim," he said with a little shrug and laughed.

It was such a beautiful afternoon, the sky was cloudless and the clear water of the Tyrrhenian invited a swim. Again, I regretted that I was not wearing a bathing suit.

I gazed at Capri, only three miles away, shrouded in haze, with the Faraglioni rocks peeping out from its side. How could I bottle this wonderful moment, I wondered, dazzled by the mystical beauty? Immediately, my thoughts drifted to the thousands of people who had navigated these waters in bygone eras: the Greek and Phoenician sailors, the merchants and masons of Amalfi, the Saracen and Turkish pirates, and the French and Spanish kings. I could only imagine what their eyes had seen in the past centuries. The sight of Capri with the setting sun behind it must be magical, I reflected, wishing for the opportunity to see it someday.

Our skipper restarted the engine, then turned the boat around. We did not return directly to Marina del Cantone but headed toward the Li Galli islands. En route, we peeked at the exclusive restaurant La Conca del Sogno, literally "The Bay of the Dream," in the hidden cove of Recommone, a popular wedding reception venue—only reachable by boat or through a narrow unpaved road from Nerano. We lingered near the little beach of Crapolla, at the base of a fjord, linked by an ancient mule track to the village of Torca up in the hills. A community of fishermen once inhabited the beach. Their shelters, called *monazeni,* are still there.

We sailed by the islet of Isca, and as we circled the small island of Vetera, I snapped another dozen pictures of the coastline and of the Galli Archipelago in the distance. It was the end of our boat tour. Fifteen minutes later we were back at Marina del Cantone. Too quickly our adventure was over, but the memory is still fresh in my mind.

Prior to returning to the villa, we enjoyed a drink at one of the terraces along the beach. Relaxing on solid ground, Aronne mentioned that he, too, enjoyed the boat ride. That night I went to bed with my arms and face sunburned.

※

The bus is pulling into the town of Massa Lubrense and stopping in front of the Church Santa Maria delle Grazie. A handful of tourists dressed in jeans and T-shirts, and a little gray-haired lady holding a large straw basket, are waiting to board while several people are stepping down, including the young woman and her darling toddler.

The elderly woman grabs the seat next to me and settles her large basket on her lap. First Grandpa, now Grandma. I wonder what she is going to do. The blue buses connecting each community in the territory with Sorrento are a great way to meet both residents and visitors. Conversations and local gossip oftentimes abound. Occasionally, I learn something that can be useful, like the name of a good restaurant.

Glancing sideways, I see the straw basket move, then hear a whimper. Does she have a baby in there? While that thought crosses my mind, a little black furry head pops above the rim of the basket. It is a black kitten with beautiful golden eyes, tiny pink nose and long whiskers. Surprised, I glance at Grandma.

"*E' per mia nipote.* It is for my granddaughter," she says with a grin.

"*E'adorabile, che ragazza fortunata.* It is adorable, what a lucky girl," I reply kindly, as the bus finally pulls away from the curb.

Massa Lubrense is the principal municipality and the largest of the territory that bears its name. Besides a couple of churches, the town boasts in its center an impressive municipio, a restored monastery, a palace from the nineteenth century, and a panoramic terrace with views of Capri and the Gulf of Naples.

Most historians believe that the name Massa derives from a sixth-century Longebard term meaning "fertile land," to which the adjective *Publica* was added in 938 to indicate that it belonged to the state of Sorrento. The adjective was replaced in 1306 by Lubrense, which derives in turn from the Latin *delubrum,* or sacred temple, in reference to the cathedral that was located on the nearby Fontanella Beach.

Throughout history the territory of Massa Lubrense lived through many periods of misfortune. The most horrific ones were in 1558, when the Turks pillaged and kidnapped 1500 inhabitants, of which only a few were ever freed by ransom, and in 1656, when the plague spread from Naples to the area, claiming many victims.

In the first two decades of the twentieth century a mass wave of immigration to the Americas took place. During World War II, a multitude of Naples' residents sought refuge in Massa. After the Armistice was signed in 1943, many returned, while others stayed. In 1944 groups of refugees from Cassino were moved here, and a small group of American soldiers came to Massa and Sant'Agata on leave. At the end of the war, a large number of townspeople emigrated to other parts of Italy and Europe in search of better job opportunities and living conditions.

X

Leaving the town of Massa Lubrense behind, I scan the landscape unrolling in front of my eyes. Not only is the coastline facing the Gulf of Naples more populated, its promontory slopes are virtually covered with extensive terraces of lemon and olive groves. Up on the sun-facing hills are acres of vineyards. The shadier banks are covered with chestnut trees, whose wood supports the trellises used in the cultivation of lemons.

The territory of Massa Lubrense produces an abundance of olive oils, red and white wines, cheeses made from the milk of locally-reared cows, and delicious homegrown vegetables. Climatic conditions, the lay of the land, a fertile soil mixed with ashes from Vesuvio's eruptions, and traditional methods of cultivation have all been contributing factors to the excellent quality of the regional produce. The most famous are the Sorrento lemons, from which the limoncello liqueur is made.

Lemon Heaven

*A*s the bus slowly proceeds downhill toward Sorrento, I catch a glimpse of an Ape truck, laden with lemons, parked along the side of the road. Standing behind it under the shade of a large umbrella, a gray-haired man is busy selling them to passersby. This is a familiar scene here in Campania, along the Tyrrhenian Sea. By the large number of lemon trees growing on terraced slopes of the Lattari Mountains, it is quite evident that we are in the land of lemons.

Fresco paintings and mosaics uncovered at Pompeii and Herculaneum reveal that lemon trees were already present in the first century A.D. In ancient times lemons were grown in small garden containers, and Romans treated them as a rare delicacy. Abundant today, they play an important role in the regional economy. Besides being the basis of everything produced on the Costiera—candies, soaps, perfume, ice cream and limoncello—lemons are an essential ingredient in many of the Campania dishes and desserts, as well as an inspiration for the local linen and ceramic industries.

The exact origin of the *citrus limonum*, or lemon, is still unknown, though it is largely believed that the citrus trees originated in the Far East where they grew in the wild. In China and India lemons were known for their antiseptic and refreshing properties, while in the Muslim world they were used as antidotes against various poisons and to fend off evil.

Greeks planted lemon trees near olive trees to protect them from parasites and used lemons as ornamental decorations and to scent their linen. By the first millennium, lemons were prevalent around the Mediterranean, especially in Sicily, Spain and Northern Africa, where conquering Arabs had introduced them.

In the eleventh century, the people from Amalfi diffused them on the isle of Capri, and two centuries later Carthusian monks planted lemon trees on the grounds of the Monastery of San Giacomo. In the middle of fifteenth century, the first commercial cultivation of lemons began near Genoa, in Northern Italy.

The demand for the citrus fruits intensified when it was discovered, quite by accident, that lemon juice, rich in vitamin C, prevented and cured scurvy, a common illness among sailors, whose diet included only flour and preserved foods during long voyages. It wasn't until the late eighteenth century that lemons started to be used for their culinary qualities, and to satisfy a growing market local farmers gradually replaced olives trees, vineyards and woodland with lemon trees.

Lemons are agriculturally produced in several regions of Italy, but those from this area are by far the finest in flavor and aroma. Two distinctive varieties are cultivated in Campania: the *Femminello Sorrentino* on the Sorrento Peninsula around Massa Lubrense, and on Capri, and the *Sfusato Amalfitano* along the Amalfi Coast. The lemon production from these territories has been granted the PGI status by the European Community. To obtain the Protected Geographic Indication stamp of approval, producers are required to apply and adhere to strict rules of cultivation.

While citrus trees generally grow in the open on flat land, the Femminello and Sfusato trees are cultivated on sun-facing degrading terraces and under trellises. Those trellises are sometimes covered with green or black netting. Fascinated and also intrigued by this unique agricultural practice, I once asked Salvatore, Danilo's uncle and manager, if it would be possible to visit a lemon farm the next time I was in the area. The following year he granted my request.

Born in Castellammare di Stabia, Salvatore has lived in the town of Sorrento for more than thirty years, and during that time he has become a respected figure in the local travel industry. I made his acquaintance a long time ago while he was touring the States and promoting Campania. We immediately connected, speaking alternatively in English, French and Italian. We spent some time talking about his region, which I was already familiar with, then later switched our discussion to the region of Umbria, for he knew it quite well, and I was anxious to discover it.

Early one fine morning we met in the lobby of the Due Golfi and together we drove to the farm of Antonino De Gregorio in the hills on Massa Lubrense. From the hotel we followed the Nastro d'Oro for about fifteen minutes, then continued along a narrow road winding through olive groves to our destination. We stopped in front of heavy black iron gates. Salvatore pushed the intercom button and we waited. Seconds later the gates opened electronically. We entered the property and parked at the edge of a treelined driveway.

As we got out of the car, a tall man in his late fifties, perhaps, with a face tanned by the outdoors, in dark blue clothing and wearing black rubber boots, stepped forward. Salvatore introduced us, and after a traditional handshake, we walked uphill toward the lemon grove, or the *limoneto* in Italian. When we reached it, I pulled out a list of questions, a small notebook and pen from my shoulder bag. For the next couple of hours or so, we wandered through the limoneto. With Salvatore acting as our translator, I asked my questions and wrote down Antonino's answers.

Prior to Italy's unification, the vast majority of the land on the Sorrento Peninsula belonged to the nobility. Such was the case with the eight-acre property we were standing on, until it was sold in 1870. Today a physician from Naples owns it. The owner and his family prefer to live in the city instead of in the countryside. Each summer, however, for a month or two, they vacation on the Peninsula. They reside on the top floor of the main house that dates back to the seventeenth century. In the owner's absence Antonino and his family manage the land. In exchange for their stewardship they live rent free in the remainder of the house. The Di Gregorios have lived on the property for more than one hundred years. Antonino is the third generation.

This was a typical lemon farm for the area, Antonino told us. The citrus trees were planted in 1870. Only twenty to thirty were still original. Most citrus trees live up to one hundred years—some even up to two hundred—but they are rare.

"Four varieties of citrus fruits are organically grown in this grove, each variety identifiable by its leaf, blossom and shape," he explained. As we strolled through the grove, Antonino pointed out the different citrus trees, gently touching the fruits as he was describing them.

"The Sfusato Amalfitano lemons have a small to medium size pointed shape, light yellow color, a wrinkled skin and an intense perfume. The Femminello lemons, often referred to as the lemons of Sorrento or Massa Lubrense, have a more elliptical shape, a thinner peel and a stronger aroma. Both types are very juicy and practically seedless," he revealed. Two thirds of the trees in Antonino's limoneto produce Femminello lemons. A few orange and mandarin trees had also been planted for private consumption.

I was particularly interested to learn about the grapefruit-size lemons I had seen in some of the local grocery stores. I had no idea lemons could grow this large until I visited the Amalfi Coast. They were incredibly huge. Some were the size of French Cavaillon melons. Curious about their flavor, I once considered buying a couple of them from a street vendor parked outside the Scavi in Pompeii, but they were too expensive, so I changed my mind. Dressed in jeans and speaking Italian with a French accent, I believed that the vendor was overcharging tourists. Later, I realized they were sold by weight instead of by the piece.

"Those are called *Cedro* or *Limone di Pane,* Bread Lemon," Antonino replied to my question. "The cedro trees were discovered by the Greeks in Persia more than two thousand years ago. They were the first citrus trees introduced in Western Europe. The tree is small with thorny branches, large oblong leaves and highly perfumed flowers. A cedro lemon is always sold with its stem and leaves. It can weight up to five pounds and have a diameter of four to five inches. Its rough peel and white inner rind are quite thick compared to other lemon varieties. Delicious marmalade and candied lemon peel are made from cedros," he added.

My curiosity satisfied, I moved on to my next question. The grove we were standing in was encased in some kind of pergola, constructed with wooden stakes at least ten feet tall, and part of the pergola was covered with black plastic netting. I asked Antonino the reason behind the trellises and the netting.

"The trellis structure is made of chestnut poles," he explained. "Chestnut trees grow wild in the woods of the hills nearby. Periodically land owners give farmers concessions to cut a certain number of trees down for new constructions or to replace existing ones. Chestnut trunks can last up to thirty years. The vertical poles that support the weight of the structure are called *Allirti* and the horizontal poles are called *Correnti*.

"Allirti are cut at one end in a pointed or spiked shape to fit into the ground, and at the other end in an angle so that they can be attached to extension poles with a leather strap. Support poles are also planted every now and then for balance. Correnti are no longer really needed for they have been replaced by iron rods. The rods are lighter and hold better.

"When I was young I used to race my brother on the correnti," he said with a sparkle in his eyes. "Like acrobats on a trapeze, we would walk fast from one side of the scaffold to the other. I won every contest, for my brother would always get confused and choose the wrong lane." He chuckled.

"Do you still climb up to the top?"

"Unfortunately, at my age, I am no longer as daring and agile as I used to be," Antonino admitted, then burst into laughter. A second later, Salvatore and I joined in.

"Lemon trees only grow at a certain altitude. They are very sensitive to extreme cold and warm temperatures, and prefer mild winters and cool summers," Antonino stated. "Their biggest enemies are the wind and hail. Strong winds like the Tramontana, for instance, can do substantial damage to the branches, the leaves and the fruit, and a five-minute hailstorm can destroy an entire crop. To protect the trees from these atmospheric adversities farmers have developed a unique system of cultivation. They build trellises over which they spread black or green plastic netting. In the past, *pagliarelle,* or straw mats were placed on top of the trellises.

"They were very picturesque but the netting is less expensive, more efficient and easier to control and deploy. The plastic nets are attached on one side of the scaffold and pulled toward the other side by cords. The *limoneti,* or lemon groves, are entirely covered during the colder months, usually from October to the end of May. They might be partially covered during the rest of the year depending on the weather conditions. Growers monitor the weather diligently. If the temperature falls below thirty-two degrees the netting is deployed," he explained.

Pointing to the weed grass growing at the foot of a lemon tree, Antonino mentioned that farmers used to keep the ground clean. They recently discovered, however, that by leaving the ground alone, it didn't get dry or burned by the sun in the summer. The weed grass, acting as a mulch, keeps the ground moist and helps with the irrigation. In the winter, it protects the tree from the red spider. The ground vegetation is removed once a year in the early spring and used as fertilizer. He warned that the earth around the tree should never be turned over, for roots sometime grow above the surface of the ground.

The mention of irrigation brought up the subject of water. "Luckily there are two springs on the property. Water is directed to the house by a small aqueduct, allowing us to care for two groves that we have here: one lemon and one olive. We are very conservative and collect water in the winter."

Zeroing in on the leaf of a tree nearby, Antonino stopped for a second to inspect it. Lemon trees are extremely susceptible to diseases, sometimes caused by insects. Microscopic creatures can do a lot of damage. Among the most disastrous are the spiders—the red, white and silver, and the cotton spiders, named for the white powder they leave behind. Yellowing leaves crunched or curled are caused by the larvae of a fly.

Up until three years ago, Antonino used to spray an insecticide, but the problem with the chemical was that it killed even the good insects, like the lady bugs, so he switched to a more organic method. He now applies a mixture of oil and water—half a liter to one hundred—to the leaves. This special oil, if lightly sprayed, seems to be doing the trick. It asphyxiates the insects and stops the larvae from doing more harm.

"We don't kill the fly; it will die naturally. Instead we spray the larvae. This must be done at the appropriate time, for if we wait too long they turn into insects," Antonino commented.

Lemon trees, unlike orange and mandarin trees, produce more than one crop per year. It is not uncommon to see blossoms, baby green fruits and ripe yellow ones simultaneously on the branches. With a favorable climate and great soil conditions lemon trees can produce up to four crops annually, and the growers have a name for each one.

The lemons harvested in September and October are called the *primofiore*, or the first flowers, after the blossoming that took place in the spring. The *bianchetti*, or the small whites, that blossomed from June to the end of July are hand picked from February to May. From August to September, a third blossoming occurs and produces the *maggiolini*, which are harvested at the end of April, and the *bastardi*, or bastards from May to September. The bianchetti and the bastardi have the best quality.

Antonino remained silent for a few minutes and my mind went to work. The next time I buy lemons at a local grocery store, I will ask for bastardi. Hmmm . . . I can't wait to see the vendor's face. He will probably think I am a crazy tourist and laugh.

On the Sorrentine Peninsula, lemons are cultivated on a total of two thousand acres, mostly on small farms of less than five acres. Antonino's grove outputs between fifteen and twenty tons per year. The Solagri Cooperative purchases his crops and those of the three hundred other growers.

"Trees used to produce a larger quantity of lemons, and growers would give a portion of the harvest to the landowners. However, recently there is just enough to fulfill our contract with the cooperative," Antonino said. After pausing for a moment, he went on to explain why his family lived on the property free of rent. "In the long run it would be more expensive for the owner to hire someone with my knowledge and workmanship. Plus it is very difficult nowadays to find people willing to work the land, for it is labor intensive. The gain from the harvest would not be enough to pay the people. I believe that one day he will sell the property. I hope that it will be to us," he added cheerfully.

As Antonino and Salvatore began to slowly edge away from the grove I found myself lingering behind for a while. I pulled out my camera and took a series of pictures. Rays of sunshine slipping through the trellises gave the lemons a golden hue. Approaching a blossom for a close-up shot, I inhaled deeply its sweet perfume. I was standing in the middle of a small lemon heaven.

While rushing to catch up with the gentlemen, I remembered that my maternal grandmother loved lemons. She owned a small neighborhood grocery store and always had easy access to the citrus fruits, even during the war. Grandma constantly cooked and cleaned with them. Growing up, I watched her squeeze the juice of a lemon onto a fish. After it was cooked, she degreased the pan with the discarded lemon.

If I had a sore throat or was coming down with a cold, she would press a large lemon and ask me to swallow the juice slowly for its soothing effect. It tasted bitter but it worked. I still do it today. In the winter she served my grandfather her special concoction of heated wine spiced with lemon slices, cloves and sugar. To her homemade jams, Grandma always added the juice of a lemon to thicken them more quickly and to maintain the original brilliant color of the fruits. If a garment had a fruit stain, she would apply a mixture of milk and lemon juice onto it before washing. For her the lemon was a cure-all and a magical household cleaning product.

Our host invited us for coffee on a sunlit terrace overlooking a large olive grove. I vividly recall thinking that in the spring the grove must be a beautiful sight when the masses of olive trees are white as snow with blossoms and the air infused with their sweet perfume.

While enjoying our beverages and a spectacular view of Capri, we discussed the health benefits of the lemons. Salvatore shared his secret for boosting his immune system. Every morning he drinks the juice of a lemon with a spoon of honey. Antonino mentioned that he occasionally enjoys a slice of cedro, sprinkled with sugar— apparently the pith of the cedro lemon has none of the bitterness of other lemon varieties. I confessed to eating a lot of lemon drops in the winter to increase my energy.

After scribbling a few words in my notebook, I left the two men to their conversation, and wandered over to the edge of the terrace to get a closer look at Capri. What would our life be without lemons? They have become so precious to our well-being, both internal and external, for not only do we take advantage of their therapeutic properties, we also enjoy their aromatic qualities.

Lemons might be small but their contribution to our everyday life is immense. Their juice, leaves, rind and essential oils are extremely valuable to several industries, notably the perfume and pharmaceutical. From Antonino, I learned that lemons should not be taken for granted, but treasured. A symbol of fidelity in love, lemons are a gift from the growers to the consumers.

On our walk back to the car I glanced at the three hundred year old country residence. The imposing three-story stone structure, flanked by cypress and palm trees, stood at the end of the driveway, facing the Gulf of Naples. Its austere simplicity reminded me of a convent. The only decorative features on the facade were the carved stone arches above three burgundy-red entrance doors and the tufa lintels on top of each window. I wished I could have seen the inside of the noble house, but we were pressed for time.

Since meeting the lemon grower, I look at lemons differently. I used to grab and go. Now I take my time. I check their rind, shape and size and wonder where they came from, for in the meantime I have discovered that there are at least forty different varieties of lemons cultivated worldwide. The largest producer is India, then Mexico. The United States is the seventh, while Italy is the tenth. The majority of the Italian lemons come from Sicily. Still, the citrus trees of the Sorrento Peninsula manage to output about 30,000 tons annually.

X

The Sita bus has now reached the outskirts of Sorrento. I quickly delve into my shoulder bag, retrieve my spiral notepad and flip through the pages to find my list of items to buy. Yes! Limoncello is on it, right below lemon soaps. I have grown quite fond of the enticing citrus liqueur and would not dream of going home without buying at least one bottle.

No one really knows for sure the origin of the delicious digestif, although several stories and legends have been presented by the Sorrentini, Capresi and Amalfitani, who all seem to be competing for its invention. The people of Capri claim that the lemon-based liquor was first created on the island. Some of the islanders attribute limoncello to the Carthusian monks, who were familiar with the distillation process of alcohol. Records from the fifteenth and sixteenth centuries show that they used to mix alcohol with fruit syrups to create elixirs.

One Caprese family believes that it was their ingenious grandmother or *nonna*, owner of a small *pensione* in Anacapri who, at the beginning of 1900, first macerated lemon peels in alcohol and syrup. She would serve the scented liqueur as an after dinner drink to her guests. Soon word of her limoncello began to spread throughout the island and amongst visitors, writers and celebrities. In the evening her establishment was often patronized by Axel Munthe, Amedeo Maiuri, Jacques Fersen and Friedrich Krupp.

Sorrento and Amalfi have their own versions of the story, of course. Some tales have sprung from the flourishing hospitality industry of the twentieth century, while others have been around much longer. Even the nuns of the Santa Rosa Convent have been credited with inventing the liqueur in the seventeenth century.

For certain, the success of the limoncello has impacted the local economy. In each town along the Amalfi Coast, in Sorrento and on Capri, souvenir shops filled with uniquely-shaped bottles abound. If you have never tried it, don't worry—vendors graciously let you sample. Limoncello always puts a smile on people's faces. I have watched hundreds of tourists enter limoncello stores with a curious expression on their faces, then exit with a grin, carrying a bottle or two.

Limoncello

The best limoncello is made with lemons plucked from the hills of the Lattari or Capri, but it is possible to achieve acceptable results with lemons found at your local super market. Limoncello should be served cold.

Ingredients:
Eight large lemons, preferably organically grown
1 (750 ml) bottle 96% pure alcohol
3 cups water
1 pound granulated sugar

Wash the lemons in lukewarm water to remove any residue of pesticides. Peel the rind and take off any remaining pith. Pour the bottle of alcohol into a gallon jar and add the lemon peels. Cover tightly. Place in a cool, dark place for twenty days. As it rests the alcohol absorbs the flavor of the lemon peels and their rich yellow color. After twenty days, combine sugar and water in a saucepan and bring to a boil. Boil for five minutes then let the syrup cool off. Slowly strain the lemon mixture through a filter into a large pitcher. Return the filtered infusion to the jar and add the cooled syrup. Place the jar back into the dark place for another twenty days. After the rest period the limoncello is ready to be bottled. Keep the bottle in the freezer until ready to serve.

Sorrento—Land of the Sirens

$\mathcal{S}$orrento is basking in the noon sunlight as I step off the bus at the corner of Via Degli Aranci and make my way to Danilo and Salvatore's office. Since I have an hour to spare before our meeting, I decide to stroll along Corso Italia and browse through the high fashion boutiques, jewelry shops and souvenir stores that line both sides of the street. Sorrento's main artery was constructed in the late nineteenth century, and as the town's main shopping street, Corso Italia is always bustling with tourists. After wandering in and out of half a dozen outlets a cacophony of foreign languages is swirling around in my head.

With seventy-five hotels, the majority of which were built in the second half of the twentieth century, Sorrento is the perfect base for Italians and foreign visitors who wish to discover all the sights of the area. While most travelers only stay for three or four days, others tend to vacation here for longer periods, as Sorrento enjoys a year-round mild climate and every season offers its own surprises.

Many European retirees return on a regular basis. Perhaps they have succumbed to Sorrento's most famous song, "Torna a Surriento," whose enchanting melody and lyrics beg a younger lover to "Come back to Sorrento." Composed in 1902 by the Napoletani brothers Ernesto and Giambattista De Curtis on the terrace of the Hotel Imperial Tramontano, it has been sung by performers as diverse as Luciano Pavarotti, Mario Lanza, Dean Martin and Meat Loaf. Elvis Presley's popular song "Surrender" is another rendition of the ballad.

In the course of time, the landscape around Sorrento has cast its spell on many travelers. The Phoenicians first used the area as a trade center in the seventh century B.C. By the fifth century B.C. it had largely been settled by Greek colonists, then successively ruled by the Etruscans and the Samnites until the arrival of the Romans, who latinized the town's Greek name of Sireon, said to be from the Land of the Sirens, to Surrentum.

The Roman patricians were the first to appreciate the beauty and the temperate climate and built their summer retreats here, several of which are incorporated in the foundations of luxury hotels. After fighting off the Goths, Byzantines, Lombards, Saracens and its neighbor Amalfi, Surrentum was taken by the Normans in the first half of the twelfth century. Thenceforth its history followed that of the newly-created Kingdom of Sicily.

Sorrento has been a popular destination since the eighteenth century with the European nobility taking their Grand Tour. Tourism increased steadily throughout the following century with visiting writers in search of sun and inspiration, among them Henry Stendhal, Walter Scott, Charles Dickens and Oscar Wilde. In the twentieth century ordinary tourists just wanted to experience the *Dolce Vita*. The people of Sorrento have a long tradition of hospitality.

As I pass the crowded Gelateria Veneruso, a young couple exits. Glancing at their three-scoop ice creams, the image of my mother flips through my mind. It's her favorite dessert. Sorrento is a paradise for gelato lovers. At least one hundred different flavors are produced fresh daily with locally grown ingredients in a dozen parlors. Some of the flavors are quite innovative. The Sorrento Moon is made with almond and lemon, the Profumi di Sorrento with orange, lemon and tangerine, and the Bongo with the mousse of profiteroles.

It is almost time for my meeting. Hastily, I stride across the street to the tour company's building, buzz the intercom to gain admittance and climb the stairs to the second floor. After a light knock on the door, I step inside a long narrow room with a row of desks on one side and bookshelves on the other. Near the entrance, the young woman who handles my individual clients is talking on the phone while making notes on a pad. When she looks up, Rossella smiles and waves hello. In the adjacent room, I spot Danilo and wander over to his desk.

"The cooking class is confirmed for tomorrow," says Danilo, grinning. "Yes, they have agreed to your request," he continues as if he had been reading my mind regarding the surprise I am planning for my group. "And your transfer back to Rome with Aronne has been approved by Angelo, so everything is in place."

"Great, thank you," I reply approvingly. Catching sight of Salvatore walking to his office, I turn to greet him. *"Ciao, come stai, e il tuo gruppo?"* He asks warmly as we kiss each other on both cheeks.

"Bene, Grazie. I have discovered that a women-only group is actually quite fun. There is a feeling of camaraderie among us and a sense of kinship when we shop." Thinking about those who were going back to Positano today I continue, "Our suitcases will be heavy when we leave. I hope that Aronne has been lifting weights." We both chuckle.

"*Brava.* Pino will be joining us for lunch," Salvatore informs me, while pulling on his suit jacket.

Pino is one of the owners of the company. Claudio, Salvatore and Peppe are the other three. The four partners grew up in Sorrento and from the mid-sixties to the mid-seventies worked together as tour guides. Last year, Claudio accompanied us. Over the course of a wonderful meal at the Antico Francischiello Restaurant in Massa Lubrense we explored the subject of historical facts versus myths. The region is certainly blessed with an abundance of legends.

While listening to Claudio, I found myself thinking that he is a gifted storyteller. He vividly narrated the legend of the origin of Sorrento, which according to the Greek historian Diodorus Siculus was founded by Liparus, son of Ausone, the king of the Italic Ausoni and the son of Odysseus and the enchantress Circe.

With great details he also recounted the tale associated with the Palms of confetti. In Sorrento and surrounding towns the beginning of the Holy Week is marked with the blessing of natural olive tree branches and branches made with colorful almond sugar-coated candies known as *confetti*. The traditional work of confetti Palms is tied to a legend.

Centuries ago on a Palm Sunday, the inhabitants of Sorrento, the Sorrentini, having been warned of an imminent Saracen raid, rushed to the Cathedral to invoke divine intervention. Their prayers were answered. A storm broke out and the Saracen vessels shipwrecked close to the coast. Only one person survived, a young slave girl who managed to free herself and swim ashore. A fisherman found her on Marina Grande and brought her to the Cathedral where she was welcomed by the Sorrentini. As a gesture of gratitude, she untied the small pouch she carried around her neck and placed it on the altar. Inside were sugar-coated almonds in an array of colors. The priest blessed them and handed them out to parishioners.

Since then, deft hands have been creating elaborate master-pieces, adding lace, flowers and embroidery to the small wire stems where confetti petals were skillfully placed. Sadly, over time the number of people dedicated to this tremendously delicate art form has dwindled, making those handcrafted by past generations even more precious. Nowadays, many confetti Palms tend to be mass produced. They are sold in bars, confetti shops and confection-aries. After the Palms have been blessed, they are given to elderly relatives, usually to the mother or mother-in-law, as a sign of respect and good luck.

)(

At the restaurant Tasso, a tall dark-haired man recognizes Salvatore and Pino and steps forward. After a quick handshake, we follow him to a round table dressed with white linen under a shaded terrace. He gallantly pulls back a wicker chair for me before turning to Salvatore to relay the day's specials. This is not the first time I notice that no menus are presented, even though they are available. Italians know what they want to eat. They discuss it with the waiter—in this case the Maitre d'—and the chef simply prepares it.

The Tasso is quite different from the family owned restaurant Antico Francischiello, which just celebrated its one hundredth birthday. Their sizes are the same but in the latter the true dilemma is choosing where to sit, relax and dine. The setting of each room is elegantly romantic. The walls are either decorated with plates or picture frames, the floor plainly carpeted or covered with floral

Vietri tiles, and the linen shades range from yellow to salmon to pink. With a frame of natural greenery, halfway between Sorrento and Massa Lubrense, and with an enchanting view of Capri, the Francischiello is an unexpected treasure.

In the center of Sorrento, a few feet from the Piazza Tasso on Via Correale, the exclusive restaurant Tasso has been open since the new Millennium. Its flowing structure is extremely versatile and able to accommodate large parties. Just a handful of paintings adorn the champagne-painted walls and the floor is entirely covered with terra cotta tiles. A couple of wooden dressers and several potted plants complete the informal decor. Focusing on the small number of patrons, we seem to have come at the right moment. Lunchtime in Sorrento can sometimes be hectic, especially when a cruise ship is anchored in the bay.

Leisurely, I unfold the linen napkin and drape it across my lap. Looking at the portrait of a bearded man I ask in French, "Who is Tasso?"

"Torquato Tasso was born in Sorrento in the sixteenth century. He was a poet," replies Salvatore as the maitre d' pulls the cork from a Feudi di San Gregorio 2006 and pours the white wine into our glasses. "Perhaps you have read his masterpiece: *Jerusalem Delivered?*" he queries, clinking his glass to mine. When I shake my head, he continues, "I am not surprised—very few people know him outside Italy."

"*Buon Appetito,*" says a cheerful young waitress as she places our primo piatto in front of us. I set down my glass and study the food. On Pino's plate is a simple pasta dish of spaghetti with a fresh tomato sauce. On Salvatore's and mine, prawns and zucchini have been added to the mixture.

While savoring the food, I listen to Salvatore and Pino's discussion about the ruins that were recently uncovered under a vacant parking lot near their office building. Although it is not uncommon for workers to unearth treasures from antiquity on a construction site, this time the whole town is abuzz with the news. The big question is, "Are they Greek or Roman?" Slowly the conversation evolves to the new artifacts found at Pompeii and to the explicit wall paintings of the suburban baths that are currently closed to the public. They were discovered in 1958 outside the walls near the Marina gate and are in the process of being completely restored. As Pino jokingly describes his visit to the baths, Salvatore and I burst into laughter. His choice of words and facial expressions make him naturally entertaining. He should have been a comedian, I realize, nearly choking on my water.

I note the tiny red hot pepper hanging from his golden neck chain, next to a Holy Cross, and ask Pino its meaning. "This is a *corno,* a horn against the evil eye," he replies, holding it. "This one is made of coral, but horns are also available in gold or silver and in different sizes. You will find them on sale in all the gift shops of Sorrento and Naples," he continues, anticipating my following question. "The amulet must be a gift to someone, otherwise it does not work. Offer only one horn or three—never two—for that person will become a *cornuto,*" he adds with an eloquent rolling of his eyes, and we all chuckle. In a similar fashion, two horns symbolize "being cuckolded" in the French culture.

Southern Italians are deeply religious and superstitious. They wear charms against the *jettatore,* or spellcaster, adorn their cars and homes with talismans, believe in lucky numbers, and celebrate their birthday as well as their patron saint's day. Mine happens to fall on the 12th of December. The people from Sorrento and neighboring towns fervently celebrate the *Settimana Santa,* or Holy Week.

Their most impressive manifestations are the processions, a tradition with roots dating back to the fifteen hundreds, if not before. In the heart of the night between Thursday and Friday, the "White Procession" winds through the historical center of Sorrento. Wearing white robes and tall pointed hoods to conceal their faces, the participants recall in majestic silence the wandering of the Virgin Mother in search of her son—betrayed, arrested and sentenced to death.

Late in the evening of Good Friday—after the liturgical functions—the "Black Procession" takes place. Store lights are turned off and shutters are closed along the parade route, plunging Sorrento into semi-darkness. Members dressed in black habits and hoods, holding languid torches and crosses, walk solemnly through the streets. In front of Our Lady of Sorrows, men carry on their shoulders an imposing wooden simulacrum of Christ. Ultimately the silence of the night is broken by a choir of two hundred. Drifting across the town, their voices echo an age-old tradition, which faith has passed on from generation to generation over the centuries.

A waiter bustles by to remove our plates. Shortly after, the Maitre d' delivers our secondo piatto, a grilled sea bass on a bed of vegetables, and refills our glasses. Intrigued by the expression *Buona passeggiata* I query Salvatore, this time in English, for an explanation.

"*La passeggiata* is an important part of our culture," he explains, leaning back in his chair. "It is an early evening Sunday ritual when families and friends gather for a gentle stroll through the center of the town. It is especially popular in the summer, when the sun is slowly setting and the afternoon heat has dissipated. Italians tend to dress up for la passeggiata. They enjoy showing off while chatting about their days, admiring window displays, and occasionally pausing to graciously greet friends and acquaintances. The practice is associated with the custom of wearing new clothes on the Thursday before Easter. Traditionally the faithful, in their new attire, would walk down the main street as part of a religious procession. In the old days men would stroll first, then the women. Today, they usually stroll in groups.

"The people from Campania refer to the passeggiata as *Lo struscio,* which in English translates to 'The strut." He laughs. "Unfortunately this local tradition, like many others, is slowly fading away. The new generation doesn't seem to appreciate them."

"This is true in many countries," I comment.

Our desserts appear—a lemon sorbet accompanied by a plate of chocolate pralines flavored with bits of orange rind. As I eagerly dip my spoon into my sorbet, Salvatore asks me if I would be interested in meeting his friend Costantino, who is a famous pastry chef. "Yes. I would like that very much. Pastries are my weakness," I reply truthfully.

"Perfect, then tomorrow after the cooking class, while your group discovers Sorrento, I will introduce you." He grins as the Maitre d' reappears to ensure that our meal and service have been to our satisfaction.

One hour later, after walking through swarms of tourists on our way back to the office, answering half a dozen of my emails on Salvatore's computer, and chatting with Rossella and Paola, her assistant, Danilo offers to drive me back to my hotel. Thinking of the alternative, a slow ride on a crowded Sita bus, I immediately accept. Maybe I will have a chance to relax on my balcony this evening. I walk out of the building with Danilo. When he stops in front of a Honda scooter, parked between two little Fiats along

Corso Italia, I am caught off guard and give him a questioning look.

"*Hai paura?* Are you afraid?" He asks, smiling.

"No, I am not. I have ridden on motorcycles before," I answer without a moment's hesitation, delighted that this day will end with an unexpected adventure. "I promise I won't hold you too tight." I laugh as he helps me with my helmet, which weighs a ton. He grins back at me.

Climbing onto the seat behind him, I instinctively place my hands around his waist and press lightly to signal that I am ready. In my mind, I suddenly see myself at seventeen, long hair flowing in the wind, wrapping my arms around my boyfriend's torso and holding on for dear life. The last time I rode a motorcycle was with my brother when I accompanied him to the Basque festival in Bayonne a decade ago.

The ride up the Nastro Verde is just as I imagined it would be—exhilarating. I dare myself to look down the hillside as Danilo cautiously skims around the bends. The open view is spectacular.

"*Non hai freddo,* you are not cold?" he asks thoughtfully, turning his head slightly over his shoulder.

"*No, sto bene.* I am fine," I reply, thankful for my sweater and his leather jacket. I glance up at the sky and notice the thunder-clouds stacking ominously over the mountains. The weatherman was correct in his prediction this morning. A storm is brewing. It is not unusual for it to rain in the hills while the sun shines over Sorrento. However, this time it appears as if it will pour over the entire Gulf of Naples.

I hold my breath as Danilo overtakes a giant tour bus, then quickly offer a prayer, grateful that there had been no oncoming traffic during his move. As we get closer to the hotel I wish for my

companions to be there to witness our arrival. To my disappoint-
ment, nobody is present as we pull into the parking lot. I let go of
Danilo and step off the bike. Raindrops are starting to fall as I wave
him goodbye and run inside the hotel.

Standing at my balcony door watching the sky, I hope that
the women have found shelter somewhere or are in their rooms
and that Danilo is all right. Maybe by now he is home. Lightning
abruptly slices through the blackened sky. I jump as a peal of thun-
der and the spatter of raindrops follow. I love to watch a storm.
Sometimes Mother Nature puts on quite a show. There is another
splash, and the rain begins to come in torrents. The drenching rain
is welcome, for it is the primary source of water for the region.
Various facilities scattered throughout the area collect the rain from
the Lattari Mountains, where it is filtered and treated before being
distributed. There is even a water treatment facility in the center of
Sorrento, right across from the Hotel Cesare Augusto.

Turning away, I settle on the bed to watch the evening news
and my favorite Italian show "Piloti," a sitcom set on the craziest
airplane in the world. The main characters are the two pilots who
fly the *Piccione,* Pigeon Airlines plane: Enrico, the captain who
moved from a prestigious company to the low-cost carrier, and
Max, the cheerful Roman co-pilot whose clumsiness spreads
mischief. There are two female attendants in bright pink and red
uniforms—the stern Silvana, who should have retired a long time
ago, and Celeste, the young, inexperienced, skinny American
blonde who is always distracted. Their satirical adventures are
hilarious. The show is the perfect end to a memorable day.

Day Six

In the Kitchen

*T*he storm had moved on by midnight. Until then, I had been unable to fall asleep. When I finally did, it was to dream of "Home Sweet Home." It is strange how the body can be in one place and the mind in another. I slide out from under the covers and walk to the balcony. Cool early morning air strokes my cheeks. Instantly, I notice that colors are more vivid. The sky is brilliant blue. The sea more majestic. The whiff of haze surrounding Mount Vesuvius has momentarily burned off, rendering it more taunting and threatening. Silently, I pray that it remains dormant for the next few days.

Turning back into the room, I dither for a while over what to wear, ultimately selecting a fuchsia top with long sleeves that can be easily rolled up and a pair of black jeans. I lay the garments out on top of the unused bed before stepping inside the bathroom. Remembering the exciting scooter ride of the previous afternoon, I smile. There is no doubt that my travel companions would have been thrilled to have been in my shoes. My husband, however, will not be so pleased once he learns about it. Yet, I would love to do it again.

Fresh from the shower and wrapped in my robe, I sit at my desk to write my thoughts in the journal I have titled *Bellissima Amalfi*. The bells of Sant'Agata's Church are chiming the seventh hour. As we are scheduled to participate in a hands-on cooking class this morning I decide to totally bypass breakfast. The menu Danilo emailed me over a month ago, requesting my approval, will be more than satisfying. After eating the results of our efforts, I doubt that anyone will even be hungry tonight.

At a little after nine I descend the stairs and stride across the lobby toward the reception counter. Since Ornella is temporarily engaged with a Dutch couple, I approach the other young woman, who is partially hidden behind a gigantic bouquet of flowers. When she glances up in my direction her lovely smile illuminates her fine features. I have often wondered where artists find their inspiration for their religious paintings. Looking at Elena, I have my answer. Among the locals. With her straight black hair tumbling down below her shoulders, her delicate oval face and long lashed deep-brown eyes, she could be the perfect model for a saint or a Madonna.

"*Buongiorno signora.* Today will be beautiful," says Elena cheerfully.

"Yes, I am pleased. Are there any stores in Sorrento that sell lingerie?" I inquire sotto voce.

"There are a couple. The Titina on Corso Italia, a few steps away from the Cathedral, and the Carmela Celentano, just around the corner on Via Giuliani," she replies with a grin.

"Do you know if they sell La Perla Collection?" I ask. Name brands are important to French and Italian women. Then after a moment of hesitation, I add, "I want to surprise my husband with something lacy."

"I am not sure, but they do carry the Ritratti and the Prima Donna," Elena answers.

"I would like to get something very seductive," I tell her, imagining the look on his face when I undress.

"I recently purchased a sexy embroidered bustier and matching panties," she confides, blushing as her attention drifts over my shoulder. Curious, I twist around to find Aronne standing right behind me, a slight smile tipping up one corner of his mouth. I laugh, wondering, how much of our conversation did he hear?

"*Cara,* I will be waiting outside," he says, chuckling and wiggling two of his fingers to indicate that he will be smoking a cigarette.

"Smoking is not good for you!" I counter.

"I know. I am trying to quit." He shrugs, spreading his arms with his hands open.

"We should be ready to leave shortly," I warn, seeing out of the corner of my eye six of the women walking toward me.

X

Upon arrival at the Sorrento School of Cooking, I look at my watch. With twenty minutes to kill before the start of class, I lead the group to the Jackie Hall where beverages are served. As we settle down on comfortable brown and white leather chairs, a twenty-something waitress appears from behind a divider. In turn, I order my usual. Minutes later she places a steaming cappuccino on the coffee table in front of me.

While listening to the women with half an ear, I glance around. For the moment the lounge is entirely ours. The classy open sprawling space, named for the First Lady who is said to have favored

Sorrento with her presence on many occasions, and whose giant picture graces one of the white painted walls, is part of a large hotel complex in Sant'Agnello, which also houses the cooking school.

The growing demand for culinary courses by gourmet travelers prompted the owner and manager of the Esperidi Resort, Raffaella D'Esposito, to venture into a new field and open a school in 2004. In a completely renovated facility, under the guidance of local chefs, students learn how to master the art of cooking regional dishes. Though our group will only participate in a one-day class, full courses from four to eight days are available. Classes are typically three hours and cover a complete seasonal menu, from appetizer to dessert and every course in between.

"Welcome to our cooking class. My name is Brenda and I will be your interpreter," announces a tall brunette with a strong British accent, after stepping through sliding doors. "Please follow me for our version of Hell's Kitchen," she invites jokingly. Chuckling at her sense of humor we trail her down a short corridor to the adjacent building.

The left side of the classroom is dominated by an oversized island covered by a gray marble slab, with a cooktop in its center and fronted on three sides by a dozen bar stools, while a long narrow table, dressed for lunch, occupies the right side, where sunlight is streaming through tall windows. Behind the island is a mini kitchen complete with a refrigerator, sink and dishwasher.

Wedged in a corner and serving as a gift shop, a china cabinet is laden with T-shirts, mugs and cooking utensils. On the small table nearby are neatly stacked magazines, piles of white aprons bearing the school's logo, flat paper student hats, and recipes printed on handouts that will be given to us at the end of the course.

Following Brenda's instructions, we slip an apron over our garments, loop the ties around our waists, don a hat and wash our hands before choosing a workstation. Meanwhile our instructor, Chef Rosaria, is bustling about, adding a whole egg and a scoop of grated parmesan cheese to each of the eleven bowls already filled with flour, and a teaspoon of dry yeast to the lukewarm water in the equal number of small plastic cups.

"Oggi facciamo primo gli Frittelle Olive e Capperi," says Chef Rosaria, catching our attention. The room falls silent. For several minutes, we listen attentively to her directions and to Brenda's translations, which occasionally overlap, before mixing the ingredients for the appetizer.

Rosaria D'Esposito, who mainly cooked for her family and friends before becoming one of the school's teachers, maintains a stern discipline during her courses. Students are here to learn specific recipes that they should be able to reproduce after they leave.

Dressed entirely in white under the school's apron, her short black hair covered with a baseball cap, she is quick to intervene and advise. Although she claims not to speak English, I believe that Chef Rosaria understands some words, for I have seen her raise an eyebrow at the wisecracks of my previous companions.

Quickly we move on to the preparation of the first course, the *Sacchetti di Pasta.* Under the chef's watchful eye, we incorporate flour, egg, a pinch of salt and a drop of water the old-fashioned way—with our hands, of course. It would be a sacrilege to make pasta with a food processor. As I knead the dough, she gives me the look, "You should know how to do this."

I chuckle. Even if this is my third attempt—my first group learned how to make *gnocchi*—I still struggle to attain the right elasticity. Glancing around the room, I realize that I am not the only one. Sighing, Rosaria grabs my dough to demonstrate the proper technique. After pressing and stretching the mass vigorously on the slab several times, she repeats the same gestures with the other women.

"This is to use on your husbands," she says seriously, handing out eleven wooden rolling pins. Bursts of laughter explode. I dust a small area with flour and roll out the dough into a rectangle, making sure to flip it around a couple of times so that it does not stick to the surface. With a fluted pastry wheel I cut little squares, spoon a dollop of cheese mixture into their centers, then pinch the four sides together diagonally to form a bag or sachet, thus the name of the pasta.

My first one is lumpy, my second falls apart, my third is a disaster. I shake my head. What am I doing wrong? If practice makes perfect, I have a long way to go! I try another one. Feeling more and more frustrated, I scan the work of my classmates. One catches me popping my flops into my mouth and giggles. My neighbor, who is deeply focused, manages to produce perfectly shaped sacchetti. Further along the work surface, four of the women have already filled a large tray. Thankfully with ten of them, there will be more than enough to eat, so I grab my camera and snap a set of pictures instead of fooling with my dough. When finished, the women ease back to let Brenda clean off the residual flour from the work top with a scraper.

Once again the room falls silent as we attentively watch Chef Rosaria prepare the sauce for the pasta. Mouthwatering aromas permeate the air. The secret to the sauce's wonderful taste, the women learn, is the glass of white wine added to the mixture of olive oil, shallot, garlic clove, locally sun-grown tomatoes and water.

"Red wine would darken the sauce," Rosaria reveals, reducing the heat to warm, letting it simmer and thicken.

During the next twenty minutes, our teacher concentrates on the main course, *Scaloppine ai profumi di Sorrento,* thin slices of beef, slightly floured, cooked in the Sorrentino styles, either in citrus juices or with mozzarella, tomato sauce and basil.

Campania is recognized throughout Southern Italy for the high quality of its cuisine, which was influenced by a long list of conquerors and occupants. In the early days, Greeks introduced olive trees and grape vines to the region. Romans promoted the planting of wheat and the drinking of wines. Later on, Byzantine and Saracen traders brought cinnamon, honey, pine nuts, almonds, figs and raisins to its shores. From nearby Sicily, through the Arabs, came the orange and lemon trees that are so prominent along the Amalfi Coast, and Turks exposed the population to coffee. Slowly adopted, it is now the Campani's favorite brew.

With the discovery of the New World, a stream of new produce was imported by the Spaniards. Neapolitans were the first to discover tomatoes, squash, potatoes, peppers, beans and chocolate. The impact of the French was mostly felt at the tables of the nobility with the introduction of the French Etiquette, culinary terms, meat dishes and fancy desserts.

Although the gastronomy of Campania has evolved over the centuries, it still mirrors the cuisine of the poor. The key to its success is simplicity. Campanians have been called *mangiafoglie,* or leaf eaters, as many of their traditional dishes include greens and vegetables. Cultivated in a rich volcanic soil, easily tillable, and heated by an average 230 days of sun a year, tomatoes, lettuce, zucchini, eggplants, artichokes and herbs reach heights of flavor.

By far the favorite vegetable has to be the tomato. It is just impossible to envision the Campania cuisine without the *pomodoro,* the golden apple. They are served practically every day of the year, in many guises. The most prized are the San Marzano, grown on the outskirts of Naples. The brilliant red San Marzano, similar to the Roma but thinner and pointier in shape, with a thicker skin and fewer seeds, are the only tomatoes that can be used for the *Pizza Napoletana.*

Campani are devoted to their pasta. For hundreds of years it was the sole diet of the poor. Nowadays, virtually everyone in the region consumes some type of dried pasta on a daily basis. The word "pasta" is actually a generic term for a variety of dried noodles that were pioneered in the nineteenth century, in the towns of Gragnano, Torre Annunziata and Torre del Greco, where a steady breeze mixed with plenty of sunshine yielded the perfect conditions for drying the dough on rods, like laundry, before the advent of industrial heaters.

In the hill town of Gragnano, "The City of Pasta," nestled between the mountain crest and Castellammare di Stabia, nine factories produce a combined total of sixty thousand tons of dry pasta a year. The Garofalo Company manufactures twenty-one different forms, some of which can be found in selected stores in the US.

Their Signature pasta is made from the finest durum wheat or *semolina* available. The most appreciated are the *elicoidali*—slightly ribbed tube pasta, the *pappardelle*—thick, flat ribbon, whose name derives from the verb *pappare* which means "to gobble up," the *farfalle*—also known as bow-ties, and the *schiaffoni*—large oval noodles that tend to "slap" sauce around on the plate, hence their name.

With the proximity of the sea, meals often include fresh fish and seafood. All along Campania's glittering coastline the Tyrrhenian abounds in cuttlefish, anchovies, baby clams, mussels, small octopus, squid, prawns and shrimp. Cooks serve them in various ways: steamed, baked, fried or grilled, as antipasto, with pasta or as a main course. Amid a vast selection of savory seafood dishes, some of my favorites are *Calamari Ripieni* or stuffed squid with shrimp, *Insalata di Mare* or seafood salad and *Zuppa di Pesce* or fish soup.

Traditional recipes containing meat or chicken are few in this area, compared to the regions of Northern Italy. They are always served as a second course and usually in a small quantity. In the old days, as eggs were too precious, chickens rarely found themselves in a cook pot, and meat was too expensive.

In the provinces of Avellino and Benevento the rearing of pigs supplies the prosciutto hams, the salamis and the sausages, which seem to be very popular. Available in many variations, the *Salsicce* are either grilled until crusty and well browned or boiled in water, and then browned. A simple dish is *Salsicce al Pomodoro*, sausages cooked in a tomato and olive oil sauce.

Campani consume a large amount of *formaggio*. As cheeses enter in the preparation of many dishes, from the antipasti to desserts, they are eaten practically every day, at every meal. Water buffalos, goats, sheep and cows graze in the Campanian countryside. Each group produces distinctive cheeses.

Arguably the most important is the mozzarella, made with the milk of the buffalos, often served as a single course or on a pizza. The other cheeses are *caciocavallo, provolone, scamorza* and *cacioricotta*. Made with cows' milk the *caciocavallo* is easily recognized by its unmistakable shape: a softball-size sack knotted with a string at the top. To cure the cheese, sacks are tied in pairs and hung on a rod over a wooden horse, or *cavallo,* like saddlebags, hence the name "horse cheese."

Provolone is a larger, denser and well-aged caciocavallo with a hazel-colored crust. With a thin straw-yellow rind, or brown if smoked, the *scamorza* has a spheroid shape and a sweet aromatic flavor. Sold immediately after processing, it's often used in place of Mozzarella.

Cacioricotta is a specialty cheese from the Cilento valley, made from fresh goat's milk or a blend of goats' and sheep's milk. Rich and creamy, shaped in a plump cylinder, the cheese is aged on wooden planks for up to four months before it's sold.

Campani are fond of desserts. The wide selection of pastries, ice creams and chocolate confections attest to their sweet tooth.

"Allora adesso facciamo il dolce, la Delizia al Limone," Rosaria declares, snapping me out of my reverie. A squeal of sheer delight escapes from one of the students. I glance in her direction and smile. "The lemon delicacy is my favorite dessert," she confesses, blushing, as Brenda sets a large tray of miniature golden-brown sponge cakes onto the marble.

Promptly Chef Rosaria reveals their preparation before launching the second phase of the recipe. In separate bowls we whisk the ingredients for the pastry cream, the limoncello syrup and the lemon cream sauce, then watch her assemble the dessert. One by one we slide to the edge of the island, closer to the chef, and diligently repeat her gestures.

"Basta!" Rosaria shouts suddenly to the woman who is getting carried away, drowning her cake with the syrup.

"Way to go!" I nod and give her the thumbs up. Our group bursts into laughter.

Now that our work is done, we cross over to the table and take a seat. With tantalizing aromas rising from the sizzling of the onion and garlic we seem to have developed an appetite and are eager to savor the fruits of our labor.

"I did not know it would be so hard to make pasta," says one of my classmates as Brenda hands us a glass of Spumante secco, the Italian version of Champagne.

"The experience was quite challenging. I was a complete failure," reveals another, meeting my gaze. Shaking my head negatively and pointing a finger to my chest I mouth, "No, I was."

"To think that in the old days women did that every day, often all day long," comments the retiree.

"Some still do today," I reply, thinking how overwhelmed I would be if I had to make ravioli instead of buying them already made. We clink our glasses and toast each other for a job well done, then turn to thank our chef, who is frying the fritters and boiling the sacchetti. She nods.

The fritters would make a great party treat, I reflect, taking small bites and sipping the white wine to wash them down. Planting my chin on the palm of my hand, I eavesdrop on the women's conversation. Gradually succumbing to the sound of their voices as they discuss husbands, children, careers and hobbies, I retreat to a memory of my childhood . . . when my Belgian grandmother, mother and aunt would be sharing in the preparation of the Holiday meals. Working together in a small kitchen they peeled, sliced, chopped, cooked and baked from the early morning until one in the afternoon, creating at least a dozen different dishes in the process.

My sister and I were responsible for setting the table. From Grandma's antique dresser we drew out an embroidered table cloth, napkins, fine china, silverware and wine glasses. Around one thirty in the afternoon, the entire family sat down to enjoy the feast. What had taken five hours to prepare would disappear in two. Afterward, while the men took their afternoon nap and we played with our dolls, the women handwashed the dishes and stored them away.

Shaking away my moment of nostalgia, I concentrate on the scaloppini. The group is split. A large number prefer the mozzarella-tomato combination over the citrus taste. Still, a handful promises to try both recipes at home to impress their spouses.

At the sound of Italian voices my attention strays to Aronne as he steps into the classroom and to Raffaella who is right behind him, holding our diplomas in her arms. "You are just in time for dessert," I point out to him as Brenda serves us our delizia and a small glass of limoncello. "Join us," I invite, but he declines, using his waistline as an excuse, which immediately extracts snickers from the women.

When we are ready to depart, I walk over to Rosaria. "It is always a pleasure to take your class," I compliment her in Italian. We kiss and hug each other. As the women express their gratitude, the chef's severe look disappears and the warmhearted person I guess her to be emerges. For a brief moment, she smiles broadly.

Frittelle Olive e Capperi - Fritters of Capers & Olives

A delicious appetizer or party treat.

For 4 persons

1½ cup all purpose flour

2 eggs

1 pinch salt

½ cup lukewarm water

1 cup grated Parmesan cheese

1 pinch black pepper

1 cup sliced olives (black or green)

1 teaspoon capers

3 teaspoons dry yeast

Cooking oil

Dissolve the yeast in the lukewarm water. Beat the eggs in a bowl. Add the flour, the yeast mixture, the Parmesan, pepper and salt. Mix. Incorporate the olives and the capers. Cover the bowl with a cloth and let the mixture rest for 30 minutes then fry.

Variation: instead of olives and capers, add pieces of ham or bacon.

Sacchetti di Pasta - Little Bags of Pasta

For 4 persons

The pasta
2⅓ cups all purpose flour
2 eggs
1 pinch salt
Drops of water

The filling
1 cup ricotta or cream cheese
1 cup mozzarella
3 spoons grated parmesan cheese
1 egg

Place the flour on a dry surface into a heap and add the eggs to its center. Mix the ingredients together to obtain a smooth dough. Add drops of water as needed. Let the dough rest for 30 minutes. In the meantime prepare the filling. In a bowl mix the ricotta, mozzarella, parmesan and egg. Roll out the dough ¼ inch thick and with a fluted pastry wheel cut out 1½" squares. Spoon the filling into each center. Brush some egg white on the edges. Press the opposite corners together to form a little bag. Cook for a few minutes in boiling water.

Salsa di Pomodoro - Tomato Sauce

Four cans (15 ounces) peeled tomatoes cut into large chunks
1 teaspoon extra virgin olive oil
1 garlic clove minced
½ small onion diced
Fresh Basil leaves
1 pinch salt, or to taste
½ glass of dry white wine
2 cups water

Over medium heat, place the garlic and onion in the middle of a large frying pan. Drizzle with olive oil. When the onion is tender and golden add the tomatoes. Add the water. Tear a few basil leaves into the sauce and add the salt. Bring to a simmer, stirring occasionally, for 5 to 15 minutes to reduce, or until the sauce has thickened. Add wine and let the sauce reduce for another 2 minutes. If necessary purée the sauce in a blender. Keep in the refrigerator for up to a week.

Scaloppine ai Profumi di Sorrento
Cutlets with the Perfumes of Sorrento

The Flavors of Sorrento
For 4 persons

    8 thin slices of beef
    ⅓ cup flour
    2 lemons
    2 oranges
    Cooking oil
    Salt
    Vegetable stock cube

Lightly bread both sides of the meat with flour. In a skillet fry the beef in hot cooking oil together with the julienned rind of the lemons and oranges. Sprinkle with salt. Add the juices of 1 lemon and 1 orange and a tip of the vegetable cube. In a cup mix the flour with the juice of the remaining fruits and add to the pan to thicken the sauce.

Sorrento Style
For 4 persons

    8 thin slices of beef
    ⅓ cup flour
    1 teaspoon unsalted butter
    8 Basil leaves…

...Tomato Sauce, *Salsa di Pomodoro* (page 255)
  Mozzarella
  Cooking oil
  Salt

Preheat the oven to 325 degrees. Lightly bread both sides of the meat with flour. In an oven proof skillet fry the beef in hot cooking oil. When the cutlets are cooked remove them and pour off the fat from the pan. Melt the butter and replace the beef. On each slice place a small piece of mozzarella, a couple of spoons of tomato sauce and a leaf of basil. Place the pan in the oven for a few minutes to let the cheese melt. Serve hot.

Delizia al Limone - Lemon Delight

Ingredients for 6 persons

For the sponge cakes - Pan di Spagna
4 large eggs
½ cup all purpose flour
½ cup granulated sugar
1 lemon, juiced to make ¼ cup.

For the pastry cream
2 cups whole milk
1 cup granulated sugar
¼ cup all purpose flour
4 egg yolks
1 drop vanilla extract
1 lemon rind

For the finishing touch
1 cup heavy cream
1 teaspoon granulated sugar
1 cup of limoncello
1 lemon
Black cherries (optional)…

...Grease and flour 2¾ oz. hemisphere or muffin molds. Beat the egg whites with freshly squeezed lemon juice to a soft peak stage. In a separate bowl whisk the egg yolks and sugar until mixture becomes light and creamy.

Then add the flour. Carefully incorporate the egg whites with the mixture by gently folding the ingredients, stirring from the bottom of the bowl. Pour the batter into the molds and bake at 325 degrees for 15 to 20 minutes, or until golden brown.

Prepare the pastry cream. In a saucepan bring the milk and lemon rind to a simmer. In a bowl, whisk sugar and egg yolks, then transfer to the saucepan, add vanilla extract and the flour. Stir over medium heat until mixture thickens. Let it cool for four hours.

To assemble

Whisk the heavy cream and sugar to soft peak stage. Add 4 teaspoons of the whipped cream to the pastry cream. Cut out the bottom of each sponge cake, leaving some of the edge and remove a portion of the center. Still holding the cakes upside down, bathe the interior with limoncello, fill them with the cream mixture, replace the bottom cover, then place them on a tray or plate. Add the remaining limoncello to the mixed cream until you obtain a liquid sauce sufficient to cover the cakes. Decorate the tops with the whipped cream, a cherry (optional) and some lemon peel julienne.

The Sweet Life

*L*eaving the women to discover Sorrento on their own, I stride across Corso Italia and stroll to the Grand Excelsior Vittoria. The sumptuous luxury hotel stands high on the cliff once occupied by Emperor Augustus' villa. Since it opened in 1834 the Excelsior has been continuously owned and operated by the Fiorentino family, who in the course of time has hosted many famous personalities, from every corner of the world, including Kings and Queens, Lord Byron, Giuseppe Verdi and the great Neapolitan tenor Enrico Caruso, who spent the last months of his life here.

At the gated entrance I smile at the guard, then continue down the gravel driveway to the oldest building of the hotel complex: La Vittoria. Though I have toured this property before, I never miss an opportunity to do it again. Surveying luxury hotels is something I thoroughly enjoy. When the occasion arises I can report on them with accuracy. This time I plan to focus my interest on the other two buildings: La Rivale and the Swiss-style chalet La Favorita, and on the lush five-acre garden filled with the sweet fragrance of citrus fruits.

After the completion of my inspection I amble toward Via Vittorio Veneto, passing on the left the Municipio, fronted by a small garden lined with orange trees, and on the right the Chiesa di Sant'Antonino, which houses the remains of the town's patron saint. At the Imperial Hotel Tramontano, I stop for a moment. Torquato Tasso, Sorrento's favorite son, was born in the west wing of the hotel, and in the Casa Tasso James Fenimore Cooper wrote his novel *The Water-Witch* in 1830.

Turning onto the tree-shaded Piazza Vittoria, I reach the Hotel Bellevue Syrene. Behind an unpretentious entry is one of the most luxurious hotels in Sorrento. Built at the brow of the cliffs, on the foundations of Roman remains dating back to the second century B.C., the hotel began as a private summer home of the Counts Mastrobuono. In the 1820s, their residence was transformed into a small hotel with thirty rooms. Heinrich Schleimann, the discoverer of ancient Troy, stayed at the Bellevue for a brief period in 1868. He described the view from his room in his diary, now in the archives of the Gennadius Library in Athens, Greece.

Although my original plan had been to wend my way down to the picturesque Marina Grande, I decide to survey the Bellevue Syrene instead. Besides, a quick glance at my watch confirms that I only have forty-five minutes before my appointment with Salvatore.

Approaching the tall man behind the reception counter, next to an impressive ancient Greek vase, I immediately present my credentials and ask him permission to walk around the premises. On his advice I wander through the delightfully appointed lounges, the indoor bar, the veranda enlivened by a piano, the internal salons featuring antique pieces mixed with bold and bright designer furniture, and the two restaurants: the intimate Gli Archi and Il Don Giovanni with its spacious interior and full-length windows overlooking the bay, before stepping into the Villa Pompeiana.

At the turn of the twentieth century, William Waldorf Astor, captured by the beauty of the location, commissioned the construction of the villa in remembrance of the Roman Empire. It is a close replica of the House of Vetti in Pompeii, with two magnificent frescoed rooms and a colonnaded terrace. It's the ideal venue for glamorous wedding receptions and gala dinners.

Emerging onto the terrace, I step up to a small table near the edge and sit down. Within seconds a cheerful young man appears to take my order. The chilly morning has turned into a warm afternoon. A gentle breeze carries the scent of flowering blossoms, and the Gulf of Naples beckons my attention. Leaning over the railing, I peer at the private sunbathing deck on the sea, dotted with sky-blue loungers and burgundy-red umbrellas.

Sorrento does not have many beaches. Hotels on the edge of the cliffs have found an ingenious way to extend their sunbathing areas by building decks over pontoons. Guests usually access them through an elevator or by an old Roman path cut into the tufa stone. Many of the dwellings along the rock are connected with the sea by subterranean tunnels, galleries and stairways. Their outlets, visible at the base of the cliffs, were often used in the past by the fishermen to store their boats.

Feeling dizzy from looking down the perpendicular drop, I lean back into my chair and scan the panoramic landscape. Suddenly I experience a keen realization that I might be sitting in the very same spot where many writers found their muse. From the penmanship of Charles Dudley Warner we first discovered Sorrento, Capri and the Amalfi Coast in his 1879 book *Sauterings*. During her stay, Harriet Beecher Stowe, the author of *Uncle Tom's Cabin,* was inspired to write her novel *Agnes of Sorrento*. Here and on the island of Capri, Marguerite Yourcenar composed her *Coup de Grace* in 1938. The acclaimed Belgian-born author is well known for her historical novels; her masterpiece *The Memoirs of Hadrian* has recently been adapted as a feature film.

Sipping from the San Pellegrino sparkling water, I glance around the terrace. Sitting side by side at a nearby table an elderly couple is gazing at the spectacular view of Vesuvio. Longing for his presence, a mental image of my husband filters into my thoughts as I watch them. After a moment, the man reaches out and tenderly puts his arm around the woman's shoulders while he whispers in her ear. She laughs. Grabbing his hand she kisses him on the cheek and they both laugh. I smile. They still seem very much in love—but then there is no age limit for romance, my maternal grandmother would always comment. She was right.

Switching my focus to the four men dining at an elegant linen-covered round table a few feet away, I immediately notice that they are impeccably dressed. Their designer suits probably cost a small fortune. The one with his back toward me is sporting an expensive gold Omega. Ranging from late thirties to maybe fifty something, they appear to be holding an intense conversation. Who are they? Business associates, G.Q. super models, Italian movie stars or crime bosses?

Without warning, the Omega man turns in my direction and grins. Oh my, what a gelato! With classic features, jet-black hair streaked with silver at the temples, dark eyes, a Mediterranean tan and a five-day-old beard, he is incredibly handsome. Hot all over with embarrassment at being caught admiring him, I look away. Delving into my shoulder bag I retrieve my notepad to write my observations on the hotel. Peaceful, refined, incredibly romantic. The view is breathtaking from all angles. Once again I smile. Checking my watch I summon the waiter to settle my bill, then head back to the Piazza Vittoria. As I near the Piazza, I see Salvatore and hurry to meet him.

While we walk through the narrow streets paved in stone, flanked by buildings with terraces and balconies, to the pastry shop, Salvatore explains that the old Sorrento still retains the Greek urban blueprint that the Romans built upon. "A plan made of *Decumani*—wide streets set parallel to the shore—and *Cardines*—narrow streets which run toward the sea, cutting the Decumani at ninety degree angles. During the Roman occupation the city was completely surrounded by walls, with five entrance gates and a series of towers strategically positioned to defend them. In Medieval times, these walls played an important role against attacks from Saracens and Turkish pirates. Sentinels would sound the alarm and the people would escape to safety.

"Unfortunately on June 13, 1558, they were not so lucky. On that fateful day, Turkish Turgut Reis, also known as Dragut, managed to enter the town, apparently with the aid of a slave from a prominent local family who opened the gate of the Marina Grande. He sacked Sorrento, Massa Lubrense and Marina del Cantone. Dragut, a lieutenant of Barbarossa, followed in his master's footsteps by continuously terrorizing the Mediterranean. In 1553 he recaptured the island and the castle of Capri. Ten years later, after looting six Spanish galleons, loaded with troops and valuable goods, he landed at the Chiaia neighborhood of Naples and ransacked it.

"Incidentally, in 1540 Dragut was captured by Andrea Doria's nephew during one of his raids and was forced to work as a galley slave for nearly four years before being imprisoned in Genoa. In 1544, when Barbarossa laid siege to the city, he negotiated Dragut's release," Salvatore continues. "The following year Dragut sailed along the Ligurian coast and revenged himself by sacking the villages of La Spezia, the Cinque Terre, Levanto and Rapallo. He was mortally injured during the Siege of Malta in 1565 and is buried in Tripoli, the capital of modern-day Libya, his home base.

"After the ferocious attack, the Sorrentini rebuilt and strengthened the walls. The work took ten years to complete and lasted until 1844, when large sections of the walls were removed to accommodate the city's expansion. The only remains still visible are on Via Marina Grande and along Via degli Aranci."

"How many people live in Sorrento today?" I query, thinking of other questions to ask him. It is wonderful having a friend as my own private guide.

"About 16,000," he answers as we enter the O'Funzionista Pasticceria.

"This is Costantino Della Pietà," Salvatore says, introducing the shop owner. We exchange greetings. From Salvatore I learn that Costantino was born in Sorrento. After graduating as a pastry chef from a culinary college, he apprenticed in the Lombardy region and on several cruise ships. In 1992 at the age of thirty-seven, Costantino and his wife took over the famous pastry store O'Funzionista, started more than a century ago on the Piazza Tasso before moving across from the Cathedral. Now in the old part of the city, they continue to produce the traditional delicacies of Sorrento using locally-grown ingredients.

When Salvatore relates that Costantino offers training courses, I grin. Perhaps on a future visit I will indulge myself and sign up for one of his classes. The long glass display is filled with earthly delights—three I recognize, the others I don't. As Costantino places small samples on a plate, he reveals their names. The cookies and chocolate bonbons bear interesting titles, *Baci di Sorrento*–Kisses of Sorrento, *Divino Amore*–Divine Love and *Pietre Lunari*–Moonstones.

Pointing to a chocolate torte with powdered sugar sprinkled on top and surrounded by almonds, Costantino says, "This is the Torta Caprese. It is a favorite of the Sorrentini."

Salvatore explains, "Napolitani and the entire population of the Campania province are very partial to desserts, and pastries in particular. Traditionally, families eat them on Sunday after lunch. If you are invited to someone's home for pranzo on a Sunday, etiquette demands that you bring a *guantiera* or a *cartoccio di dolci*. The small cardboard box or tray filled with sweets is a gift of affection and appreciation."

"I was raised with a similar tradition and still practice it today. On Sundays and religious holidays my family enjoys a fruit pie after the noon meal. When we are invited to someone's house, we always bring a dessert, and that goes for any day of the week," I say as we sample some of Costantino's confections. *"Delizioso,"* I compliment. The bite-sized pastries not only dazzle the eye but the palate as well. *"Come é dolce la vita,* how sweet life is," I exclaim, and we all laugh.

It is growing late. After thanking Costantino, I walk back with Salvatore to the Piazza Tasso where we say our goodbyes. I completely forgot about the lingerie. Hopefully I will find something in Rome. The members of my group are straggling into the Piazza where I told them we would meet. Two, five, eight, nine—one is missing. Scanning the area, I spot her at the streetlight around the corner, waiting to cross Corso Italia. Seconds later, I look again. Unbelievable! One moment she is there, the next she is gone. Where did she disappear to? It is easy to find a missing person in a small town, usually in a gift shop, but in a city the size of Sorrento, where do I begin? There are hundreds of gift stores here.

The other women offer to help in the search. Anxiously, I pace the pavement glancing in all directions. Suddenly I see her and breathe a huge sigh of relief. She looks a little frazzled—as if she has been running. Then I notice what she is toting and I burst out laughing. At the last minute she bought herself an extra suitcase!

At the sound of my name, I whirl around. Aronne is pulling to the curb. *"Va bene?"* he asks, opening the sliding door. I motion to the suitcase. He chuckles, then loads it into the back of the van.

"Raccontami," Aronne says, shifting gears to move with the traffic. "Tell me, how was your afternoon in Sorrento?"

"Incredibilmente dolce," I reply, thinking of the Omega man and the wonderful treats I devoured.

"That good!"

I roll my eyes and we both laugh.

Babà al Limone

Before becoming one of Campania's most popular pastries, the babà was already a famous French dessert. Its invention is credited to the twice dethroned king of Poland Stanislaw Leszczynski, father-in-law to Louis XV of France, who married his daughter Marie in 1725. According to a legend, the exiled king, living in Lorraine and finding the local cake too dry, dunked it in a glass of Madeira and enjoyed it so thereafter. Another version recounts that when Stanislaw brought back a pastry from one of his voyages, it had dried up. Apprentice pastry chef Nicolas Stohrer soaked the cake in sweet wine, then enriched it with raisins and vanilla cream. The new dessert was dubbed Ali Baba by the king, who was fond of the tale "A Thousand and One Nights". When Nicholas followed Marie to Versailles he discovered that the preference went to Jamaican rum, the latest imported from overseas. Five years later, he opened his pastry store in Paris, still to be found at number 51 rue Montorgueil, where he baked the babà in the shape of a mushroom or a chef's hat.

Subsequently, the "Ali" was dropped from its name when a ring shape was introduced with fruits in the middle. The babà made its appearance at the Bourbon Court in Naples under its original form, thanks to the wife of King Ferdinand IV. Kept abreast of Parisian fashions by her sister Marie Antoinette, Maria Carolina introduced a number of French desserts and terms to Neapolitan cooking. The babà with limoncello is the most recent evolution and the current hottest trend. It is served plain, or with whipped cream topped by a sour cherry.

...

...Ingredients for ten small portions.

For the cake mixture:

1¾ cups all purpose flour

5 teaspoons dry yeast

1/3 cup lukewarm water

3 teaspoons granulated sugar

5 eggs

3 ounces unsalted butter, softened

1 lemon peel, grated

1 pinch salt

Apricot Jam (optional)

For the infusion:

3 cups water

1 cup granulated sugar

1 lemon

½ cup Limoncello or Rum

To ½ cup of flour add the yeast dissolved in the lukewarm water. Mix. Make a small loaf shape and leave it to rise in a warm place for 30 minutes. Incorporate the yeast mixture to the remaining flour, salt and lemon zest. Using an electric mixer, beat the eggs in a separate bowl. Slowly stir the eggs into the flour mixture. Add the sugar. Incorporate the butter (room temperature). Knead vigorously after the butter is absorbed for several minutes to obtain a smooth, soft dough. Then leave it to rise for 40 minutes or until the dough has doubled. Grease and flour the molds and fill them halfway. Bake in a preheated oven at 325° for 15 to 20 minutes or until golden brown. Remove the babà from the molds and let them cool...

...For the syrup bring the water, sugar and lemon peel to boil. Let it simmer for five minutes, then add lemon juice and limoncello, and chill. Soak the cakes in the infusion. If desired, glaze the babàs with an apricot jam to give them a shinier appearance.

Torta Caprese - Capri Torte

This recipe is for the chocolate lovers.

Ingredients for two tortes
9 ounces unsalted butter
9 ounces dark chocolate
9 ounces peeled almonds
5 eggs (room temperature)
1 cup granulated sugar
¼ cup powdered sugar
⅓ cup limoncello (optional)
Lemon zest (optional)

Roughly grind the almonds in a food processor. Melt the chocolate with the butter. In a separate bowl beat the egg yolks with the sugar until light and creamy, then add the chocolate mixture. Incorporate the almonds, limoncello and lemon zest. Whip the egg whites to a soft peak stage. Slowly fold the whites into the batter in two additions. Line the base and sides of two 9-inch round baking molds with wax paper or baking parchment. Butter and flour the lining. Fill the molds halfway and bake at 325 degrees for 35 minutes or until a tooth pick inserted in the center comes out clean. When cool, unmold upside down on a serving plate, remove parchment or wax paper, and sprinkle powdered sugar on top.

Pastiera

The pastiera is an Easter classic, although nowadays the dessert is available year round in most pastry stores. The pie is made from an ancient recipe passed down through generations, with everyone putting their own spin to it. The taste of the pastiera varies slightly among families as they secretly guard their recipes, each claiming to be the owner of the best or the most traditional one. Fierce competitiveness exists, even between mother and daughter, as they argue about its ingredients and preparation.

The rich ingredients are a reminder of the past when Romans, Arabs and the merchants of Amalfi would bring their bounty of new-found spices and flavorings to the shores of Campania. The most distinguished ingredient is the whole wheat grains used in the filling. In ancient Rome, they represented the earth's return to fertility, while Christians associate them with Easter's rebirth. The preparation of the dessert is simple, however it does require a little time and patience. The recipe calls for whole wheat grains, but barley or rice could be substituted.

Prepare the grano, or wheat pudding

1 cup of whole wheat berries (alternative: rice or barley)

1½ quarts whole milk

1 lemon peel

2 teaspoons granulated sugar

2 teaspoons unsalted butter

1 pinch cinnamon

1 pinch salt

2 drops vanilla extract…

…Wash the wheat berries, then boil them in water for 20 minutes. Leave them soaking overnight. The following day strain the berries. In a large saucepan combine them with the milk, butter, lemon peel, cinnamon, salt, sugar and vanilla. Bring to a boil, then gently simmer for 2 hours or until the milk is absorbed. Stir the mixture constantly as it thickens to a creamy texture. Remove the lemon peel and transfer to a bowl to cool.

Prepare the pastry cream.
2 cups whole milk
1 cup granulated sugar
¼ cup all purpose flour
4 egg yolks
1 drop vanilla extract
1 lemon or orange rind

In a saucepan bring the milk and lemon rind to a simmer. In a bowl, whisk sugar and egg yolks, then transfer to the saucepan, add the vanilla extract and the flour. Stir over medium heat until mixture thickens. Let it cool for four hours.

Prepare the pasta frolla or pastry
1½ cup all purpose flour
½ cup granulated sugar
3 large egg yolks
5 ounces unsalted butter at room temperature
1 pinch salt
1 teaspoon limoncello (optional)…

...In a large bowl mix the flour, sugar and salt. Cut in the soft butter and incorporate until the mixture resembles a coarse meal. Mix in the egg yolks and limoncello (optional). Place the dough on a lightly floured surface and knead it just enough to obtain a cohesive and soft ball. Cover with plastic wrap and place it in a cool place for an hour. After the pastry dough has rested, roll it out between two pieces of baking parchment or wax paper to form a round dough ¼ inch thick.

Butter and flour a 9-inch round springform mold. Peel off the top sheet and turn the pastry into the pan allowing the extra dough to hang over the edge. Peel off the remaining sheet while fitting it.

Prepare the farcitura or filling
15 ounces fresh ricotta cheese
½ cup granulated sugar
1 cup mixed candied lemon and orange peel
Pinch cinnamon
2 teaspoons orange juice
Grated rind ¼ lemon
2 large egg yolks
6 egg whites
Pinch salt
Grano (page 273)

Pastry cream: In a large bowl thoroughly mix the ricotta, salt, sugar, lemon rind, orange juice and cinnamon. Add the egg yolks one at the time, then the candied fruits, the cooked grano and the pastry cream. Separately beat the egg whites until stiff as snow. With a spatula, gently fold the whites into the ricotta mixture. Pour or spoon the mixture into the mold, cut off the extra dough. Form a ball and roll it out....

...Cut ¾ inch wide strips with a fluted pastry wheel. Place the strips in a crisscross pattern over the filling to form a lattice. Bake in the oven at 325 degrees for one hour, or until a knife inserted in the edge comes out clean. The filling will puff up during baking and retract when it cools. It will turn lightly brown while the strips will only turn slightly beige. Let the pastry cool thoroughly, sprinkle powdered sugar on top, then place in the refrigerator for 12 hours.

Sfogliatelle Santa Rosa

The queen of the pastries on the Amalfi Coast is undoubtedly the *sfogliatelle,* created according to legend by a nun of the Santa Rosa Convent in Conca dei Marini from leftovers. The traditional shell-shaped sweet is made with a soft, flaky dough, similar to phyllo, filled with a mixture of ricotta, semolina, cinnamon, eggs and some candied fruits. The word sfogliatelle means multi-leaves, layered on top of each other. The Santa Rosa is one of its cousins, filled instead with a custard cream and topped by a black cherry in syrup. Although the savory treat is generally made by trained hands, it is possible to obtain satisfactory results with a pasta machine.

For a dozen sfogliatelle

Ingredients for the dough
2½ cups all purpose flour
1 cup water
2 teaspoons honey
10 ounces lard or unsalted butter
1 teaspoon salt

For the filling
2 cups whole milk
1 cup granulated sugar
¼ cup all purpose flour
4 egg yolks
1 drop vanilla extract
1 lemon rind
Black cherries (optional)
Powdered sugar…

...Prepare the dough. On a clean surface create a well with the flour. Add the water, salt and honey. Mix from the center, lifting the flour from its edge to create a soft dough. Continue adding the remaining flour to form a firm dough. Knead for 5 to 10 minutes, then wrap the dough in plastic and refrigerate it for 2 hours.

Rolling and layering the dough. In a small pan melt the lard or butter. Roll the dough in the shape of a long sausage. Cut it into four pieces. Flatten each piece with a rolling pin. Using the pasta machine, crank out gradually each piece to obtain a very thin layer. If necessary, cover the dough with parchment paper. Roll each sheet of pastry, brushing it with the melted lard or butter. Cover the rolls with plastic and refrigerate for 24 hours.

Prepare the pastry cream. In a saucepan bring the milk and lemon rind to a simmer. In a bowl, whisk sugar and egg yolks, then transfer to the saucepan, add vanilla extract and the flour. Stir over medium heat until mixture thickens. Let it cool.

Take out the chilled pastry rolls and cut 1/2 inch slices. With your fingers dipped in the remaining melted lard or butter, press into the center of the slice and begin pushing the layers out to form a cone or cup. When all the cones have been shaped, fill them with the pastry cream. Fold the edges over to resemble a shell and place them on a tray covered with parchment paper. Slightly brush them with lard or butter and bake at 350 degrees for 15 minutes or until they are golden. Add a dab of pastry cream on top and a black cherry (optional). Sprinkle the pastries with powdered sugar. Best savored warm.

Day Seven

The Coastal Villages

*A*s I open the drapes, a stream of sunlight greets me with the promise of another beautiful day. So far, with the exception of the rain storm two evenings ago, we have been fortunate with the fall weather. Feeling well rested after a full night's sleep I am ready to embrace our last day on the Amalfi coast.

To my surprise, upon entering the hotel lobby, I discover that my entire group is already there waiting for me. My watch assures me that I am not running late, but actually twenty minutes early. What is going on? Did they all fall out of bed? Oh yes—the previous afternoon I did suggest leaving earlier to spend more time at a fabulous ceramic shop along the way to Ravello. I smile. Apparently everyone jumped on the idea.

I cross over to the reception desk to reconfirm our dinner reservation with Ornella. "Dinner at seven-thirty. No problem," she assures me. I hear a familiar voice: *"Ciao Bella."* Strolling toward me is Aronne, his eyes faintly amused for he has just discovered that we are all ready to go. *"Che succede?"* He grins, pointing to the group.

"It is amazing how fast women will move with the right incentive. In this case, it is a visit to another ceramic shop." I laugh.

"Allora andiamo," he calls and we follow him out the door to the van.

While Aronne pulls out of the hotel parking lot, I flip the microphone on and review the day's program—Ravello in the morning and Amalfi in the afternoon. Within minutes we are once again on the coastal road SS163, labeled by the locals as the *Amalfi Giro* for its thousand turns. The women express their delight at seeing Positano again. Their short visit will not soon be forgotten nor will the Casola Factory that we just passed.

After rounding a few bends, we are granted a spectacular view of the village of Praiano, clinging vertically to the green slopes of a promontory below the mountain San Angelo a Tre Pizzi. In comparison to its glamorous neighbor, Praiano is a treasure of discreet, narrow winding streets lined with whitewashed two and three story villas, intimate gardens, churches, small hotels and quaint restaurants.

Praianesi refer to their town as *il cuore della Costa Amalfitana,* the heart of the Amalfi Coast, for it lies nearly equidistant from two of the most famous towns on the coast: west of Amalfi and east of Positano. Its unique geographical position guarantees splendid views of both, plus brilliant sunrises and fiery sunsets.

Originally a small fishing village by the sea—a fact clearly indicated by its ancient name *Pelagianum,* or "Open Sea"—Praiano was forced to relocate higher up the mountains to fend off Saracen attacks. Its expansion did not begin until the eleventh century, when Dukes from the nearby Republic of Amalfi decided to build their summer residences here.

While driving through the center of Praiano, a small traffic jam grants us a moment to admire the splendid Chiesa San Gennaro with its blue and white majolica tiled cupola—the most beautiful along the coast—and the bell tower that dates back to the end of the eighteenth century. Built in 1589 on an existing twelfth century structure, and completed in 1602, the golden-yellow Baroque church, with white ornamental details on its facade, stands at the edge of the large square overlooking a cobalt sea.

In the evening, locals gather on the Piazza San Gennaro, as well as in the front of the sixteenth century Chiesa di San Luca Evangelista, in the upper part of the village. The citizens of Praiano live in a tight-knit community. They come to meet friends, to talk about the weather and to chit chat. News and gossip are exchanged on a daily basis. Markets and festivals are held on both squares. The two most important are the Fiesta di San Gennaro, celebrated on the first Sunday of May, and on September 19th, and the Fiesta di San Luca Evangelista, Praiano's patron saint, celebrated on the first Sunday of July, and on October 18th.

Praiano's most traditional seafood dish proves that Italians do occasionally eat potatoes. *Totani e Patate* is prepared with squid, locally-grown tomatoes and potatoes, smothered in olive oil and white wine.

Shortly after whizzing by the Marina di Praia, a popular sea resort on the outskirts of Praiano, squeezed between two rock walls at the mouth of a ravine, Aronne points to a natural stone formation at the edge of the road that resembles a Madonna holding her child. Farther along, we catch a glimpse of the *presepe* in the Grotta del Diavolo before cruising through a tunnel.

The creator of the elaborate nativity scene of the "Grotto of the Devil," is Maestro Michele Castellano, a native of Praiano. He started the project ten years ago after the completion of a smaller nativity scene on the main road between Praiano and the Marina di Praia. Both are modeled after his home town. Every miniature item was personally handcrafted by Mister Castellano: the houses, churches, fountains, the small clay figures, even the lights. Each

Christmas, a small ceremony is held at the grotto as the local priest blesses the infant.

The concept of the nativity scene began in Italy in the thirteenth century. Saint Francis of Assisi is credited with having created the first live one in 1223, while the Tuscan-born architect Arnolfo da Cambio first carved one from wood in 1280. The idea took root. Around Christmas time, churches began to feature nativity scenes made of wood or terracotta figures set against a simple painted background.

Nobles and wealthy patrons caught on and started to commission their own presepe from renowned artists, who eventually expanded the setting to include elements from the countryside and other figures. The same craftsmen introduced the use of wire mannequins stuffed with *stoppa,* or fiber, on which were mounted exquisitely painted terra cotta feet, hands and heads. The *presepi* were so elaborate with richly dressed characters that they became a status symbol. In the nineteenth century, poor families began to craft their own crèche with papier maché and terracotta miniatures that represented their daily lives, including shepherds, farmers, vendors and tradesmen.

Presepi are very popular in Southern Italy and none more so than in Naples, where an entire street is dedicated to them. In the small workshops of the pedestrian Via San Gregorio Armeno, in the historic part of town, skilled artisans, using centuries-old techniques passed from one generation to the next, build crèches of various sizes, from the simplest to the most intricate.

Some are so spectacular that they resemble miniature movie sets with ruins, ponds and grottos. In tiny stores merchants sell everything from complete nativity scenes to individual characters— traditional, historic and modern—made of plaster, wood and terra cotta, ranging from one to fifteen inches in height. During the

Christmas rush, the Via San Gregorio is so crowded that officials enforce a one-way system. Hundreds of people come to admire the artists' new creations and to buy pieces for their own presepe.

After driving through a series of short tunnels, Aronne is slowing down to afford us a quick peek at the natural Marina of Furore, also known as the Fjord of Furore, which is dominated by a cluster of small dwellings once occupied by fishermen. From the main road the fishing hamlet can be reached through a steep stairway of two hundred steps. The main village of Furore, with a population of about 900, lies high above the fjord in a spectacular position along the slopes of the Vallone del Furore. In bygone days it was called the *Terra Furoris,* or the "Furious Land," deriving from the fury of the sea during stormy nights, when raging waves crash against the limestone walls of the canyon in a frightening, deafening sound.

The property I rented with my husband several years ago is among the scattered houses of Furore, perched on a terrace overlooking the sea, between two medieval parish churches and a short walking distance from a quaint family-owned restaurant.

I recall that, upon our arrival, we were met by the owners, a lovely couple in their mid-thirties. The husband gave us a quick tour of the house before handing over a set of keys. He was extremely appreciative that I spoke Italian, for his English was very limited.

The house was large enough to accommodate six persons comfortably. The rooms were tastefully furnished in the typical Mediterranean style with Vietri tiles throughout. The kitchen was fully-equipped and quite large by European standards. The parking spot assigned to the house, a concrete ledge extending from the side of the road, was challenging if not downright scary, and I was grateful for the fact that it was my brother-in-law who parked the car every night. With my driving skills, I probably would have been hanging over the edge.

Our days would always start and end in the same fashion—by eating and drinking on the balcony. Every day, we watched a glorious sunrise and a dazzling sunset. At times, it was impossible to distinguish the sky from the sea, giving us the impression of floating somewhere in between. Silence reigned in Furore except for the timely tolling of the church bells and the occasional warning tune of the Sita buses as they drove along the zigzag road through the village to Agerola.

Although we mostly purchased our groceries in the towns we visited during the day, we often stopped by the tiny grocery store below the house to buy our wines for the evening. The shop owner, a heavyset man with a thick mustache, always graciously assisted us with our selection. Seeing that we were interested in trying some fine vintages, he would take the time to enlighten us about the different varieties of wines produced in the area.

On two occasions, while driving through the hills of the Lattari Mountains, we stopped at the picturesque Agerola to buy bread and cheese. The small town in the middle of a wide green valley, 1970 feet above sea level and surrounded by three peaks, was founded in the third century B.C. by refugees from Salerno. Shortly thereafter, they were conquered by the Romans, a fact confirmed by the discovery of numerous ancient Roman artifacts in the area. As people settled, they began to clear small fields, an action that probably gave the town its name, for *Ager* is Latin for "Field." From the Middle Ages up until the mid-nineteenth century, Agerola was an important silk and wool production center.

With a population of about eight thousand, Agerola is known as the *Città del Pane,* "City of Bread" for its traditional breads of rye and wheat. *Pan biscotto,* the twice-baked bread, can be stored for up to a month, and the *Taralli,* ring-shaped dough with a texture similar to a breadstick or pretzel, are entirely made by hand following age-old recipes. Sweet or savory Taralli have become a favorite snack in Southern Italy. Agerola is famous for its cattle and sheep, which produce some of the best cheeses in the region.

Since Furore and Agerola see very few tourists, we found the inhabitants there to be genuinely friendlier and more patient than in Positano or Amalfi. They smiled as we alternatively spoke among ourselves in English, Dutch and French, the last of which they sometimes understood. A few words at least. Furore was peaceful and heavenly. Our only regret was that we should have reserved the house for two weeks instead of one, for in seven days we barely touched the surface of the Amalfi Coast. We did not have enough time to enjoy some of the walks along the "Path of the Gods" that started right in our backyard.

X

Aronne, applying a slight pressure on the brakes, interrupts my thoughts. We are slowly coming to a standstill behind a huge German tour bus. I look at Aronne questioningly. He points to a red car the size of a matchbox, parked on the side of the cliff in a narrow stretch of the road. Amazing! Of course its owner is nowhere to be seen. He is probably sunbathing on a secluded beach below. What was he thinking? At least he had the presence of mind to turn in the car's sideview mirrors. Although the Fiat 500, or the *Cinquecento,* the Italian ancestor to the Smart car, is less that ten feet in length and four feet wide, its mere presence is still enough to interrupt the normal traffic flow. After a couple of minutes the road is clear; the tour bus has managed to squeeze around the curve without a scratch, and we are moving again. I ask Aronne if he has ever "kissed" a car. He chuckles, then responds that he only kisses women. "I am sure you do!" I retort, laughing.

Aronne pulls into the parking space in front of the Piccadilly ceramic shop. It is nearing nine-thirty. Before alighting from the van, I remind everyone that they can leave their sweaters and large bags behind. All they need is their credit cards.

As we enter the store, I cannot refrain from smiling—the women are reacting as if they have just stepped into a candy store. Their eyes glimmer with delight and a string of oohs and aahs float through the air.

The Piccadilly is the largest ceramic shop along the Amalfi coast. It carries the broadest selection of exquisite hand-painted items of the highest quality, such as individual tiles, panels, decorative plates, dinnerware and accessories, vases, planters, umbrella stands, bowls, Capodimonte figurines, fruits and floral compositions. Books related to the Amalfi Coast and Campania, DVDs, CDs and jewelry are available as well.

The store is operated by the sons of Mario Criscuolo, who founded the business sixty years ago. Mario began in a small workshop dug right out of the limestone cliffs in the small village of Conca dei Marini. For good luck he named his business after the London commercial center of Piccadilly. This proved to be a good choice, for he gradually expanded. Recently, the upstairs workshop was transferred to another location, and a coffee bar was added to the ground floor, near the entrance.

As it is customary for large tour buses to stop at the Piccadilly, the store can sometimes be chaotic. I am pleased to note that on this early morning it is almost empty. Ceramiche Piccadilly is not a shop where you just browse. You need to make some serious decisions, for the choices can be overwhelming, and not having to fight a crowd is lovely, indeed.

In Piccadilly, I always manage to get into trouble. Even though I mentally promised myself beforehand that I would not buy anything, my resolve is weakening by the minute. There are just too many exquisite temptations around me.

When I step up to a large display of decorative plates to study their intricate pattern, Aronne appears at my side and asks *"Ti piace qualcosa?"*

"Si tutto, everything," I reply, sighing. He laughs, then reminds me that the previous year I purchased a large plate with the profile of a young Renaissance woman in its center.

"Yes, I remember. It is hanging in my living room. I am interested in buying a companion plate but cannot make up my mind," I explain. With his help, I narrow down the selection to three, then choose a particular one before moving on to look at tiled panels. There I quickly pick out a marvelous six-piece fruit composition on a green and orange background as a present for my sister, and an identical one for me.

After the charges have gone through on my credit card, I walk around in search of the women. Three of them are deciding which planters to buy, while another one is standing in front of the Capodimonte fruits and vegetables.

The famous Capodimonte brand owes its origins to Bourbon King Charles VII and his wife Queen Maria Amalia of Saxony. Together, they established the Royal porcelain factory of Capodimonte in 1743, next to their Naples summer residence, on "Top of the Hill," hence the name, in direct emulation of the porcelain being produced by the Queen's relatives at Meissen. The King, an avid collector of the masterpieces produced by the creative Neapolitan artists, displayed them in his Palace, which today houses the Museum of Capodimonte.

While the old Capodimonte style included porcelain figurines, plates, clocks and modeled flowers in baskets and vases, the new Capodimonte is represented by decorative ceramic lemons—individuals or stacked in a pyramid—and various fruit combinations and vegetable arrangements. In Southern Italy and in Sicily, tradition dictates that on their wedding day, brides and grooms gift their parents, aunts, uncles and siblings with Capodimonte presents.

After wandering through the upper floor and observing the other women deeply contemplating several purchases, I decide to join Aronne at the coffee bar. Standing next to him is Antonio in a black suit and pristine white shirt. A few years ago, Antonio drove my group to Paestum in place of Aronne, who was attending a wedding at the time. He is touring with a honeymoon couple from Florida who just arrived yesterday from Rome. "They are only staying for two nights at la Sirenuse, so I have a twelve-hour day," he comments.

"Are they trying to see the entire Amalfi Coast in one day?" I ask incredulously.

"Yes, if you can call it that, for all they do is smooch in the back seat," he replies, rolling his eyes.

"Well, at least you don't have to fend off eleven middle-aged women," Aronne comments, grinning from ear-to-ear as he hands me a cappuccino.

"Surely you are not complaining?" I tease, sliding my free hand up and down his arm.

Turning to Antonio, Aronne says, "You see what I mean?" and we all burst into laughter.

Soon both chauffeurs return to their vehicles. Savoring my coffee, I watch the women finalizing their purchases. It is close to ten-thirty! Time sure flies when you spend it shopping. Back in the van I take the microphone and ask, "Are you glad we got here early?" A resounding "Yes" explodes in the air, followed seconds later by a collective chuckle.

X

As we resume our journey, the road widely curves around the Bay of Cape Conca. On the slopes above us is Conca dei Marini, a hamlet of little white houses immersed in lemon orchards and olive groves. At the entrance of the village, on top of a gigantic open cave, looms the eighteenth-century Dominican Convent of Santa Rosa, where the nuns invented the delicious creamy Sfogliatelle Santa Rosa dessert. On the eastern side of the bay, at the headland of the promontory is an Aragonese tower, built in the sixteenth century to guard and defend the village from Turkish attacks.

On the western side, below the state road, is the Grotta dello Smeraldo, the Emerald Grotto, discovered in 1932 by the local fisherman Luigi Buonocore. In the Bay of Conca the sea assumes brilliant shades of blue and green. As the turquoise water invades, its reflection casts a mysterious emerald glow on the walls of the cave, which inspired its name.

Inside the enchanting cavern is a cathedral of stalactites and stalagmites with an underwater Vietri ceramic nativity scene, placed there in 1956 by skin divers. The impressive grotto, measuring ninety-eight feet in length, 197 feet in width and seventy-nine feet at its deepest point, is accessible for a small fee from the road by an elevator, a long scalinatelle, or by boat from nearby towns.

When circling the bay, the magnificent Marina of Conca dei Marini becomes visible. Clinging to the rocks, several structures remind us of the village's commercial past, based almost exclusively on the sea. On the beach is the small Chiesa di Santa Maria della Neve, the Church of Saint Mary of the Snow. Each year on August fifteenth, a naval procession sails from Amalfi to the Marina to celebrate the Saint's special day.

Rounding the next curve, we pass a splendid white villa perched on a narrow piece of land, nestled in lush greenery, with views of the sea. The fifty-five room villa is said to belong to Sophia Loren and her late husband, Carlo Ponti. While many celebrities simply vacation here, a few actually own homes in the area.

Finally, after a succession of bends in the road, Amalfi is revealed. The splendid panoramic view of the white and yellow buildings crowned with red roofs never fails to impress me. The town that gave its name to the entire coast is, without a doubt, one of the most fascinating in the region of Campania. Reaching for the microphone, I begin to relate its glorious past.

"Historians believe that Amalfi was founded in the fourth century A.D. by a group of Roman families who, while bound for Constantinople, were forced to seek shelter along the coast during a violent storm. A legend offers a slightly different version. It recounts that the village was settled a century later by a group of Romans from the village of Melphi, in the neighboring region of Basilicata.

"After the collapse of the Roman Empire, certain parts of Campania fell to the conquering Lombards, while other parts were annexed to the Byzantium Empire. Under the protectorate of the Duchy of Naples, which had been established by the Byzantines, Amalfi began to flourish. By the eighth century, the town had asserted its independence and developed a powerful naval fleet.

"In 838, the Lombards succeeded in capturing Amalfi and deported half of its population to the town of Salerno, which they controlled. A year later, the people of Amalfi rebelled, killed the Lombard leader and regained their freedom. This last sequence of events encouraged the surrounding communities to join the town in its renewed independence, and in the process a new republic was born, with Amalfi as its capital. The Duchy of Amalfi encompassed the entire territory between Sorrento, Salerno and the Lattari Mountains.

"In 849, Amalfi defeated the Saracen pirates, who were constantly raiding the coastline, and in exchange for their services the republic was granted, in 866, dominion over Capri by the Duke of Naples. From then until the early twelfth century the Republic of Amalfi was to know a golden era. In spite of several encounters with the Saracens, Arabs and Lombards, trade with the Orient and Eastern Mediterranean ports flourished and enriched the city.

"In 958, the first Doge was elected by Amalfi's aristocracy. The republic drafted a constitution and minted its own currency, the Tari, which means "freshly coined." Trade regulations and maritime laws were established and laid out in an official document entitled the *Tavole Amalfitane*. The Amalfi Tables were so important that they prevailed until the seventeenth century. A fifteenth-century manuscript copy of the tables is displayed in the Civic Museum in the town's municipio. The Republic of Amalfi was able to retain its independence under the Norman rulers when they settled the area in 1073. However, it lost it entirely when the town was sacked by its rival, the Maritime Republic of Pisa, in 1135, and subsequently conquered in 1137."

Just as I pause to collect my thoughts at the entrance to Amalfi, a swear word escapes from Aronne. *"Scusi?"* I exclaim, genuinely astonished, for I have never heard him curse out loud before.

"I forgot you understand Italian." He grins.

"Working with Italians, I learned quite a string of bad words." I smile in return.

"Pazzi, they are crazy," he grumbles, " I am just irritated by a bunch of teenagers who for the last kilometer have been trying to weave their scooters in front of us. Between the Sita buses and the

tour buses, there is barely enough room to spare on this stretch of the road." He sighs while driving through the arch of the Piazza Gioia.

"Surely you must be accustomed to their moves by now?" I ask, thinking that in comparison to him, tense tourists sit on the edge of their seats when they ride this winding road. Aronne is saved from answering my question by a phone call. *"Pronto! Si mi dica,"* I hear him say to his earphone.

As we loop around the Piazza, hordes of daytrippers are alighting from a dozen tour buses. They appear to have stepped off a cruise ship, for they all carry the same cream-colored bags. Amalfi, like Positano, is uncomfortably crowded in the morning. I prefer to wander through its streets in the afternoon, after the majority of the tourists have left.

Ascending the Corso delle Repubbliche Marinare, I point to Amalfi's cemetery, a long arch-colonnaded structure built in the rock, high above the town. The cemeteries of the Amalfi Coast are often positioned between the sea and the sky, closer to heaven. Such is the case for the cemeteries of Amalfi, Positano and Ravello. Above Amalfi's cemetery are the remains of the Torre dello Ziro, which occasionally served as a prison. The ruins are a testimony to the fact that Amalfi was once completely enclosed by a wall and defended by castles, most of which were constructed by the Normans.

Leaving Amalfi behind, we climb up a short promontory, round the headland and reach the village of Atrani. The tiniest community in Southern Italy lies at the entrance of the Valle del Dragone, the Valley of the Dragon.

"Atrani is linked historically to its neighbor. In the time of the Republic, it was the residential quarter of the nobles and aristocrats, and Doges were ceremonially crowned in the Chiesa del San Salvatore. Atrani, which is only five minutes away from the bustling Amalfi, is picturesque and tranquil. Life revolves mostly around the small Piazza Umberto I, below the Chiesa," I reveal as we head toward Ravello.

Ravello – City of Music

*A*t the seaside village of Castiglione, Aronne leaves the SS163 to climb the winding mountainous road to Ravello. The most romantic and refined town on the Amalfi Coast lies on top of a rocky spur between two valleys: the Valley of the Dragon and the Valley of the Reginna. The scenery of the Valley of the Dragon is amazingly beautiful. Complete silence reigns inside the van. Our eyes are focused on the terraced landscape, the quaint hamlets, the scattered ruins, and the hundreds of vineyards and lemon and olive groves that cover the slopes of the Lattari Mountains.

The higher we drive, the more impressive the vision and, with each mile, our heartbeats accelerate. Flipping the microphone back on, I break the silence. "If you haven't already fallen in love with the Amalfi Coast by now, you definitely will when you discover Ravello. I promise you a *Coup de foudre.*" Next to me, Aronne smiles and nods in agreement.

"Turning to the historians once more, it seems that Ravello was founded in the fifth century by Roman colonists escaping from invading Barbarians. The village developed considerably in the ninth century as it became economically and politically linked to the Republic of Amalfi.

"In the beginning of the eleventh century, the population increased when a group of nobles and wealthy merchants from Amalfi, rebelling against the authority of the Doge, moved to Ravello and elected their own. Their action earned the town its name, as Ravello is said to derive from the Latin word *Rebello*. The city prospered thanks to a flourishing textile industry and an intense trade exchange with the Arabs and Byzantines. After Amalfi was sacked and Ravello pillaged in 1137 by the Pisans, trade suffered and the town slowly began to decline. It finally rebounded in the last century, when Ravello became part of the Grand Tour."

At the entrance of Ravello, Aronne pulls to a stop, as cars are not allowed inside. Still dazed by an amazing twenty-five minute ride, we walk along Via Boccaccio to the center of town and continue on to the Villa Cimbrone by following well-posted signs.

The steep climb to the Cimbrone is through a narrow pathway lined with ceramic shops, boutique hotels, private houses and intimate villas. Stepping upward, we rapidly feel the effects of aging, lack of exercise and too much Italian food, for our legs are getting heavier and heavier. Finally, after resting a few times to get control over our heart rate and breathing, we reach the villa, purchase our tickets and set out separately.

The history of the Villa Cimbrone is quite interesting. Like many of the villas along the Amalfi Coast, it probably dates back to the Roman times. The name originates from the rocky ridge it stands on, known in Latin as a *Cimbronium*. Records show that from the eleventh century until the seventeenth, the estate belonged to a sequence of prominent and wealthy families. For a while the Cimbrone was even integrated into the nearby Convent of Santa Chiara, thus the papal coat of arms at the top of the old entrance.

At the end of the nineteenth century, Ernest Willam Becket, an English nobleman known as Lord Grimthorpe, discovered the patrician villa during his Grand Tour and fell in love with it. He purchased the estate in 1904 from the Amici family of Atrani who had inherited it in the previous century. Lord Grimthorpe immediately set out to restore the property with the help of Nicola Mansi, a tailor from Ravello whom he had met in London. At his death, the villa passed to his son. Then in 1960 the Villa Cimbrone was sold to the Vuillemier family, who turned it into a five-star hotel.

A long list of famous visitors, mostly English, stayed at the Villa Cimbrone when it was owned by the Beckett family, among them were Winston Churchill, the Duke and Duchess of Kent, Virginia Woolf and Graham Greene. David Herbert Lawrence wrote numerous chapters of *Lady Chatterley's Lover* at the villa. Fellow French writers André Gide and Paul Valery were also among the guests, as well as the American author Tennessee Williams. The fact that the actress Greta Garbo and the conductor Leopold Stokowski had a secret love affair at the Cimbrone is engraved on a marble plaque that hangs on the hotel's facade.

While the women meander through the splendid gardens of the Villa Cimbrone, I walk over to the Cloister near the hotel's entrance to look at a stone carving representing the Seven Mortal Sins. I missed seeing it the last time I was here. After taking a snapshot, I stroll along the Avenue of Immensity, under the shade of a vine-covered pergola with dripping golden grapes, to the Pavilion of Ceres, the goddess of harvests, and beyond to the Terrace of Infinity.

Once again, I find myself drawn to the magnificent panoramic view from the belvedere—a view etched in the minds of lovers of the Amalfi Coast the world over and that enticed Gore Vidal to buy a house in Ravello in 1972. He recently sold his beloved *Rondinaia,* "Swallow's Nest," which had been built by Lord Grimthorpe for his daughter in 1920, to a private investor.

I lean over the stone parapet, breathe in the fresh air and stare dreamily at the sun's reflection in the blue sea. A luxury yacht is gliding across the horizon toward Sorrento. Can people on board see me? I am standing one thousand feet above the sea. Still, I wave.

Out of the corner of my eye, I catch a movement at the end of the balcony and turn away from the view. Several of my companions are standing next to the classical marble busts that line the balcony, waiting to be photographed. Their chuckles fill the air as they pose. I manage one last glimpse at the Gulf of Salerno and the divine coast before I retrace my steps and exit the Villa Cimbrone and its manicured gardens.

A short distance from the villa, I pause and glance over a lovely multi-level terraced vegetable garden. With a small knife, an elderly man is busy harvesting lettuce and bright red tomatoes. Sensing my presence, he looks up and greets me with Buongiorno, to which I reply in kind. The northern corner of the garden is partially covered with a trellis from which pumpkins and giant zucchini are dangling. The locals call those *cocozze* and *cucuzzelle* in Napoletano. The zucchini are cut and boiled, then eaten with lemon, or mixed with other vegetables to make a *cianfotta:* a Southern Italian vegetable stew.

In another section of the garden, two men, partially hidden by still-green foliage, are picking deep purple grapes, fat with juice, from a pergola. Arbors and gazebos on hillside terrain are a feature often used in this area since flat lands are in such short supply. Wherever it is possible, farmers take advantage of the space above them.

Beyond the garden is a sweeping vista of the Valley of the Dragon. Within its center is Scala, the most ancient village on the coast. Once a fortified town with two imposing castles and a flourishing religious center, Scala was destroyed on several occasions by invading armies. It's now a sleepy little place nearly devoid of tourists.

Further along the path, I peek, on one side, at the colorful garden of the Hotel Villa Eva, which features a lovely mural of Eve at the end of a tree-lined walkway and on the other side, three steps down, at the pink Hotel Villa Maria. The entrance of the former country mansion is shaded by a trellis, which in springtime is blanketed by fragrant, dropping, pure white wisteria.

Ravello is elegant throughout, even down to the smallest details, as stylish hand-painted numeric ceramic tiles designate each house along the narrow pathway. Their similar design represents the most classical landmark of Ravello: the twin domes of the Chiesa dell' 'Annunziata, viewed from the gardens of the Villa Rufolo. Nowadays, the church is used as a conference hall.

As our time in Ravello is short, I walk quickly past the fourteenth century Monastery of Santa Chiara with its adjoining small romanesque church and the Convent of San Francisco, founded by the Saint himself in 1222, before finally reaching the Piazza del Vescovado—the town's main square.

A handful of visitors are waiting to enter the Villa Rufolo, where every July a Wagnerian Music Festival is held in honor of the German composer who visited Ravello in the spring of 1880. The villa was built in the thirteenth century, next to a Norman tower, by the Rufolo family, one the richest and most influential merchant families in Ravello at the time. The sumptuous residence passed through several hands. Having been totally neglected, it was purchased in 1851 by Francis Neville Reid, a Scottish botanist and expert in art, who completely restored it to its initial splendor.

It was in the luxuriantly landscaped gardens of the Villa Rufolo that Richard Wagner found inspiration for the scenery of the Magic Garden of Klingsor in the second act of his opera *Parsifal*. Five centuries earlier, Giovanni Boccaccio, who was visiting the Amalfi Coast during his stay in Naples, became so fascinated by the Rufolos that he related the tale of one of its members in his masterpiece, *The Decameron*.

As I stride across the piazza, two little dogs catch my eye. They are sitting a few feet away from an outdoor café, one black and one brown, derrière touching derrière and facing in opposite directions. Their pose is amusing, I can't help but smile. In my mind, I imagine their conversation.

"If you watch my back, I'll watch yours!" says the black dog.

"Fine by me, glad to return the favor," replies the brown dog. I wish that my companions could see them.

Overlooking the piazza is the Cathedral San Pantaleone, built in 1087 at the initiative of Nicolo Rufolo, head of the powerful family, and consecrated by the town's first bishop, Orsi Papice. Its facade has three ancient portals. The center bronze door, dating back to the twelfth century, is the most spectacular one, for it is composed of fifty-four panels with figures sculpted in relief. The main features inside the cathedral are the white marble pulpit resting on six twisted columns finely decorated with gold mosaics and supported by lions, and the chapel of San Pantaleone, which houses the reliquaries of the blood of the saint to whom the cathedral is dedicated.

The steps of the white-painted Duomo are decorated with purple flowers, and a large group of fashionably-dressed men and women are waiting at the bottom—a sure indication that a bridal couple is about to make their appearance. Traditionally, after the ceremony, all guests and members of the wedding party wait outside the church to see the bride and groom emerge. It is a very special moment that no Italian wants to miss.

Just as I aim my camera to take quick shots of my elegant surroundings, the newly-wedded couple exits the cathedral and a great cheer arises from those assembled, disrupting the usual quietness of the town square.

Stepping closer, I focus my attention on the couple. The bride is exquisite. Her black hair coiled back in a French knot reveals dangling pearl earrings, the only pieces of jewelry, besides her wedding ring, to grace her olive complexion. Her gown is absolutely stunning—a strapless leather bodice from which flows a tulle skirt draped with Venetian lace and accented at the waist by a large leather belt with a sterling buckle. In her left hand, she is carrying a basket filled with white freesias.

The groom is equally fabulously dressed in a dark designer suit, probably Armani, an ivory shirt and a sky-blue tie with a boutonnière pinned to his lapel. In his arms is an adorable six-month old *bambino* dressed in a darling white outfit and matching booties.

Just a second—let's rewind. Blinking several times, I ask myself: "Do I really see a baby, or is it my imagination?" Apparently not, for he is still there giggling, quite happy between his proud parents—a future gelato by the handsome looks of his dad.

Wending my way to the tourist office, I encounter a Japanese bridal couple. Silently wishing them all the happiness in the world, I quickly snap their picture as they walk gracefully toward me, arms wrapped around each other's waists. Their allure and shyness remind me of the Peynet lovers' drawings that were published in French magazines in the seventies.

Both are entirely in white. The groom is attired in a coat-length white tuxedo and the bride in a strapless silk lace gown. He grasps in his right hand a lovely bouquet of white roses, while she holds up her billowing skirt with her gloved left hand. Around her lovely neck is a pearl necklace with a single tear drop. Unlike the Italian bride, the Japanese bride is wearing a long tulle veil.

With a refined elegance, a choice of Moorish or Byzantine-styled venues and an abundance of spectacular views, Ravello is the perfect backdrop for a dream wedding. Italians and foreigners alike choose to get married in the serene and romantic atmosphere of the town elevated between the sea and the sky.

Civil weddings are performed in the municipio, a charming Mediterranean town hall with a small garden. Catholic weddings take place in the cathedral, although other churches are available, as well. Since Italian law does not allow for civil or Catholic weddings to be officiated outside the normal premises, only symbolic ceremonies are performed outdoors.

Couples from the Amalfi Coast and the Sorrento Peninsula usually go through the process of a civil wedding a few weeks before the religious ceremony. The formal ritual is then followed by a simple lunch or dinner with the immediate family members: parents, brothers and sisters. On the day of the religious wedding, the groom and his mother enter the church first. The bride follows on the arm of her father. At the altar, the father entrusts his daughter to her fiancée and the ceremony can begin. A lengthy and copious lunch or dinner affair, consisting of five to nine courses, to which the entire family, down to the youngest child, and friends, are invited, follows the mass.

During the festivities, which may continue well unto the wee hours of the morning, the bride and groom present their guests with a *Bomboniera,* a party favor filled with confetti to which an imprinted ribbon with the couple's name and wedding date has been attached. The long-standing tradition of offering a gift to each person or family serves both as "thank you" for their good wishes and support, and as a keepsake. Typically, five candies are included in a bomboniera, representing happiness, health, fertility, longevity and wealth. Confetti are sometime wrapped in a combination of tulle, organza and ribbon to create an intricate flower arrangement, and, in certain families, a Capodimonte bomboniera is also given.

After collecting a small bundle of brochures on Ravello and dropping by the Enoteca Mansi to purchase an excellent Greco di Tufo to take home, I check my watch. Since I still have some time to myself, I decide to stroll through the Via San Giovanni del Toro. In the Middle Ages and the Renaissance, it was the quarter of the local aristocracy.

Today, the Via can be considered "The Street of Glamour," for in the last century three of its noble residences have been turned into renowned deluxe hotels. The Hotel Caruso occupies the former eleventh-century Palazzo D'Afflitto and the twelfth-century Palazzo Confalone houses the Hotel Palumbo, while next door the Arabian-style Hotel Palazzo Sasso was once owned by the prosperous Sasso family from Scala.

Ambling down the street, I fantasize about the possibility of someday adding my name to the long list of illustrious guests that have stayed at those prestigious hotels. They came from every corner of the world. In the course of time royal families, presidents, writers, filmmakers and actors have all visited Ravello. Richard Wagner and Francis Neville Reid, who arrived on mule back in the nineteenth century, left their autographs in the golden book of the Hotel Palumbo. In 1943 Allied officers rested at the Caruso after the landing in Salerno. In the Sasso, Eisenhower planned the attack on Monte Cassino, and John Huston, Humphrey Bogart and Gina Lollobrigida resided here in the fifties while they filmed the movie *Beat the Devil.*

I would thoroughly enjoy occupying one of the luxurious suites of any of those hotels for a few days and being pampered by their staff. My mind is rapidly visualizing what a dream it would be. I imagine myself having breakfast on the balcony, looking at the sun playing on the crystal-blue sea underneath. My husband would be here to share it all with me. We could celebrate an important anniversary or have a second honeymoon. Of course, a new wardrobe would surely be needed, for I could hardly walk into a luxurious lobby wearing a simple pair of jeans and a plain top. A good excuse to visit Chico's.

Suddenly, the sound of a car engine pulls me out of my reverie. I swing around in time to see a black limousine slowly driving toward me. Moving out of the way, I keep an eye out for any celebrity or VIP that might be vacationing in Ravello. According to the Ravellotime's latest issue, that I picked up at the tourist office, Richard Gere and his wife were recently spotted at the Villa Cimbrone.

As I resume my stroll, the village bell begins twelve chimes for mezzagiorno. Fifteen minutes remain before Aronne returns. Counting the number of chimes in the midday warning signal, I hurry my steps, descend Viale Wagner, circumvent the outdoor cafés on the Cathedral Square and stride onward to Via Boccaccio. Before stepping through a long tunnel, I catch glimpses of the vestiges of the ancient wall and defense towers that centuries ago surrounded Ravello. History books recount that during the Norman domination and Frederick's reign, the town was protected by three castles nearby: the Castle of Trivento, Fratta and Sopramonte.

For avid hikers and for those who wish to discover the territory, a number of fabulous cliffside pathways, some dating to the Roman times, link Ravello to the neighboring hillside villages and seaside towns. Instead of taking an always-crowded Sita bus to and from Amalfi and Minori, why not step through terraced lemon orchards and picture perfect small hamlets, passing ruins of textile and olive mills, churches and monuments, which are witness to the historical grandeur of the area—all this while trying to absorb unexpected views at every turn. The footpaths are clearly signposted and detailed maps are available at Ravello's tourist office.

Aronne is waiting at the designated spot. Before joining him I quickly enter the post office in the vicinity and buy half a dozen stamps.

"Tutto a posto?" he asks me as I open the passenger door.

"They are right behind me," I reply, glancing in the direction I came from and seeing my companions trickling along like a parade of penguins. Some are carrying large shopping bags—a sure sign that they stopped in yet another ceramic store! They are impossible to resist.

As I stand four feet away from the van, close to a railing, looking downward at the spectacular view of the towns of Minori and Maiori, one the women approaches me. "You are correct. I lost my heart here. Someday I hope to return with my husband," she comments.

"Yes, Ravello is special." I nod approvingly.

Back in the van as Aronne pulls away from the curb, I smile to myself. Once again, Ravello has worked its magic.

Amalfi – Former Queen
of the Mediterranean

*T*roops of tourists are walking back to their tour buses as we enter Amalfi through the Porta della Marina and make our way to the restaurant Risto on the small Piazza dei Dogi, just a short distance from Cathedral Square. Emerging from a narrow passageway, I immediately spot Elisa, who is busy clearing one of the outdoor tables. Recognizing me she gasps joyfully and lifts her arms in welcome. "Has it been a year already?" she exclaims in Italian, for she does not speak English. I nod. "*Quanti siete oggi,* how many are you today?" she asks as we kiss each other lightly on the cheeks.

"*Undici,* eleven" I reply. Hurriedly she pushes three tables together to form a long table to accommodate our group. "*Prego,*" Elisa points to the chairs and we sit down under the shade of umbrellas. Disappearing inside, she quickly returns with menus, baskets filled with freshly baked bread, and several bottles of water. Feeling a hand on my shoulder, I look up. "*Sei retornata,* you came back," comments her husband Giovanni warmly. I nod again, smiling. "*Benissimo. Siete tutti benvenuti.* Wonderful. You are all welcome," he says to everyone, then retrieving a notepad from his apron pocket, he begins to take our orders.

The Rispoli family opened their restaurant nearly a decade ago. Elisa prepares the pasta daily by hand while Giovanni cooks. Occasionally, one of their sons helps in the kitchen. Their menu features traditional dishes made from family recipes handed down through generations.

My brother-in-law discovered this hidden gem while wandering through small alleys and narrow stairways. At Risto that first time we enjoyed a three-hour lunch. Two-hour lunches are the norm on the Amalfi Coast, for one delights in the food as well as in the view. Charmed by the genuine Italian atmosphere of the small square with fresh laundry hanging from balconies, we had spent our extra hour nursing the house limoncello and chatting with the owners. Of course, after that first delightful experience, every time I visit Amalfi, my feet find their way back to Risto.

The house special today is one of my favorites: *Scialatielli ai frutti di mare,* long pasta served with green olives, minced parsley, peppers, shellfish and fish. Simultaneously, three of the women order the special, five prefer the ravioli filled with ricotta cheese, served with a fresh tomato sauce, and the remaining two select a mixed salad, but quickly change their minds and order the Caprese salad instead. Confused, Giovanni glances at me over the rim of his red glasses and asks me to reconfirm our selection. I smile. We have totally addled the poor man. I clarify our choices and request a couple of bottles of the house wine before he escapes to his kitchen.

It feels so wonderful to be back in this peaceful corner of Amalfi. In the old days, the Piazza dei Dogi, the unique example of medieval urban architecture in the town, was called the Piazza dei Ferrari, for blacksmiths plied their trade in this location. Four churches stood here once, but all are now deconsecrated and incorporated into private dwellings.

"This is our last lunch on the Amalfi Coast," I announce sadly as Elisa serves us our meal. "Let's toast it." Suddenly, as we raise our glasses, a melodious voice breaks the quietude of the Piazza with a popular Italian song. "It doesn't get any better than this," I remark, looking for its source and realizing that it originates from a restaurant nearby. "Lunch on the piazza serenaded by an Italian tenor—who could ask for more?" All agree.

As I listen to the women's conversations while savoring the delicious food, one of my grandmother's favorite quotes springs out of the memories of my childhood. Grandmother was a woman who lived through two world wars and lost a son in the last one. "Seize the moment, absorb the joy," she used to tell me. Closing my eyes for one second, maybe two, I follow her advice.

"Tutto bene?" asks Giovanni minutes later.

"Si, è molto buono. Grazie," I reply, as the women nod approvingly.

A short time after the women have left me to experience Amalfi on their own, I bid farewell to Giovanni and Elisa, promise them to return, and walk back toward the town's main square. I glance briefly at the ancient Palace of the Piccolomini, at the corner of the Passage dei Ferrari and the Piazza di Duomo. The grand mansion was the residence of the Dukes of Amalfi from 1461 to 1568 and the scene of the tragic story behind *The Duchess of Malfi,* a macabre play written by the English dramatist John Webster in the early seventeenth century.

The tale captures the life of Giovanna d'Aragona. In 1490, at the age of twelve, she was married to Alfonso Piccolomini, the son and heir of the Duke of Amalfi. Two years after her husband's death, the Duchess, then nineteen, ruling in the name of her son, secretly married her steward Antonio Bologna. When the Duchess' brothers learned of it some years later, they persecuted the couple. Bologna was assassinated in an ambush. Giovanna and their children were imprisoned in the Tower of Amalfi and strangled.

Reaching the Antichi Sapori d'Amalfi I step inside. Around the store, shelves are stacked with a myriad of bottles of limoncello, lemon and raspberry creams, and lemon-flavored jams and candies. I grab a few bags of lemon drops to offer as gifts, then walk to the counter to sample the limoncello. With an alcohol content of thirty-three percent, it is by far one of the strongest sold on the Coast. I set the empty cup back on the counter and eye the prepackaged boxes on the floor nearby. Each contains three bottles. How heavy are they to carry around, I wonder. Sensing my hesitation, the saleswoman graciously offers to keep my purchase behind the counter while I sightsee. I promptly accept.

In the middle of the lively Piazza Duomo, I pause for a moment to admire the impressive sight of Amalfi's glorious Duomo, one of the finest cathedrals in Southern Italy, at the top of a large flight of sixty-two steps. Its construction began in the ninth century over the site of a paleo-Christian temple. The structure was subsequently modified several times. In the tenth century it was enlarged and in the thirteenth century the Cathedral assumed a Moorish-Byzantine-Norman style, a style completely Amalfitan. Renovated again in the 1500s and in the next century, it was completely remodeled in the eighteenth century. The present day geometric facade with black and white stones, golden mosaics and a magnificent gallery with three tiers of interlacing arches was built in 1891, after the previous facade had collapsed.

The bronze portal adorned with inlaid silver work, the first to appear in Italy, was cast in Constantinople in the eleventh century and donated to the town by Pantaleone di Mauro Comite, one of the rich Amalfitan merchants who founded the Order of the Knights of Saint John in Jerusalem. This religious and military organization, whose emblem is Amalfi's white eight-pointed cross, was created to assist pilgrims in the Holy Land. The first Grand Master of the Order, which would later evolve into the Order of Knights of Rhodes and the Knights of Malta, Gerard Sasso, was born in Scala.

Adjacent to the Cathedral stands the Campanile. Built between 1180 and 1276, the bell tower still retains its original Romanesque style in the lower part and Moresque features in the upper part.

The Duomo is well worth the entrance fee. The Baroque interior of the newest structure of the Cathedral, with a richly-carved, gold-painted ceiling, is majestic. It would not surprise me to learn that during masses Amalfitani often stare at it, for I did when I sat down on one of the wooden pews. In the crypt, a bronze statue of the Apostle St. Andrew, Amalfi's patron saint, stands on the main altar while his remains, brought here from Constantinople in 1208, are preserved in a silver urn underneath. The oldest structure, the Church of the Crucifix, was restored in 1994 to its original Romanesque style. It now houses a museum where marvelous frescoes were uncovered and medieval and religious treasures are displayed. The most beautiful part of the Cathedral is the Cloister of Paradise, with its slender white columns and entwined arches reflecting the Arab influence on the people of Amalfi.

Every four years, on the first Sunday of June, the steps of the Cathedral and the Piazza di Duomo are transformed into a theater of pageantry as the city hosts the historical regatta, an event that honors the four ancient Maritime Republics of Italy. The first Regatta was held in Pisa in 1956. Since then, each year in turn, the cities of Genoa, Pisa, Venice and Amalfi have evoked with great pomp a salient episode in their history. The two main features of the event are the procession of three hundred and twenty members, eighty participants per Republic, followed by the rowing contest of the galleys.

The Amalfi pageant recalls the city at the height of its period of greatest splendor, around the eleventh century, and celebrates the wedding of the duke's son with a noblewoman of Norman origins. Represented in the parade are the various classes of the Amalfitan society of the time. The bridal couple is escorted by knights and maids of honor, by the duke surrounded by pages, the Knights of Saint John of Jerusalem, followed by consuls, ambassadors and merchants. Drummers, archers, armed soldiers and sailors close the procession, which departs from Atrani. A small collection of their sumptuous costumes, faithfully reproduced in the Moorish, Byzantine and Norman styles, made of linen, silk, brocade and damask, are on display in the Civic Museum.

The race is held on the Sea of Amalfi in a straight course of two thousand meters (6561 feet), with the starting line at Capo di Vettica. The vessels are approximately thirty-six feet long, weighing close to 1770 pounds and painted in the traditional colors of the four cities—blue for Amalfi, white for Genoa, red for Pisa and green for Venice. On the poop deck is a castle representing their city and on the bow is a golden figurehead, symbol of the

Republic—a winged horse for Amalfi, a dragon for Genoa, an eagle for Pisa and a lion for Venice. Each boat is powered by eight oarsmen guided by a steersman. In 2008 Amalfi hosted the regatta, and its team won the race.

Equally interesting to my photographic eye is the Fontana di San Andrea, the Fountain of Saint Andrew, at the edge of the Piazza, built in 1760, also known as the people's fountain. At the feet of an almost-naked statue of the saint carrying a cross, children are playfully refilling their bottles with the water spilling from the breasts of a mermaid, while their parents are engrossed in a map. Children being children, they instantly switch to the game of splashing each other, and the parents have to intervene.

Satisfied with my snapshots, I leave the piazza behind and amble through Amalfi's main street, which follows the course of the River Chiarito that was covered over at the end of the thirteenth century. The pedestrian Via d'Amalfi is bursting with colors, from the faded shades of pink and ochre-painted four-story buildings with flowering vines climbing up their facades and balconies overflowing with greenery, to the hundreds of lemons piled in pyramids and the baskets filled with oranges displayed in the stalls of small grocery stores, to the dried hot red peppers—the Italian Natural Viagra—covering their facades, and to hand-painted ceramics and oil paintings exhibited outside the souvenir shops and art galleries.

At the Annazio Grocery, I enter. Looking around, I realize how much I will miss the feel of a family-run store. Although convenient, supermarkets tend to be impersonal. Over the deli counter in the back, whole legs of cured ham are hanging from the ceiling. Hundreds of bottles of wine are lined up against the right wall, waiting to be selected by customers, and a dairy cooler occupies most of the opposite wall. The center aisle is stacked with pasta on one side and limoncello bottles in a variety of sizes and forms on the other. On the floor below are boxes of soaps in the shapes of lemons, oranges and apples. To satisfy my fondness for the fresh fragrance of citrus oil, I quickly fill up a basket with two dozen lemon and orange soaps and step up to the cash register. Once outside, I resume my exploration.

Now and then, as I peer through a web of whitewashed alleys with barrel-vaulted ceiling and look up steep stairways that sometimes lead to a side street, a dead end or a private home, I catch a glimpse of the medieval Amalfi.

Nearing Via Pietro Capuano, the street narrows considerably till it reaches the Piazza Spirito Santo. The small square of the Holy Spirit was once the extreme limit of the town. On the right is the Donkey's Head Fountain, or *Capa é Ciuccio* in Napoletano, named for the donkeys that used to drink here while transporting the ironworks to the city. On the left are the remains of the cloister of the Church of the Holy Ghost.

Running parallel to the Via Capuano is the Supportico Rua, the ancient *Ruga Mercatorum,* the covered street of the Merchants. In Medieval times spices, exotic perfumes, precious fabrics and rugs, imported from the Orient and Africa by the merchants of Amalfi who traded the wheat and the wood of Campania for them, were sold here.

Beyond the archway "Faenza," named for the artisans who in the sixteenth century produced ceramics that rivaled those of Faenza, and the ancient Arab quarter is the Museo della Carta on Via della Cartiere. Opened in 1969, the museum is dedicated to the art of papermaking, a process discovered by the Arabs and perfected in the Arab town of El-Marubig. Thanks to its intense commercial relationship with the East, Amalfi was the first town in Europe to manufacture the *bambagina* paper in the twelfth century.

The creamy smooth stationary that became known as Amalfi paper was made from a mixture of recycled cotton, linen and hemp rags and mountain water. Considerably thicker than parchment, Amalfi paper was used for the documents of the Dukedom and Diocese and by the Royal courts of Italy throughout the Middle Ages and the Renaissance. The luxurious paper continued to be made by hand until the eighteenth century, when with industrialization, machine production began.

In the mid-nineteenth century, when papermaking was a flourishing industry, more than two dozen mills along the Chiarito Valley were producing the high-quality paper. Of those, only two mills remain: the Cavaliere and the Amatruda. Sadly, they are struggling to survive. Even though nowadays the paper is mainly used for weddings, baptisms, communions, important works and for the correspondence of the Vatican, demand is dwindling. Should they close, the valley will be forever silent and Amalfi will have lost another one of its ancient activities. Travelers passing through have a chance to save the industry by purchasing a small quantity of the stationary for themselves or as gifts.

Further up is the Vallone delle Ferriere, a protected nature reserve created in 1972. The valley takes its name from the ancient iron mines, which were in operation from the fourteenth century up until the beginning of the twentieth. In the factories that provided employment to the surrounding towns, minerals were worked, brought by ships from Elba, Puglia and Calabria, and carried up the valley by donkeys and mules.

Only a small number of tourists get a glimpse at Amalfi's past. Daytrippers don't have enough time to venture out this far. Those who stay in the area discover a handful of ruins amid a lush valley covered with typical Mediterranean flora, small streams and waterfalls that at one time supplied the factories.

I ponder the idea of venturing a little further out, but a quick glance at my watch warns me that I would not do the valley any justice. I retrace my steps. Before reaching the Piazza Flavio Gioia, I retrieve my limoncello, then stop at the Savoia Pasticceria Gelateria, at the corner of Via Matteo Camera. Walking into the pastry shop is like stepping into a confection paradise.

My eyes travel the length of the glass display case that features a large selection of pastries, an array of fruit-shaped marzipans, a mountain of candied orange peels and a tray of raspberry, lemon and vanilla-flavored *Fondenti*. These sugar delicacies are rarely seen. They were highly favored by my grandmother. Resisting the sweet temptations, I move over to the second glass case, which holds tubs of rich Italian gelato in a tantalizing selection of flavors. Minutes later I emerge from the shop with a double cone of one of the best limone ice creams in Amalfi.

Crossing Corso delle Repubbliche Marinare, I notice one of the women sitting on a bench at the edge of the pebble beach and stroll in her direction.

"I am overwhelmed," she admits as I approach her. "There is so much to see."

I nod, and sit down. Suddenly, as I am about to ask her if she toured the inside of the Cathedral, band music bursts into the air. Simultaneously, we turn to find its source. Below the bronze statue of Flavio Gioia, who is reputed to have perfected the sailor's compass in the fourteenth century, a small school ensemble is playing. Slowly, residents and visitors alike gather to listen to the late afternoon entertainment. For a brief moment, I linger to enjoy the medley. Then, since my companion offers to hold my limoncello, I decide to walk to the end of the pier for a last glance at Amalfi.

Lounging on the beach, girls in bikinis and men in tiny swim trunks are toasting in the sun. Sprawled on a towel and chaise lounge, a topless young woman is captivating the attention of a group of Asian men. They elbow each other jokingly, nearly falling over the rim of the concrete dock trying to get a closer look. I find humor in their behavior and cannot hide a smile. In the past, members of the Grand Tour gaped at statues and paintings of naked breasts. Today the real thing is on display. Amazing how times have changed and society has evolved. Five hundred years ago women were running for their lives, for fear of being kidnapped and enslaved; now they are exposing themselves for all the world to see.

A few feet away, fishermen are knotting their nets, which are continuously being damaged by submerged rocks along the coast. Oblivious to the crowds of spectators, their trained hands move patiently while they chat in the local dialect.

Turning my attention to the town, I study the panoramic landscape in front of me. This view often appears in box-office films. At the western side, perched dramatically on a cliff and suspended between a flawless blue sky and the dark Mediterranean below, is the recently refurbished luxurious Grand Hotel Convento. Formerly known as the Cappuccini Hotel, it was a favorite with the Grand Tour travelers. Erected in 1212 on the site of a small church, the hotel was initially a monastery entrusted to the Cistercians. When they abandoned it, it passed into the hands of the Cappuccini. The belvedere of the hotel is famous for the gorgeous vista, one of the most portrayed on the Amalfi Coast.

Continuing eastward, clinging to the hillside below, is the perpendicular Vagliendola neighborhood, accessible from the Piazza dei Dogi through the western gate of the city, the "Vallenulla," that leads to the Via Annunziatella. In its center, plastered to the mountain, is the Church of San Biagio, for a long period a property of the Abbey of Monte Cassino.

Further below, along the waterfront, at the start of Via Camera, are the remains of the Arsenal of the Republic. In its heyday, merchant ships and warships were constructed on the closed dockyards of Amalfi, Atrani and Minori. Those built in Amalfi were the finest and fastest of their time, with up to one hundred twenty oars, and highly valued by the Aragons who confiscated them to fight the French Angevins. On November 24, 1343, a tidal wave destroyed a third of the coastline and all of the ports. Amalfi's ancient waterfront actually lies under today's waves.

Along Corso delle Repubbliche Marinare, the golden building with the city's characteristic terra cotta tiled roof encompasses the town hall, the Civic Museum where the Amalfi Tables are kept, the library, the tourist office and the Church of Saint Benedict. On its facade, a ceramic panel by Diodoro Cossa illustrates some of the important phases in the urban development of Amalfi.

At the eastern edge of town is the Hotel Luna. From the nearby Saracen tower, a splendid view of Amalfi rewards those who reach it. Glancing higher, above the tightly packed dwellings is the monumental cemetery and, on top of the bluff, are the ruins of the Castle of Scalelle with the high Tower of Ziro, where Giovanna d'Aragona was locked up before being executed.

As I stare straight across at the Cathedral tower, at the bare precipice of rock behind it and at the verdant slopes of the mountains beyond, Sarah Brightman's song "Time to Say Goodbye" is running through my mind. I sigh. This week is slowly coming to an end. After bowing to the former queen, I amble with regret back to the piazza.

Within minutes of reaching it, our chauffeur pulls into the same spot where he dropped us off earlier and opens the side door electronically. The women step forward to climb on board. Across the street a female police officer is signaling us to move quickly, for parking is not permitted in this area. Tired yet exhilarated, the women hurry to store their last purchases and take their seats. Once I am strapped in, Aronne drives on, turning west into the traffic. Rummaging through my shoulder bag, I retrieve a CD of my favorite Italian songs and hand it over to him. Seconds later we are singing the chorus of "Volare" in unison.

The sun is riding low over the horizon, enveloping the coastline in a dark shade of grayish-blue, almost black, mist. Powerful last rays are penetrating the van through the windshield. With a hand flip, Aronne lowers the visor to block their blinding glare. While soaking in the sunset and listening to the music, we are fast retreating, each to our own thoughts.

Ciao Amalfi

*T*he first light of dawn is creeping over the gulf, pushing aside the moon and the blanket of stars that I gazed upon only hours before. The chair on which I sat then is now glistening with a fine dew. Stepping closer to the railing of my terrace, I close my eyes for a moment to memorize the view. Time is elusive on the Amalfi Coast. Even though our activities were leisurely paced, this week has flown by with incredible speed. Pulling my blazer on to fend off the morning chill, I find myself wishing I could stay longer. I will miss the dynamics of this group.

Just thinking about the very lively meal we shared last night puts a smile on my face. I don't know if Italian men are God's gift to women, but they certainly are to the women in my group. The charming, playful, funny and irresistible men we encountered in the last seven days have made our trip unforgettable.

After we reached the hotel, I barely had enough time to change and pack before the dinner hour. Dashing about, I undressed, showered, blow-dried my hair, applied fresh make-up, brushed my teeth, slipped into a pair of black tailored pants and donned a lavender-colored silk blouse. As I was retrieving my suitcase from under the bed, the phone rang. It was Danilo to give me last minute instructions for our airport transfer in Rome. Seconds later, Salvatore called to wish me a safe trip back home. When my arms were loaded with clothes, the phone rang again. It was Ornella's turn to remind me to tell everyone to check out that evening instead of in the morning. I had just hung up when the ringing commenced anew. Dumping everything on the bed, I once again reached for the receiver. One of the women was wondering if I had any bubble wrap to spare. I did and would bring it downstairs to the restaurant. For a split second I debated about unhooking the phone, but a glance at my watch told me that I had only three minutes to step into my black pumps and walk out the door.

My group was already at the table when I sat down. Almost immediately, the Maitre d' appeared. *"Buonasera,"* he greeted us joyfully. He explained the menu, detailed the ingredients and preparation of the dishes and recommended wines that would accompany our selection. Shortly after taking our order, a waiter began to serve the food and we started to eat.

Looking around at the elegantly dressed women who had shared the past eight days with me, I asked, "Now that you have experienced the Amalfi Coast, what is your favorite town and most delightful memory?"

"Wow! That is a difficult question. I need some time to reflect on it," replied the retiree, after taking a deep breath. Her answer did not surprise me. The images floating in her mind were too new. In a few days they will be sorted out into the "liked, enjoyed, loved, long to see again" categories and the preferred one will probably be used as a screensaver on her computer.

"The ceramics were fabulous," exclaimed the woman to my left, extracting a chuckle from all of us. She was by far, to the delight of the store vendors, the one who had purchased the most.

"Let's drink to the master artists of Campania," I said, lifting my glass for a toast.

"And to the wonderful cooks, our chauffeur Aronne, and to our spouses for holding down the fort while we are having fun," she blurted out.

"I still remember the thrill of my gondola ride in Anacapri," revealed the woman to my right, reminding me of my own adventure. "I am definitely coming back with my husband. He is a hike junkie," she continued, then added, raising her glass, "We should cheer the wonderful moments we have had."

When the *Spumone*, a special Italian dessert made with layers of pistaccio, vanilla and strawberry ice creams, representing the colors of the Italian flag, was served, the woman with her back toward the window asked her neighbor, "Do you remember the charming waiter in Positano?" The other one nodded.

"Oh, yes. He was such a gelato," she answered swooning. An outburst of laughter filled the air. Reminiscent of my days in college, for the next twenty minutes we remarked on the handsome men we had encountered in the last few days, exposing and defining their appealing features, and we raised our glasses to the most sexy ones.

"To the gelato sisterhood," I exclaimed, lifting my glass once again. Everyone quieted down. I repeated it and, as each woman latched on to the idea, she burst into laughter. Swept away by their enthusiasm, I joined in. What did I start, I wondered.

By the end of the meal, we must have clinked a dozen times and attracted curious stares from every guest in the dining room.

Some looked a little envious. Even the Maitre d' and waiters smiled at our joie de vivre.

Back in my room I kicked off my shoes, finished packing, poured myself the last of the Capri wine and settled on the balcony. Peering at the twinkling lights of Sorrento, I found myself reflecting on the land that had inspired so many to write. My mind must have pondered the subject all night long, for I slept restlessly.

This morning I have no doubt that these writers fell under some kind of spell. Maybe they stared for such an extended time at the horizon that they were bewitched. Legions of travelers who whisk down from Naples or Rome, guidebook in hand and prompted by the desire to see the archeological ruins of Pompeii, drive along the Amalfi Coast, buy a load of beautiful ceramics, perhaps take a speedboat to Capri for the day, and then whisk away again, are untouched by the siren call of the area. It seems enough to them that they write "amazing scenery" in their journals and hurry off to new sites and more famous towns.

However, the visitor who comes here and remains long enough to get entangled in the land's enchantment soon finds himself losing the will to depart. The longer you stay the more difficult it is to leave. The writers who lingered here week after week and month after month uncovered what guidebooks in their enumeration of the delights of the region do not touch—the romance of the land, the warmth of its people and the genuine way they draw you into their lives. Without realizing it, their stories weave themselves into your memory, and you feel the urge to compose. Here authors find their muse.

)(

Reluctantly, I tear my eyes away from the view, silently vowing to return, and walk inside the room. My radio alarm on the night stand reads seven-thirty. I still have time for a light breakfast. The last one in Campania. Half an hour later, after two croissants and two cups of coffee, I lift my suitcase off the bed. Actually, lift is not the appropriate word, for it weighs a ton. Awkwardly, I slide the oversized bag down the side of the bed and flip it over onto its wheels.

In my carry-on, I store the last of my belongings, journal, notes and toiletry bag. In Rome I will have to transfer those cosmetic products to my checked luggage. That will prove to be an interesting challenge. I cannot resist a chuckle at the image of myself sitting on it, trying to close the zipper. Gathering up my raincoat, shoulder bag and camera, and grabbing the handles of my carry-on and suitcase I march to the door, thrust it open, roll them down the hallway to the elevator, place them inside and press the L button, then quickly descend the stairs. In the lobby, people are waiting to ride it. Excusing myself, I slide in front of them, and as the door glides open, reach for my luggage under their startled looks and raised eyebrows. I smile. Yes, I did it again.

"*Tutto a posto?*" asks Aronne, who is standing next to me as I hand over my electronic room key to Ornella. I nod. Lifting my suitcase, he swears. "*Porca miseria.* This is heavy. What is in it?"

"Since I am not sure when I will come back, I bought extra soaps, limoncello, books and other things," I reply, grinning. "Mine is probably the lightest compared to the others. I have a hunch that the women will have taken great care to keep you in shape," I warn, squeezing his biceps.

"By the time I have stowed them away I may not be feeling my arms or my back again," he jokes, touching the nape of his neck, and we both laugh.

Turning my attention to Ornella, I thank her for the wonderful service, say my goodbyes to the staff and follow the women outside. I watch Aronne close the back doors of the van, then flex his shoulders and arms. Grimacing, he glances in my direction. Again, we burst into laughter. After taking last minute group pictures in front of the hotel, we step on board. Minutes later Aronne pulls out of the parking lot.

While listening to my favorite Italian singers, Albano, Laura Pausini and Zucchero, I gaze at the unfolding scenery on our way back to the Eternal City. Tomorrow four of the women will continue by train to Florence for a three-night stay, and the rest of the group will fly back home. Already the Bay of Sorrento is out of sight. Soon this week will just be another memory. Until next time.

Ciao, ciao Amalfi . . .

Author's Notes

Dear readers,

I hope that you have enjoyed this book as much as I have loved writing it. While researching the history of Campania and the sites we visited, I found conflicting information. I have tried to be as diligent as possible in reporting accurate dates and sequence of events. Any mistake is mine alone. I have used August 24, 79 A.D. for the eruption of Mount Vesuvius, which is the date registered in many of the guide books. However, as scientists continue to analyze the site, recent evidence has surfaced confirming that it actually took place on October 24, 79 A.D. I have also chosen to include the Italian name of certain land masses as well as their various appellations when describing them. For example, the Sorrento Peninsula and the Sorrentine Peninsula represent the same territory.

Should you journey to the Amalfi Coast, I expect that you might drop in on some of the businesses mentioned in this narrative. As they hold a special place in my memory, it is my fervent wish that you see them the way I did. But things change. Nothing stays the same, which makes each trip truly unique.

Acknowledgements

While writing is a solitary endeavor, I received a great deal of assistance along the way. I am deeply grateful to Linda and Wayne Knepper, Nancy Miller and Marjorie Meeks. My appreciation also goes to Laura Davis, Patricia Fry and Leona Grieve for their editorial suggestions. My thanks, too, to Nita Greene for her kind attention to details.

A special note of gratitude to Warren Leach for helping me with the maps. Many merci to my sister Carine Cattrel for her drawings and for putting up with me as we validated the recipes.

Mille grazie to my Italian friends for their cordiality and openness. I am indebted to Salvatore Capuano whose generosity with his time and knowledge shaped the content of this book.

A warm thank you to Judy Bolton at the Louisiana State University Libraries in Baton Rouge for helping me with the research of the life of Lieutenant Colonel John McKowen. I am obliged to Nino Miniero at the Sorrento Tourist Office, Rosalba Irace at the Praiano Tourist Information Office and to the Tourist Offices of Capri, Positano, Amalfi and Ravello for answering my numerous questions.

Finally, I want to thank my husband for his encouragement, support, patience and the hilarious moments we shared during my seemingly endless writing journey.

Bibliography

Boccaccio, Giovanni. *Decameron*. French translation Livre de Poche, 994.

Bora, Salvatore. *A Brief Historical Guide to Capri*. Edizioni La Conchiglia.

Cafiero, Antonio. *Sorrento and its Delicacies*. Franco Di Mauro Editore, 2007.

Cerio, Edwin. *The Masque of Capri*. Edizioni La Conciglia, 1999.

De Vero, Giampiero. *The Coast of Amalfi*. Andrea de Luca Edizioni, New Edition.

McKay. Alexander G. *Houses, Villas and Palaces in the Roman World*. Baltimore and London: The Johns Hopkins University Press, 1988

Rizzotti, Tullia. *Capri Blossoming*. Editorial Giorgio Mondatori, 2003.

Schwartz, Arthur. *Naples at Table - Cooking in Campania*. Harper Collins Publishers, 1998.

Stowe, Harriet Beecher. *Agnes of Sorrento*. Ams Press Inc. New York 1971, reprinted from the 1890 edition.

Trower, Harold Edward - British Consular Agent at Capri. *The Book of Capri*. Emil Prass Editor Naples, 1906.

Vassalluzzo, Mario. *Naples and Campania*. Cografa Publisher, 2003.

Warner, Charles Dudley. *Sauterings*. General Books Publication 2009, reprinted from the 1879 edition.

Special Collections of Louisiana State University. *McKowen-Lilly-Stirling Family Papers*, MSS-4356.

Lente Pede - excursions in Sorrento Peninsula and Amalfi Coast Confine Edizione, 2007.

Paestum, the Temples, the Museums. Casa Edite Bonechi, 2007.

Amalfi. Casa Edite Bonechi, 2005.

Sorrento. Casa Edite Bonechi, 2007.

Naples, Sorrento & the Amalfi Coast. Hunter Publishing Inc. Travel Guide, 2006.

Italian Trade Commission, Government Agency. *Campania Tiles.* www.italiatiles.com.

Filmography

Beat the Devil
1953 Black and white movie directed by John Huston. With Humphrey Bogart and Gina Lollobrigida. Partially filmed in Ravello and on the Amalfi Coast.

Voyage to Italy
1954 Black and white movie with George Sanders and Ingrid Bergman. Scenes of Pompeii, Cumea, Naples and Capri.

It Started in Naples
1960 Comedy starring Clark Gable and Sophia Loren. Shot on the isle of Capri and in Sorrento.

Le Mepris
1963 French drama with Michel Piccoli and Brigitte Bardot. Filmed in Rome and Capri.

Vanille Fraise
1989 French comedy starring Sabine Azema & Pierre Arditi. Filmed on Capri.

Only You
1994 Comedy with Marisa Tomei & Robert Downey Jr. Scenes of Rome and Positano.

Bread and Tulips
2000 Italian comedy with Lucia Maglietta and Bruno Ganz.
The beginning of the movie was filmed at Paestum.

Under the Tuscan Sun
2003 Based on the book by Frances Mayes. With Diane Lane.
Scenes of the Amalfi Coast, Positano and the Sirenuse Hotel.

A Good Woman
2004 With Helen Hunt and Scarlett Johansson. Scenes of Amalfi,
Atrani and Ravello.

Brian Sewell's Grand Tour of Italy
2006 Mini-series about the 18th century "Grand Tour."
Scenes of Naples, Pompeii and Paestum.

Des Racines et Des Ailes sur Naples
2008 French Documentary filmed in Naples, Scala, Capri
and Sant'Agata.

Glossary

Italian words			
Albergo	Inn	*Che*	What
Alimentari	Grocery store	*Chiesa*	Church
Allora	Then	*Cuore*	Heart
Andiamo	Let's go	*Denominazione*	Denomination
Amoretti	Cupids	*Diavolo*	Devil
Antipasti	Appetizers	*Dragone*	Dragon
Bacio	Kiss	*Duomo*	Cathedral
Bambino	Baby, masculine	*Fermata*	Bus stop
Bambina	Baby, feminine	*Fervore*	Fervor
Bella	Beautiful, feminine	*Formaggio*	Cheese
		Furore	Fury
Bello	Beautiful, masculine	*Fusto*	Hunk or attractive man (literal translation oil-drum)
Bomboniera	Box of candy		
Buongiorno	Good day		
Buonasera	Good evening	*Gelateria*	Ice cream parlor
Cara	Dear, feminine		
Caro	Dear, masculine	*Gelato*	Ice cream
Cavallo	Horse	*Gelati*	Plural
Confetti	Sugar coated almond candies	*Giro*	Tour
		Grotta	Grotto or cave
Ciao	Hello and also goodbye	*Grande*	Grand
		Grazie	Thank you

337

Limoneto	Lemon grove	*Scalinatelle*	Romantic way of describing a flight of little steps
Limoneti	Plural		
Limone	Lemon		
Marina	Harbor		
Mozzare	To cut off	*Scavi*	Excavations
Municipio	Town Hall	*Secondo*	Second
Nonna	Grandmother	*Signora*	Lady
Nonno	Grandfather	*Signore*	Mister*
Nipote	Grandchild, niece, nephew	*Spiaggia*	Beach
		Regio	Neighborhood
Palazzo	Palace	*Totano*	Squid
Pane	Bread	*Totani*	Plural
Panino	Sandwich	*Vallone*	Valley
Passeggiata	Stroll		
Pensione	Inn or family hotel		
Piazza	Square		
Piazzetta	Small square		
Piatto	Course, dish		
Pranzo	Lunch		
Presepio or presepe	Nativity scene		
Presepi	Plural		
Primo	First		
Salute	Health		
Salsiccia	Sausage		
Salsicce	Plural		
Scalinata	Flight of steps		

* The "e" is dropped when the word is followed by a name or surname.